LEADERSHIP SYSTEM

SYSTEM

2.0

IMPLEMENTING

INTEGRATED ENTERPRISE EXCELLENCE

Rachele, Thanks for your input to this ooky reviews, & Spreading IEE word! [signature] 9-15-20

FORREST W. BREYFOGLE III

MW00529630

Copyright © 2020 by Forrest W. Breyfogle III

Published by Citius Publishing, Inc., Austin, Texas: www.citiuspublishing.com

All rights reserved. No part of this book may be reproduced by any mechanical, photographic, or electronic process, or in the form of audio recording; nor may it be stored in a retrieval system, transmitted, or otherwise be copied for public or private use—other than for "fair use" as brief quotations embodied in articles and reviews—without prior written permission of the publisher.

Limit of Liability/Disclaimer of Warranty: While the publisher and author have used their best efforts in preparing this book, they make no representations or warranties with respect to the accuracy or completeness of the contents of this book and specifically disclaim any implied warranties of merchantability or fitness for a particular purpose No warranty may be created or extended by sales representatives or written sales materials. The advice and strategies contained herein may not be suitable for your situation. You should consult with a professional where appropriate. Neither the publisher nor author shall be liable for any loss of profit or any other commercial damages, including but not limited to special, incidental, consequential, or other damages.

For general information about our other products and services, contact us at www.SmarterSolutions.com.

Paperback ISBN: 978-1-7352882-2-2
E-book ISBN: 978-1-7352882-3-9

Cover Design by 100Covers.com
Interior Design by FormattedBooks.com

OTHER BOOKS BY FORREST W. BREYFOGLE III

TABLE OF CONTENTS

FOREWORD

For decades, Forrest Breyfogle has been creating and writing about processes that companies have embraced. Fortune 100 companies to small and emerging businesses have greatly benefited from his thoughts and teachings. While Lean Six Sigma concepts continue to be his foundation, Forrest is continuing to move the edge toward better measurements and scorecards. His wisdom leadership has grown with each passing year. He thinks beyond the traditional corporate dashboard.

What if companies focused on root causes that lead to higher quality and lower costs? What if companies abandoned traditional incentive compensation that often leads to destructive behaviors? What if companies adopted and embraced an enlightened approach to measurements that focused on things that really matter?

In this book, he approaches questions like those I have asked above with new energy and innovation. Forrest has always been convinced that there is a better way to lead and manage businesses. He continues to be committed to fresh ways of looking at complex issues and of challenging people to think outside their comfort zones.

I have known Forrest for twenty years and have known of his work for much longer. I am amazed by his intellect and drive to make things better. I believe you will experience the same wonder when you read his book.

Earl Maxwell
Retired CEO of St. David's Foundation and Retired
Leading Partner of Maxwell Locke & Ritter LLP

PREFACE

There are some major *elephant-in-the-room* business management issues that no one seems to be addressing. In my opinion, this not-talked-about elephant is an underlying component of many past and current, frequently encountered organizational business management issues. Resolution to these problems requires that organizations do things differently. This book deliberates on many common-place business management issues that can lead to unfavorable, if not destructive, organizational behaviors and what to do to resolve the problems.

This book provides a no-nonsense next-generation business management system that minimizes the risk of organizations doing bad things. Besides, the described methodology provides direction for establishments to move toward the achievement of the 3Rs of business; that is, everyone doing the Right things and doing them Right at the Right time.

This book, written as a novel, describes an enhanced business management system called Integrated Enterprise Excellence, which has an abbreviation IEE, pronounced I-double E. The IEE system offers much flexibility, including a means for effectively managing an organization remotely.

IEE provides a comprehensive 9-step system that CEOs, Presidents, General Managers, executives, managers, leaders, practitioners, and others can use to resolve *elephant-in-the-room* management issues such as:

- Business goals not being met.
- Scorecards leading to harmful, if not destructive, behaviors.

- Persistent day-to-day firefighting problems.
- Business strategies that are very generic and/or difficult to translate to organizational work environments.
- Lean events and other improvement projects that consume a lot of resources often do not offer a quantifiable benefit to the business as a whole.
- Lean Six Sigma process improvement deployments that have improvement projects, which are either not completed in a timely fashion or make substantial financial claims that are questionable.

Whether documented or not, an organization has processes for executing work. These processes have output responses (Ys) and inputs (Xs). This relationship can be expressed mathematically as $Y=f(X)$; that is, a process Y response is a function of the Xs that impact a process-output response. Organizations often give focus to managing the Ys without giving much attention, if any, to improve the Xs or the process that can lead to the enhancement of a process's output response. Y-Management can lead to very harmful organizational behaviors, including playing games with the numbers to make situations appear better than they are.

Leadership often has the desire to improve an organization's key performance indicators (KPIs) or to achieve its objectives and key results (OKR) quickly. This metric performance enhancement aspiration can lead to the setting of specific, measurable goals for a future time-period. However, often these measurement objectives are arbitrarily set with no mention about improving the underlying processes that can lead to performance measurement response enhancements so that there is long-term, business-as-a-whole benefit. A meet-the-numbers style of running a business is Y-Management and can result in many forms of unfavorable organizational behaviors and lack of sustainability. IEE provides a system for overcoming Y-Management issues.

In this book, Jorge and his wife have an automobile accident. Jorge's wife is critically injured in the accident and transported to a hospital near where the accident occurred. This hospital has many process problems, which could impact her survival. During his wife's recovery, Jorge reflects on what he did at his Harris Hospital to address similar business performance metrics and process improvement needs. This book describes many details for implementing IEE in a variety of organizations.

This book's storyline includes many application situations for IEE; however, there are more IEE concepts and metric reporting applications that need sharing in this writing. Rather than bog down the book's storyline, Appendix A contains additional application illustrations of IEE techniques and information.

Instead of merely providing a theoretical description of IEE and its benefits, included also is a description of how organizations can use an Enterprise Performance Reporting System (EPRS) software methodology to implement the described IEE techniques.

BOOK OVERVIEW

Many traditional business practices give focus to the achievement of vague but well-intended executive-retreat-developed strategic statements that often have wording like 'expand production capacity' or 'develop global logistic capabilities.' Common-place business management methodologies that target the execution of hard-to-get-your-arms-around, organizational-handed-down strategies can lead to harmful, if not destructive, behaviors.

Everyone should be well aware that organizations need to improve and adapt to survive. Because of this aspiration, a business may undertake a process improvement program such as Lean or Six Sigma; however, often, these process improvement program undertakings are not long-lasting. The reason for this occurrence is that, when leadership undertakes a program self-assessment, they often find that they cannot see a tangible, big-picture positive financial impact from the conducted process improvement program's efforts. Far too often, process enhancements from an improvement program occur in silos, where there is little if any positive impact on the big picture.

This book also describes organizational issues that commonly occur with tried-but-not-so-true techniques like strategic planning, the balanced scorecard, red-yellow-green scorecards, table-of-number reports, hoshin kanri, and Lean Six Sigma programs.

The tools in an automobile mechanic's toolbox can be handy. However, a mechanic must know not only how to use their tools individually but also be able to apply the right tool correctly at the most appropriate time when addressing a vehicle issue. Similarly, many business management and process improvement tools can be very beneficial; however, not unlike an automobile mechanic, the people in an organization must know when and how to use specific tools for the management and improvement of an organization. This book provides a roadmap for the wise utilization and execution of business management and improvement tools, both at the enterprise and process-improvement-project level.

This book describes the benefits and usage of the 9-step Integrated Enterprise Excellence (IEE) business management system. Among other things, IEE provides a means to create and report 30,000-foot-level operational and satellite-level financial performance metrics, which separate common-cause variation from special-cause events. When only common-cause variation is present in a process-output response, the IEE high-level 30,000-foot-level performance-metric reporting methodology utilizes data from the recent-region-of-stability of a process's output response to provide a predictive statement estimate. When a provided 30,000-foot-level futuristic statement is undesirable, this metric enhancement need *pulls* for the creation of a process-improvement project. This IEE approach for improving a Y response gives focus to enhancing the associated Xs and processes that impact the magnitude of a Y's response level.

Appendix B, Web page 13 provides access to software for creating 30,000-foot-level and satellite-level reports described in this book. The author intends to have a *no-charge* licensing fee for this software.

Organizations can use the described Enterprise Performance Reporting System (EPRS) software to provide automatic updates to high-level IEE value-chain performance metric reports throughout the business, as described in Chapter 6 of this book.

This book presents a blended analytical and innovative approach for creating an organizational enterprise improvement plan (EIP). An EIP graphic shows 30,000-foot-level IEE value-chain metrics that, when improved through a process-improvement project, will enhance an organization's overall satellite-level reported financials. In IEE, all IEE value-chain metrics are to have an owner who is responsible for the performance metric's response and associated process enhancement efforts.

The many provided website linkages provided in Appendix B offer much additional how-to information about the application of the described techniques, including application software for applying the methodologies.

COMPARISON OF IEE TO OTHER SYSTEMS

Figure 0.1 provides a comparison of the IEE system to taught methodologies in a typical MBA program and traditional organizational deployments of Six Sigma, Lean, and the original balanced scorecard methodology.

Comparison of Systems

SELECTED ATTRIBUTES ++: Attribute included +: Partial/incomplete Inclusion -: Not included	Integrated Enterprise Excellence (IEE)	Typical MBA Program	Traditional Six Sigma	Traditional Lean	Original Balanced Scorecard
Defines process for improvements at operational/project level	++	-	++	++	-
Defines a process for improvements at enterprise level	++	-	+	+	-
Derives improvement projects from enterprise value chain metric performance needs	++	-	-	-	-
Uses DMAIC process to implement process improvements	++	-	++	+	-
Integrates enterprise scorecards, strategic planning, business improvements, and control using 9-step IEE system	++	-	-	-	-
Supports standardized graphical representation of selected data (dashboard)	++	+	-	-	+
Aligns enterprise level business metrics (satellite-level) and operational metrics (30,000-foot-level)	++	-	-	-	-
Includes process for definition of rational metrics that are aligned at operational and enterprise level	++	+	-	-	-
Includes process for distinguishing between "common cause" and "special cause" problems so as to eliminate firefighting	++	-	-	-	-
Uses a traditional approach for business management and/or making process improvements	-	++	++	++	++

Figure 0.1: Comparison of IEE to other Systems

This figure summarizes the benefits of IEE; however, as highlighted in the table, the IEE business management system is different. This book describes and highlights the benefits of these differences.

READER'S AND LISTENER'S GUIDE

For the audio version of this book, the book's figures, acronyms, glossary, and references can be downloaded from SmarterSolutions.com/iee-audio-book2-supplemental-material. Figures in this supplemental material are larger than those provided in this book. Readers of this book can use this additional information to examine a figure's smaller printed details more closely.

When explaining IEE and its benefits in this book, there are references to a few figures and web page links. To avoid disrupting the book's flow by referencing a figure number or another portion of this book for each refer-

ence occurrence, readers and listeners of this book can use the following to locate the referenced information.

- IEE one-minute video: Appendix B, Web page 1 (video link)
- IEE overview article, "Positive Metrics Poor Business Performance: How does this happen?": Appendix B, Web page 2 (PDF copy)
- IEE 9-step business management system: Figure 6.3
- IEE value chain at Harris Hospital: Figures 6.4—6.14
- IEE value chain in non-profits, school districts, government, and for-profit companies: Chapter 9
- EIP (Enterprise improvement plan) example: Figure 6.15
- Capturing Voice of the Customer: Appendix B, Web page 7
- Characteristics of Successful IEE Master Black Belts and IEE Black Belts: Figure 4.3; Appendix B, Web page 15 (PDF copy)
- Enterprise Performance Reporting System metrics (EPRS-metrics) software: Appendix B, Web page 13 (30,000-foot-level metric-reporting software)
- Enterprise Performance Reporting System IEE (EPRS-IEE) or (EPRS) software: Appendix B, Web page 14 (IEE system software that includes IEE value chain with automatic metrics updating)
- IEE Deployment at Harris Hospital with EPRS software: Chapter 6
- SmarterSolutions.com additional information about IEE methods: Appendix B, Web page 11
- Over 80 'IEE implementation experiences and discussions,' not included in the novel's storyline: Appendix A
- IEE implementation books: Appendix D

This book references computer hyperlinks. Access to these links could be through a desktop computer, notebook computer, tablet touch screen, or smartphone. A *click of a mouse* or some other variation of the word *click* describes navigation through these hyperlinks.

AUTHOR COMMENTS

Process improvement and other business practitioners often state that IEE concepts look great, and they believe their organization could benefit much from utilizing the methodology. These individuals then continue saying that the problem that they have is that IEE concepts need to be presented to people much higher in their organization's hierarchy than where they reside.

To address this valid point, in addition to an e-book and paperback book offering, an audio-book version of this book is available that IEE proponents can suggest to others. Business leadership, executives, and others who have constraints for book-reading time might listen to this book on their commute to and from work or during exercise workouts.

Another frequent question is how to receive more information about implementing IEE. Appendix B provides more than twenty website links for additional information about the implementation of the IEE techniques described in this book. Appendix D includes books that provide IEE, how-to methodology implementation details.

This book is a derivative work of *Lean Six Sigma in Sickness and Health* (Breyfogle and Salvekar 2004). Also, this novel is a continuation of the Harris Hospital IEE implementation story initiated in the book *Management 2.0: Discovery of Integrated Enterprise Excellence* (Breyfogle 2020).

The organization, Harris Hospital presented in this book, is fictitious. As the author, I have created many situations that need a smart resolution. The described circumstances may have fabrication in the book's storyline; however, I have observed all the basic presented scenarios at some point in time in my career.

Randomly generated data were used to create the illustrative metric reporting figures.

ACRONYMS, GLOSSARY, REFERENCES, AND REGISTERED MARKS

The glossary and acronyms sections of this book provide reference material for increasing the understanding of unfamiliar statistical and non-statistical terms. The reference section of this book offers additional resources for the reader or listener of this book.

Integrated Enterprise Excellence, IEE, Enterprise Performance Reporting System, Satellite-level, 30,000-foot-level, and 50-foot-level are registered service marks of Smarter Solutions, Inc. In implementing the programs or methods identified in this book, authorization is granted to you to refer to these marks in a manner that is consistent with the standards set forth herein by Smarter Solutions, Inc., but any and all use of the marks shall inure to the sole benefit of Smarter Solutions, Inc. Smarter Solutions is also a registered mark of Smarter Solutions, Inc.

AUTHOR

The author solicits your comments and improvement suggestions for this book. He is also available to discuss the application of the described techniques, which is his passion.

Forrest W. Breyfogle III
Smarter Solutions, Inc. (SmarterSolutions.com)
Forrest@SmarterSolutions.com

1
THE ACCIDENT

"What a beautiful Saturday," Jorge Santos exclaimed to his wife as he sped along the two-lane highway, one hand on the wheel and one elbow out the window.

"Couldn't agree more," his wife Sandra replied, smiling at his enthusiasm as she looked out onto the passing scenery, "75 degrees with a light breeze—a perfect day for golf."

Jorge wrapped her small hand in his, and they drove on in silence, appreciating each other and the beautiful day ahead. They had been living it up the past year, or so, Jorge reflected, spending more and more time together. A big part of that credit went to his hospital's Integrated Enterprise Excellence (IEE) Implementation. His job as Senior Vice President of Harris Hospital had become a lot less stressful and a lot more rewarding since they had implemented the IEE business management system. Both profitability and customer satisfaction were up, which made him look great. The smoother running operation also meant he had more time to spend with his wife and friends on the golf course!

On top of all that, his friends now call him *the Professor*, a title humbly accepted as a compliment. It all began when he started casually telling them about IEE on the golf course over three years ago. Eventually, they had decided to push for implementing IEE at their own companies, and it was as much a success for them as it had been for Jorge. Now they were all reaping the rewards together.

Just then, his thoughts were interrupted by a semi-truck coming from the other direction, which blew past them on the narrow highway, rocking the happy couple's car.

Sandra gasped, "Holy cow! That was close!"

"Sure was!" Jorge agreed, scowling at the disappearing truck in the rearview mirror. "That guy ought to be more careful. These old two-lane highways are so narrow. You've your seatbelt on, don't you?"

Sandra tugged at the belt around her chest, "Got it. Jorge, look at this next car coming—he's *awful* close, isn't he?"

Jorge saw the car too, and Sandra was right—his left tire was practically rolling right down the double yellow line in the center of the two-lane highway. It made him more than a little uneasy, so he slowed down and got as far over to the shoulder on the right as he could without letting his tires hit the gravel. The oncoming car was a black sedan, and when it was about 100 yards away, Jorge saw that it had begun to swerve into his lane a little, then a little more.

Sandra gasped. The rest was in slow motion for Jorge as he watched the approaching car weave violently back and forth, tires smoking. Jorge slowed to almost ten miles an hour and pulled onto the gravel shoulder of the road, but the car swerved at them like a heat-seeking missile. The last 100 yards closed in a blurry flash of screeching metal. Jorge caught a glimpse of the driver the final second before impact—it was a woman, middle-aged, slumped over the steering wheel, seemingly unconscious.

Jorge leaned back and gripped the wheel as the sedan slammed into them head-on with a horrendous crash, and then everything went black.

Jorge awoke to a young woman who shook him lightly by the shoulder, "Are you okay? Mister, Mister, can you hear me?"

Jorge realized that his eyes were open long after he opened them. He was in shock. He wondered why the woman's eyes got so big when he first raised his face to her. Why did she cover her mouth like that? The sound of her voice outside the smashed car door window faded away then. Everything became quiet and still. His heartbeat and breathing were the only things he could hear in the next moments.

The airbag in the steering wheel had deployed during the crash and now lay deflated in his lap—a thin blanket of powdery white plastic, marred only by a few dark red droplets of blood. The sight of it made him aware that something was running warmly, quickly, down his forehead. He touched his fingers to the wound he found there and winced. Acrid smoke from the airbag deployment filled the air. Voices slowly worked their way into his consciousness.

He looked next to him and saw Sandra lying limp in her seat, seatbelt still secure, deflated airbag rustling against her unconscious form. The airbag lying across her legs was red—very red. A blast of adrenaline washed through his system as he recognized the redness as blood, and concern for his wife overtook everything else. She was unconscious and injured about the head and face. He wasn't a doctor, but he'd worked in a hospital long enough to know that head and neck injuries are the most dangerous. Jorge struggled to free himself from his seatbelt so that he could lean over far enough to check her breathing.

As though from far away, but now getting closer and closer, he heard the woman outside the window pleading with him, "Mister, don't move her! Don't move her! The ambulance is on its way!" He heard the sirens approaching in the distance.

He put his ear to her mouth and could just barely feel her warm breath. He took her wrist in his hand and pressed her pulse. She was alive.

"Good," he thought, "that's good," and he assured his unconscious wife, "You're gonna be ok. You're gonna be fine."

A trickle of blood crept into the corner of his eye.

He cursed and looked into the partially shattered and dangling rearview mirror to see how badly he was hurt. That's when he first saw the long, deep gash running across his forehead, so deep that he thought he could see some bone down there, and then he turned white and passed out for a second time. Although he'd worked in a hospital for years, significant amounts of blood still made him a bit squeamish.

"Sir! Sir!"

Jorge's eyes flickered as he struggled with consciousness. The first thing that Jorge did was look to his right and saw that his wife was not in the seat next to him.

"Where's Sandra?" he asked groggily, still disoriented.

3

"She's being put into the ambulance," said the paramedic, a large balding man with a grave but compassionate face and a deep, steady voice. He held a compress to Jorge's forehead.

That was when Jorge noticed that his car door had been removed, which was how the paramedic was able to lean over him. Then he saw the red and white ambulance lights, and the blue and red police lights, flashing dimly in the daylight. He realized that he must have lost some time somewhere.

To spot Sandra, he looked past the highway patrol officers looming behind the paramedic, taking notes in small pads, talking on radios. The smell of burnt rubber again filled his nostrils, and the squawk of police radios filled the air. Finally, he saw Sandra, just twenty feet from him, on the other side of the tow truck and police cars, as she was being loaded into the back of an ambulance.

"Is she going to be all right?" he asked, attempting to get out of the battered car.

The pear-shaped paramedic held him firmly in place. "Easy," he said, "Not so fast. She's sustained some serious injuries, but she's breathing, and she's got a strong pulse. We're taking her to City Hospital…"

"City? No, no…we go to Harris Hospital…"

"Sir, Harris is more than a half-hour from here. City Hospital is only ten minutes away, and we've already called it in."

Jorge didn't like it, but the paramedic was right. Time was of the essence. He had an uneasy feeling, though, about going to City Hospital. It wasn't that he'd heard anything necessarily bad about the place; it was more that he knew that Harris was so good, especially after the implementation of the IEE business management system. "I want to go with her in the ambulance."

"You're her husband?"

"Yes."

"Okay. Your head wound looks superficial. You'll need some stitches, but it looks okay. Can you stand up?"

"Yes, I think so."

"Okay, take it slow."

The paramedic helped Jorge out of the car. Now that his adrenaline was kicking in again, Jorge felt as though he had just downed an entire pot of coffee. "I'll check you for a concussion in the ambulance, but you seem all right."

"As long as we do it on the way, that's fine by me," Jorge said with determination, and they made their way through the crowded accident scene to an ambulance parked along the shoulder of the highway. Jorge braced himself on the rear ambulance door when he got his first full sight of Sandra on the gurney, IV tubes coming out of her arms, clothes, and skin darkened with blood, delicate eyelids closed as in a deep sleep.

He felt the paramedic's firm, steady hand on his back, "You okay?" he asked.

Jorge shook off his fear and nodded sharply, then began to pull himself up into the ambulance.

"Hold on one second, sir," said the paramedic who was already inside and attending to Sandra, "Let me just get her locked in before you climb up."

As Jorge waited impatiently, he looked around to see if he could get a glimpse of the driver who had hit them. Then he saw another ambulance parked just past the police and fire truck, further down the highway. Its emergency lights were off. Two other paramedics walked towards it, wheeling a gurney with a black body bag on it across the rocky shoulder of the road.

"Is that the other driver?" Jorge asked the paramedic outside his wife's ambulance with him.

The man followed Jorge's gaze to the body bag, and bobbed his head grimly a few times, "Heart attack." he answered. "She was probably gone before she even hit you."

"Okay," the paramedic inside the ambulance waved him in. "Let's go."

Jorge took a deep breath, grabbed the rear door of the truck, and pulled himself up.

2 WHAT BAD PROCESSES MEAN TO GOOD PEOPLE

At the hospital, Sandra was unloaded efficiently by the paramedics and met at the doors by the triage team. Jorge trailed along behind. In the ambulance, technicians determined that Jorge suffered only from a deep laceration to the forehead, caused possibly by some flying debris during the accident, but there was no concussion. Sandra, on the other hand, was in serious but stable condition.

When the triage team met them at the hospital's emergency entrance, Jorge was relieved. At first glance, Jorge's well-trained eye for emergency department procedure and military-like efficiency gathered that everything was as it should be.

The on-duty physician and triage nurse team hustled Sandra down the hall on her gurney, hovering around her on all sides. As they ran towards the trauma room, they called out her vitals. The doctor ordered medications and gave commands in an urgent yet controlled voice.

Jorge walked briskly along beside them, "I'm here, honey," he called to Sandra. "I'm right here."

Suddenly, someone gripped Jorge by the arm and pulled him aside.

His eyes locked on the triage team surrounding his wife; in the back of his mind, he became aware that someone was calling to him, telling him that he couldn't go any further and preventing him from moving forward. The triage team did not stop, and Jorge watched them disappear down the hall, rolling his wife towards what he assumed was the trauma room.

"Sir," came a voice next to him, "Sir, please stop. I need to ask you some questions."

It took some effort for Jorge to peel his eyes off his wife's retreating path, but he finally did. He looked over to see who had him by the arm and met the furrowed, blue-eyed gaze of a strong woman in her mid-forties wearing an all-business expression. It was a triage nurse. Jorge saw her nametag, which read Melanie Watson, RN. He stopped struggling against the registered nurse's firm grip. He knew from his dealings with the battle-hardened emergency department (ED) triage nurses of Harris Hospital that he had as much chance of getting past her as he had of winning the Pulitzer Prize for interpretive dance.

"No," Jorge told her in anticipation of her questions, "She's not on any medications. No pre-existing medical conditions or allergies to any medications. Our regular physician is at Harris Hospital—Doctor Jack Gray. He has all our records. Um gosh, I'm having a hard time thinking right now. What else can I tell you that'll help?"

She said, "That's enough for now. We can get anything else we need from her medical records at Harris," handing him a clipboard with forms specific to liability releases, medical history, and insurance coverage, "but I do have some papers for you to fill out."

"Sir," Nurse Watson said hurriedly as she backed towards the ED doors, "If you fill out the paperwork we've given you, that'll be sufficient for us to treat your wife, Sandra. We'll have everything needed to give your wife the best emergency care possible. The best thing you can do for her is to wait and let the doctors do their job. We've got an outstanding team here. Now please excuse me—I'm needed in the trauma room."

Jorge wasn't worried about the quality of their team; he was sure that they were dedicated, caring professionals. It was their *processes* specific to the medical and surgical departments that would be required to treat Sandra's injuries that worried him.

"But...what if there was something that...something important that I've forgotten, or didn't know about..." he must have sounded frantic, was possibly even incoherent to some degree. He could read it all over Nurse Watson's face.

But he let her leave him without further protest, a sinking feeling building in his stomach with every step she took. Oh, how he wished they had been taken to Harris Hospital instead. He should have insisted that they go to Harris! But it was too late. Nurse Watson was right. All he could do at this point was get out of the way and let the City Hospital system work. Jorge didn't like it, but it was Sandra's only chance. He tried to be optimistic but quickly failed when he turned and wandered down the hallway towards the hospital ED waiting room.

"This place is a mess!" he thought as he looked around.

The bright white tile hallways were lined with stretchers that looked yellowish in the fluorescent light. One of the patients lying there had what looked like a severe head wound. The others on the stretchers were unconscious, hooked up to IV's, some moaning in discomfort.

In the waiting room itself, in the two rows of blue shell chairs that looked like they were out of the 1950s, was a variety of patients who had made it to the ED on their own. In one corner was a mother with a wailing baby. A college student sat with a compress held to the side of his face, head tilted back and to the left. Another young man sat alone with a blanket around his shoulders, shivering. And there were others, many others: a pregnant woman, a man with a cut leg, and several elderly couples. They weren't waiting patiently, either. It seemed as if they had long ago abandoned any pretense of a positive outlook. Most seemed troubled and dissatisfied.

Not to mention, Jorge thought as he surveyed the hive of activity around the nurses' station that the staff seemed stressed out and rushed—it looked as if they hadn't planned on being so busy that sunny Saturday afternoon and were understaffed. Triage time was slow, even though some of the nurses were running from one task to the next.

Jorge picked a nurse and watched her perform what seemed like one task, yet she had to run twice from one side of the room to the other to get some object that was vital to that task. Jorge shook his head slowly. He worried that these small inefficiencies were only the tip of the iceberg and was now seriously questioning the ED's ability to give his wife the best treatment possible.

He shook it off. "Got to stay calm," he told himself.

He redoubled his efforts to be positive and took a seat back in the ED waiting room. There was nothing he could do at this juncture to help City Hospital perform its job any better, he reasoned to himself.

The system they had was the system they had. He just had to get out of the way and let it work. But underneath that, he couldn't help but think that, as soon as it was safe, he would have Sandra transferred to Harris Hospital.

He filled out the forms that the Triage nurse had given him, writing down everything that might be helpful to the team, and simultaneously cursing the hospital for not running a tighter ship.

He also thought of Sandra, who was probably lying somewhere in an operating room (OR) prep room, bandaged and perhaps immobilized, IV tubes coming out of her arms. He wished he could be with her instead of out here in the triage area of the ED, feeling so helpless and trying in vain to be positive. Then, over the loudspeaker, he heard, "Trauma Team to OR, Trauma Team to OR."

Uh oh. Jorge knew what that meant and closed his eyes in stolid disbelief. Jorge presumed that the ED staffing had only one Trauma Team, and they were busy, so they had to page the on-call Trauma staff. On a sunny Saturday afternoon like today, it was a good bet that at least one of the doctors needed to operate on Sandra was out hitting the links about now. Hadn't he been going to do the same thing himself? He only hoped that they kept another OR prepped and ready to go so that when the team arrived, all they would have to do is scrub up and get to work.

Jorge finished and turned in his paperwork, then began pacing the hallway. It didn't take him long to realize that he should probably contact family—their son, Sam, for one. Sam was in Boston doing an internship for a financial company, but Jorge knew their boy would fly home at a moment's notice if he knew his Mom needed him. Then there was his wife's sister, Helen, who lived in the same town as they but was out of town for the weekend on vacation. Jorge had a younger brother, who lived in Asia with his family, working for a company there, but there was no sense in calling him—it would take him a day just to get here. That was it for close family members. Both his and Sandra's parents had passed away years before. He debated whether or not he should call and worry Helen and Sam, but decided that, just in case, he'd better call. If he didn't, and something happened…

He walked through the hospital's emergency room and exited the building for privacy. He then looked up his son's number on his cell phone and hit the speed dial. He sagged when he got his answering service after three rings. "Sam," he said at the tone, unsuccessfully attempting to keep the worry out of his voice, "it's Dad…"

He paused, cleared his throat. Did he want to leave this message on his son's answering machine? Finally, he just said, "Call me when you get in. Everything is…ok. But, please call. It's important. Bye."

He clicked off the phone, then dialed Helen's number.

An automated voice spoke after one ring. "The customer you're trying to reach has traveled out of the coverage area. Please try your call again. Thank You."

Frustrated, Jorge clicked off the phone. Should he begin calling friends? What could he tell them? He didn't even know anything about Sandra's condition yet. He decided there was nothing friends could do for him at the moment, except try to console him. He didn't want to be comforted at the moment. He decided to stay focused on Sandra and do what he could to help her. He thought it might be strange, but he didn't want a lot of people patting him on the back and telling him right then that it was all going to be okay.

Finally, he decided to try to contact everyone again once Sandra was out of surgery, and he knew more. Feeling better with this decision, he wandered back to the ED waiting room, tuned out everything around him, and sank alternately into prayer and deep thought. Jorge did not know how much time had passed when suddenly he felt a firm hand grip him by the shoulder. He came out of his trance and looked up into the bright blue eyes of a woman dressed in a green gown with a green hair cap—a surgeon.

"Mr. Santos?" she asked.

Jorge was afraid, "Yes, that's me," he told her, "Is she…"

"She's stable," the surgeon said, "My name is Doctor Miller, and I'm the trauma surgeon who'll be operating on your wife. Her wounds are serious, but she's got strong vitals. That's a good sign, but we haven't been able to operate yet. Our on-duty Trauma Team is now operating on another patient. Since we're not sure when they'll finish, we've paged the on-call Trauma Team and are prepping the OR."

Jorge sighed at the confirmation of his worse fears, "How long do you think it'll take to get everything ready?"

The surgeon's eyes were steady, "Mr. Santos, we're moving as quickly as we can, but we have to wait until everything is ready. It shouldn't be long now. I'll send a nurse out to let you know when we've begun operating."

"Okay, thank you, doctor."

"Hang in there."

The doctor left, and Jorge went back to pacing. Fifteen minutes later, the doctor came out to talk to him again. Hadn't she said she would send a nurse?

"Dr. Miller, is there something wrong?"

"No, sir, everything is still fine. I just wanted to let you know that the plastic surgeon needs to be paged."

"Great!" Jorge thought. "Another process that hasn't been mistake proofed and isn't robust to the normal variation from its input variables."

Dr. Miller went on, "Your wife has sustained some injuries to her nose and teeth," she explained, "and we want Dr. Monk to be there when we operate."

"Okay. How long until he can get here?"

"It won't be long. Don't worry. Dr. Monk is very good—the best."

The doctor smiled and gripped him firmly by the shoulder once more, "We'll tell you as soon as we know something," she said. Then she turned and went back through the OR doors.

A new wave of anguish washed over Jorge as he thought about the precious time this further delay would cost his wife. No matter how caring and confident the trauma surgeon sounded, Jorge knew that every minute that slipped by worsened his wife's chances for a full recovery.

Two hours later, a nurse came out of the OR to tell Jorge that surgery had begun and that he could move to the OR waiting room if he wanted.

Jorge wandered through the hospital hallways, following the colored arrows on the floor that led to the OR waiting room. When he finally found the OR waiting room after two wrong turns, he joined the other waiting-room occupants: several small groups of distressed families who huddled together in the small, blue-carpeted room. A television was on in the corner, tuned to some kind of mid-afternoon game show, but no one was paying attention.

The surgery seemed to take forever. During this time, Jorge drank coffee and worried about the speed of lab tests and x-rays or if the hastily-prepared OR would be adequately equipped for doctors to operate. He fretted because of the lack of error-proof systems in their processes. What if Sandra got the wrong kind of sedation or blood? Simple, but devastating, mistakes like that could certainly occur when adequate checks and balance procedures are not followed.

There were even cases of patients having the wrong limb amputated—and how easily something like that could be avoided! In his hospital, for example, they simply gave a marker to amputee patients so that they could indicate to the doctors where to cut; and that was just one example of the kind of basic but cost and effective quality improvements that hospitals were now incorporating. Jorge hoped that this hospital was religiously following these types of procedures. The IEE system had led his hospital towards implementing this type of error-proof practice throughout not only operations but back-office processes as well.

Eventually, Jorge was able to calm himself enough to sit down and begin waiting in earnest. Hours later, the trauma surgeon came out to see him. She was still in her gown and cap, mask hanging limply around her slender neck.

Jorge rose to his feet as she entered the room, heart-thumping, "Is she all right?"

The trauma surgeon allowed herself the briefest of smiles, "The surgery was successful. She's stable."

"Thank God!" Jorge softly exclaimed, aware that he was being watched by others in the waiting room who might not receive such good news that day.

"Yes," the surgeon replied, "but we're not out of the woods yet. We'll need to keep her for a while. Tomorrow morning the neurosurgeon will look at her head wound. The pulmonologist/intensivist specialist will look at her lungs. Also, we need to run some tests. The lab is running under a heavy load today, so that could take a while."

"Okay," Jorge nodded, undeterred from taking a positive outlook, "but the prognosis is good?"

"Yes, but I don't want to give you the impression that she's totally in the clear, Mr. Santos. There could be damage that we haven't identified yet. For the moment, things look good. We'll know more in the morning when the specialists arrive. Okay?"

Jorge nodded soberly, "I understand. Thank you, doctor."

He did understand. The doctor was doing her job. She didn't want him to get his hopes up in case something happened, though more than anything, he wanted her to declare victory over his wife's injuries.

Minutes later, he was talking to the recovery room nurse to find out where his wife was going to be moved. He was told that he would have to wait until she got a room before he could see her. He was afraid to see her in her wounded condition, but desperate for it nonetheless. At first, the nurse—a very thin woman with a kind, but beleaguered look on her face—wasn't able to give Jorge any information at all because his wife hadn't yet been assigned a bed. A cup of coffee later, she told Jorge that his wife would be transferred within the hour to room 1215, but that he shouldn't go up there just yet in case something changed.

"Do bed assignments out of recovery room change often?" he asked.

"It's happened," the worn-out nurse told him flatly.

And it happened again. Sandra's bed assignment was changed or pushed back three more times in the next forty-five minutes. Jorge was chomping at the bit and severely irritated through the entire process. Finally, an hour and a half later, Sandra was put into a room for the night.

3 SEASON OF DISCONTENT

Jorge went up to Sandra's assigned room as soon as he was given the go-ahead. When he got to the room, his wife had not yet been wheeled in. He spent some time with the nurse, who was to be in charge of his wife, as she prepared the room for Sandra's arrival.

Her name was Nurse Barnes. She was a tall woman with bright red hair done in curls. She made Jorge think of the character *Flo* from the popular 70s sitcom *Alice*. It was about three waitresses who worked in a diner for the tough-exterior-but-heart-of-gold owner named Mel, who was their boss, cook, friend, and sometimes father. Flo was the sassy one, always telling the customers to *kiss her grits*.

"Sugar," she said to Jorge after they introduced themselves, "you have got to be just plum exhausted. I heard they moved her on you three times!"

When Jorge confirmed this, he opened the floodgates for a mini-rant from Flo, "Well, I tell you what, that's hard. The problem is these specialists. Oh, they're good—when you can get a hold of one because they are so busy. Sometimes we've to put people in beds just because the specialist won't be available until the next day to make the diagnosis. So what happens? Well, I'll tell you what happens: we run out of beds, that's what. Then when somebody like your wife comes along who really needs a bed, we'll have to scramble. I tell you, it's a nightmare."

Ten minutes later, Sandra arrived in the room. She was conscious but very groggy. She was hooked up to IV tubes in both arms, bandaged about the head and face so that only her mouth, eyes, and the tip of her nose were visible. In a way, Jorge was thankful that he didn't see his wife's face when she was so severely injured. He didn't know if he could take it. As the orderly and Nurse Flo hooked Sandra up to a variety of monitors, the rhythmically-beeping machines eradicated the eerie silence in the room. Jorge held Sandra's hand, and they whispered to one another for quite some time, as a couple will in that situation.

"I'm tired," Sandra told him, "but don't leave me."

"Course I won't leave, Sandra. I'll stay right here."

"Did you bring the Chinese?"

"The what?"

"The orange duck," Sandra whispered sluggishly through her bandages with a thick tongue.

Jorge looked up at Flo, "What's she talking about?"

"It takes a while for the sedation to wear off," Flo explained to him in a whisper. "It's normal if she's a little disoriented for a while. Does she like Chinese food?"

"No," Jorge leaned into the nurse, "that's just it—she hates it! Especially Duck! Gave her food poisoning once."

Flo shrugged and whispered, "I've heard stranger things. S'cuse me now a minute, hon."

She moved around to the other side of Sandra's bed and leaned over her patient to introduce herself. Then she said to Sandra, "Can ya tell me if yer in a lot of pain, sweetheart?"

"Not too bad," Sandra answered her, trying to sound courageous.

"You sure you're not just saying that so you won't worry this fellah beside you here? Who's he, anyway?" Flo teased her, "You want me to get rid of him for you?"

"Oh, no," Sandra whispered, and Jorge thought he could see the hint of a smile at the edges of her mouth. "He can stay."

"Well, okay. But you've to promise to tell me if you're feeling too much pain, okay?"

"Yes," Sandra agreed weakly.

"You better promise us that, Sandra," Jorge put in.

"Okay," she said.

Flo smiled, "Good—it's settled then. Well, Jorge, I think she's going to need some rest, so don't keep her up all night, y'hear?"

Jorge found himself smiling now, something he wouldn't have thought possible in such a situation.

A few minutes later, Jorge watched as Sandra's heavy eyelids drooped, and she fell asleep. Flo had left, and Jorge was alone with her in the room. He pulled a chair from the corner up to her bedside and turned on the TV to watch something that could help pass the time together. He commented on the shows, hoping his small talk would make her feel comfortable and at ease in her slumber.

At one point, he turned the TV down, took out his cell phone, and tried to call their son, Sam, again. He wanted to share with someone the news that Sandra was out of surgery and was doing well, but he still got Sam's answering service. Before the tone could sound, he disconnected. There is no sense in leaving another message. He tried Sandra's sister Helen again, too; he got the same message as he had before.

So he gave up and settled into his chair; however, try though he might, Jorge couldn't sleep. He wished the specialists were there to tell him whether or not Sandra was going to be all right—not tomorrow morning, but now. He again wished the accident had happened closer to his hospital, where he knew and trusted the way that things were done.

Jorge reminded himself to keep his anger in check. It wasn't any doctor's or nurse's fault, but the system they followed had some flaws. He reminded himself that he had probably participated in just such a system, subjecting who knows how many families to this level of frustration at Harris Hospital, back before they had adopted an IEE approach and changed things for the better.

Now more than ever, he knew the real value of those systemic changes.

4 BUY-IN

Author Note

Described in this chapter is an IEE deployment initiated with a CEO. However, often an organization does not want to pursue an IEE deployment's initiation with a CEO, president, or general manager sponsorship, but instead thinks it would be better to begin an IEE implementation in one department and grow from there. With this approach, there is the belief that once there is a demonstration of the benefits of IEE in one department, other departments will get onboard.

I have found that this IEE pilot-department-test-and-grow-from-there approach does not work. Since IEE is a business management system, any IEE evaluation assessment must be made at a comprehensive business-management level. However, relative to a pilot-assessment, IEE could, for example, be implemented and assessed in one corporate division and then later leveraged to other divisions.

The level of an IEE implementation and assessment needs to be high enough in a business that there is someone responsible for the deliverables of an entire IEE value chain.

Rather than trying to sell a CEO, president, or general manager on the benefit of IEE, it is desired that this organizational leader wants and asks for the implementation of the IEE system in his or her business.

Those who see the benefits of IEE could informally suggest to others that they look into IEE and its benefits by listening to this book on their home-to-work commute or when exercising. One book-listening event could multiply into many people appreciating the benefits of IEE after hearing the audio-book's methodology explanation. In time, an organization's CEO, or another organizational leader, might listen to this book and then ask for assistance to implement IEE in his or her organization.

For additional thoughts on how-to techniques to present the IEE business management system to others, see Appendix B, Web page 18.

That night, Jorge continued tossing and turning in the uncomfortable chair next to Sandra's bed as he thoroughly examined every conceivable outcome of this present situation. It was a grim reminder of what poor quality meant in a hospital. On the other hand, whether it was a hospital, a restaurant, or a factory when the quality of a process suffered, you could be sure that somebody, somewhere, was also suffering as a direct result—to a greater or lesser extent, of course. Getting a lousy steak at a restaurant was nothing compared to a botched surgery, but neither was desirable. And hey, what about food poisoning? If a restaurant had an inadequate system for preparing food, someone could get sick. A botched surgery might kill you, but a bad case of food poisoning would make you wish you were dead, as Sandra had repeatedly attested during the Chinese Duck incident. Businesses had been sued and gone belly-up over less, the direct result of an incapable process; that is, a process that does not regularly produce results consistent with specification requirements or customer expectations.

Finally, Jorge drifted into that state of being that is neither sleep nor wakefulness. Jorge's thoughts swept along subconscious, undirected currents. He settled into one uncomfortable position in the hospital chair. He grasped his chair while drifting back a couple of years to when Harris Hospital had begun its implementation of the IEE system.

Jorge remembered how he had become aware of IEE through the Internet and his first conference call with an IEE implementation consultant. He also recalled how he could relate to his discussion with Ron, the consultant, during a less-than-hour conversation. The business scorecard issues described in a linked-to IEE one-minute video (Appendix B, Web page 1) and Ron's walkthrough of the high-level IEE descriptive "Positive Metrics Poor Business Performance" article made so much sense(Appendix B, Web page 2).

Jorge recollected that, after viewing this video and article, he was immediately sold on the IEE methodology. However, he did not have a clue about what he should do to implement IEE in his hospital. He pondered how someone could ever get his leadership colleagues to buy into such a methodology.

Ron then stated that approaching a leadership team collectively to get an overall consensus before proceeding with an IEE implementation would take a very long time and have little chance of success. With an approach that strives for a group-consensus before initiation, the IEE implementation proposal could be *cut off at the knees* by only one dissenting person. Ron then stated that what was needed for an IEE organizational initiation was the go-ahead from a Company's CEO, president, or general manager.

Jorge then mentioned that for their situation, this person would be Harris's CEO, Janice Davis.

Ron then highlighted that not only was an IEE endorsement from the CEO needed, but the organization's leader, must personally agree to participate in utilizing IEE techniques.

"For example," Ron had said, "your CEO needs to transition from examining and requesting performance metrics in a table-of-numbers or a red-yellow-green scorecard format to an IEE measurement report format."

Ron then made a memorable statement to Jorge about why this IEE implementation requirement was so necessary. There had been many process improvement initiatives initiated by companies over the years that have not withstood the test of time. The question was why, since most organizations need to improve to survive. Ron then pointed out that the reason for this lack-of-initiative occurrence was that there had been a significant disconnect.

Ron continued, "CEOs may have a process improvement program deployed in their company, but at the same time aren't changing how they and their leadership team view performance metrics. Leadership has typically continued to examine performance metrics and the setting of goals utilizing tables-of-numbers or red-yellow-green scorecards. When an organization's targeted focus is the achievement of a performance number at a particular point of time, perhaps also referencing a past time-period reported-number, the resulting behavior is inconsistent with process-flow and process-improvement thinking. For long-term success with a process-improvement initiative, this fundamental meet-the-numbers organizational policy needs alteration.

"The way IEE addresses this disconnect is first by creating an easy to use metric reporting format, so that leadership and others throughout an organization will transition to high-level process output response measurement reporting and thinking. The IEE system then provides a methodology to determine where and how to execute improvement efforts so that there're performance metrics enhancements that benefit the big picture."

Jorge then recalled how he and Ron had discussed how best to approach a conference call with Janice, Harris's CEO. It was essential to build a constructive dialog with Janice. It was desirable to ask Janice questions that would lead to a better understanding of her organizational pain. Ron believed that the IEE system could help resolve most business-management discomfort, but Janice must first understand and then convey to us what the most pressing issue or issues were in her world.

Ron and Jorge decided that they wanted to start the Janice conversation with the IEE one-minute-video, then walk through the "Positive Metrics Poor Business Performance" article, as Ron had done earlier with him.

They decided to include two additional items in this Janice meeting. One of these added items was a current reporting of how the hospital viewed its financials. The second item was an IEE satellite-level report of monthly profit margins or perhaps earnings before interest, taxes, depreciation, and amortization or EBITDA over two years. During the meeting, Ron would present a comparison of Harris's current financial reporting methodology to an IEE approach for the same set of business financial data. Anticipation was that the IEE reporting methodology for this same metric would be eye-opening to Janice.

A non-disclosure agreement would be signed between Ron and Harris Hospital to avoid any potential down-the-road issues. After formalizing the non-disclosure agreement, Jorge agreed to send Ron, in two days, a spreadsheet of the previous month's Leadership Financial Statement Summary and the hospital's monthly profit or EBITDA numbers for the last five years.

They agreed that Jorge would call his CEO and say: 'Janice, I've uncovered an enhanced business management system that would benefit every department in our organization, but maybe no one as much as you. This Integrated Enterprise Excellence (IEE) system will give you so much more visibility into our organization and into effective tools to drive us to improve our processes. All I'm asking is 60 minutes of your time to explain the system and its benefits. I believe that these 60 minutes will be the best investment of your time for the entire year.'

A quick call from Jorge to Janice conveying this agreed-to message resulted in a scheduled next-week, one-hour conference, first thing in the morning. They planned an early morning time so that the session would not get pushed out because of some unexpected event or crisis that might need Janice's attention.

Jorge and Ron had toyed with the idea that, instead of a conference call, Ron would be physically present for this CEO conversation, which would have been the best option; however, schedules would not permit a face-to-face meeting. Hence, to have a timely get-together, they defaulted to setting up a remote video conference call.

Later, Jorge distinctly recollected all the details of the conference call meeting. Jorge presumed that his precise recall of what happened in the conference call was because of his excitement in that he had never experienced anyone's buying into a new concept as quickly as Janice had.

In the conference call, Ron did not attempt to sell Janice on IEE. Instead, Ron asked many questions to uncover any organizational pain that she might be experiencing, which the IEE system could help resolve. Focus in the discussion was to determine if Janice believed that IEE techniques were a good fit and would provide needed benefits to Harris and its bottom-line.

Author Note

The following discussion illustrates the application and benefit of IEE in a US for-profit hospital; however, IEE methodologies and its performance metric reporting system are applicable to most, if not all, organizations.

Chapter 9 provides information on how-to-apply IEE techniques in non-profit organizations, schools, governmental agencies, and for-profit industries.

Many references are made to 30,000-foot-level and satellite-level reports. Readers and listeners of this book can use Enterprise Performance Reporting System metrics (EPRS-metrics) software to easily create similar reports for their data. My plan is to offer a *no-charge license* for use of this software (Reference Appendix B, Web page 13).

As planned, Ron first uncovered Janice's description of her pain issues. Ron then facilitated discussion around the framework of having Janice access on her computer the one-minute IEE video and then talking to the figures in the "Positive Metrics Poor Business Performance" article, as he had earlier done with me.

A few of Janice's candid comments and discussions that were most memorable during the conference call were:

- "I can relate to the scorecard issues that the video describes! Tell me more about how IEE resolves the video-described problems!"

- "I've never seen any listing of *Effective Management Attributes* like those presented on page 2 of this article. These are very relevant inquiries. We've issues with the achievement of all the listed items, especially scorecard reporting and organizational improvement efforts! If IEE has the means to solve all these issues at the same time, I'm all ears."

- "I understand that common causes of variation are those causes that are part of the process as currently designed and deployed. This concept is crucial to internalize because it has significant implications in our process improvement efforts.

- "The first part of a glossary definition for 30,000-foot-level metric reporting made so much sense. I appreciated the cheat sheet that Ron gave us for this metric definition, which stated: 'Reporting of a process output response or business metric from a high-level viewpoint. In this elevated performance report, short-term variation from the natural variation of input variables will result in an individuals chart or charts that view these fluctuations as common-cause variations. This metric has no calendar boundaries, and data from the latest region of stability is used to provide a predictive statement for stable processes. An undesirable 30,000-foot-level prediction statement suggests that the associated metric's process needs improvement.'

- "Wow! I've seen similar reports to all the four scorecard illustrations in the article. Table of numbers reporting and red-yellow-green scorecards have hurt my eyes for years. I found it alarming that one person could reach one conclusion from a scorecard report, while someone else could conclude something utterly different from the same report. I agree with Ron's comment about there being a scorecard reporting *elephant in the room* that nobody openly discusses."

- "For me, the how-to conversion of percentages in a table to a 30,000-foot-level performance metric reporting needs a few clarification points. However, I'm excited about IEE's high-level metric reporting methodology. I can see the benefits of this form of reporting when compared to what we're currently doing at Harris with our scorecard reporting approach."

- "Ron, our hospital needs to internalize this essential point. That is since Harris's current red-yellow-green scorecards, and table-of-numbers reporting doesn't provide a predictive statement, our current performance management is not unlike trying to drive a car by only looking at the rearview mirror."

After Ron's walk-through of the "Positive Metrics Poor Business Performance" article's figures, Janice gave a resounding "yes" when asked whether she would like to see the results from an examination of Harris's financials from an IEE perspective.

Ron then stated that he had looked over Harris's monthly Financial Statement Summary. He then noted that EBITDA seemed to be the primary measure of the hospital's operating performance.

Janice's response was yes that EBITDA was Harris's primary financial measure. Janice continued by saying that, among other things in this report, there's a comparison of our current hospital's monthly EBITDA to year-to-date budgeted numbers. There's a discussion about EBITDA and the additional information in this monthly summary report during our regular weekly, monthly, or bi-monthly Leadership Team, Finance Committee, and Board of Directors Meetings. Achievement of budgeted EBITDA numbers is the basis for Leadership's monetary bonuses.

Ron's then commented that the budgeted summary-report values were mainly expectations or goals. He then inquired about the methodology used to create these expectations- or goal-values.

Janice gave an affirmative response that budgeted values in the report were goals or expectations for the metrics. She also noted that a publicly-traded corporation owns Harris and sets the performance-metric expectations in this Financial Statement, which Harris Hospital is to achieve.

Ron then said that the Harris Financial Statement Summary for October indicated that EBITDA was $14.2 million or 1.0% over budget and $0.2 million or 1.2% over October of the previous year. He thought that these numbers, which were colored green in the report, were viewed as a good measurement response; however, EBITDA year-to-date was $137.9 million, which was $3.1 million or 2.2% under budget and $0.9 million or -0.6% under the EBITDA amount from the previous year. A summary from all these numbers was that EBITDA in October performed consistent with budget, but the year-to-date numbers were not looking as good relative to achieving year-end goals.

Janice agreed with these statements, adding that leadership was not feeling good since their year-end-bonus prospects might not happen because of these numbers. Janice's leadership team wanted to negotiate with the mothership company about adjusting next year's budget values downward so that next year bonuses would happen as they had in previous years.

Ron continued by saying that he was not surprised by Harris's leadership desires. He then stated that the Harris Financial Statement Summary also listed several reasons for the current level of EBITDA performance:

- The volume of Admissions was down by 1.9% and colored red in the report.
- In-patient Surgeries were up by 3.1% and colored green in the report.
- Emergency department visits were down by 1.9% and colored red in the report.
- Service Mix with Managed Care and Medicare was down by 0.4% and colored red in the report.
- Cash Expense was 4.5% over budget and colored red in the report.

Ron then asked Janice what the organization did with this summary report.

Janice responded that leadership spent much time trying to uncover why reported-out-numbers for a particular month were higher or lower when compared to a budget value for the specific measurement. Also, everyone worked to do what it took to make the numbers relative to the budget-targets better for the next month.

Ron, as a follow-up, suggested that Harris could increase its 'Volume of Admissions' metric for next month if it increased the percentage of emergency department (ED) visits that resulted in hospital admission.

Janice quickly responded that Harris would not do such a thing because encouraging more admissions than necessary from ED visits would be unethical.

Ron said that that was good to hear; however, he pointed out that not all organizations take this right-thing-to-do attitude relative to the creation and achievement of metrics and their goals, as often reported by the news media.

Ron continued by asking, "Isn't it true that with your current hospital processes, Harris has no real control over the number of 'Volume of Admissions,' 'In-patient Surgeries,' 'ED visits,' and 'Service Mix with Managed Care and Medicare?' It would seem to me that the only one in this list of metrics that Harris could have some control over relative to achieving a favorable EBITDA is 'Cash Expense.' Do you agree?"

Janice responded that she agreed that the only metric which the hospital could control was 'Cash Expense.'

Ron's response to Janice was that all of these metrics typically had common-cause variation associated with them, including 'Cash Expense.' He continued, "Because of this type of variation from the output of processes, Harris does not, in reality, have any control over the precise number that'll occur next month. However, there's something that the hospital might do to achieve an enhanced month-to-month mean response for all these metrics, which could result in a significant enhancement to a mean-monthly-reported, satellite-level performance metric reporting for EBITDA.

"To accomplish this metrics improvement objective, Harris would need to create IEE process improvement projects for 30,000-foot-level metrics identified for enhancement in the hospital's enterprise improvement plan (EIP), per the 9-step IEE system methodology. This overall methodology for improving metrics relevant to enhancing the business as a whole is consistent with the IEE system summarized figures in the 'Positive Metrics Poor Business Performance' article.

"I'd think that one EIP identified measurement that could enhance a mean-monthly-reported value for EBITDA, through the execution of an IEE improvement project, would be Harris's market share of total hospital revenue generated for its region-of-service.

"To improve this market-share metric, a created process-improvement team would surely give focus to enhancing Harris's marketing process of the services that the hospital currently offers. The desire from this effort would be to make Harris Hospital the location of choice for ED visits, in-patient surgeries, and other services. It'd seem that this project would give focus on making Harris's offerings more attractive than those of other hospitals in the region for referring physicians, ambulance drivers, and individuals for both elective and non-elective medical hospital procedures.

"Statistical evidence for a process metric's enhancement occurs when a 30,000-foot-level individuals chart for the hospital's market share has a staged-shift to a better-performance value during the same period as the project's process improvement implementation. The 30,000-foot-level accompanying probability plot can provide an estimate for a new, enhanced market-share response estimate.

"Rather than focusing on the creation of explanations for individual percentages over budget goals, which can change over time, an IEE financial reporting gives focus to undertaking the improvement of processes that enhance the mean satellite-level report's value for EBITDA."

Ron then stopped himself and said, "Perhaps I'm getting ahead of myself. Let's step back and examine the monthly EBITA satellite-level report that I created from the last five years of Harris data given to me" (See Figure 4.1).

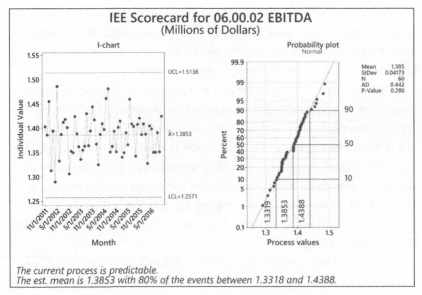

Figure 4.1: IEE Satellite-level EBITDA Report

Ron then stated, "The individuals chart on the left side of this two-chart EBITDA satellite-level reporting provides a statistical assessment which indicates that this hospital performance measurement has been stable for the past five years. This time-series monthly financial-metric tracking offers evidence that the measurement-response variation for EBITDA over the past five years originates from common-cause-variation of the system's processes.

"The normal-probability-plot on the right side of this report provides a methodology for determining a statistical-best-estimate expectation for month-to-month EBITDA unless something were to change. The statement below the report's charting provides a futuristic estimate for mean-monthly EBITDA to be 1.38 million dollars with an expectation that 80% of monthly EBITDA values will be between 1.33 and 1.44 million dollars.

"Your current methodology for reporting Harris's financials leads to people making statements for the up-and-down movements of these common-cause monthly measurement values. These proclamations may be valid or not, but offer little, if any, worth in the encouragement of what to do differently to improve future performance from this stable process.

"This satellite-level report provides supporting evidence that Harris is not experiencing the amount of over-time financial improvements that you might think is occurring. This report indicates that the mean monthly value for EBITDA from this hospital's satellite-level individuals chart has not shown any statistical increase in the past five years.

"I'd think that the compilation of all these monthly reports, with all the investigation that must occur to create the metric-change causal statements, must take a substantial amount of time. To reiterate, from my vantage point, I'm having difficulty visualizing, in general, specific actions that are beneficial to the organization as a whole coming from your current form of performance-measurement reporting.

"Also, do you see how this form of reports is not any different from the red-yellow-green scorecard report that's discussed in the 'Positive Metrics Poor Business Performance' article, including all the associated issues with these scorecards?"

Janice's eyes widened and then remarked, "I see the similarities between Harris's performance measure reports and the previously discussed red-yellow-green scorecard example, with all its issues. Ron, you're correct in speculating that the effort expended to create our 60-plus page monthly financial report is enormous. One department in Harris spends a considerable amount of time and resources compiling all this information, including investigations for the up-and-down measurement change causal statements.

"This Satellite-level report presents a very different and scary picture of what's truly happening to the financial results at Harris. I'm confident that the Harris leadership team won't like this chart. This report indicates that we've not made any EBITDA improvements at Harris for the last five years. I, with my leadership team, have been conveying to our board of directors that Harris has made many improvements; however, this chart indicates that we've not been successful in increasing the hospital's EBITDA measurement. Presentation of this chart's information to Harris's board of directors could negatively reflect on both my hospital's leadership team and me."

Ron responded by saying, "Harris's leadership received point-in-time goals from the owners of the hospital. This management goal-setting approach is a common practice across all industries. This meet-the-numbers, goal-setting approach is an attempt to manage the Ys of an organization in the relationship $Y=f(X)$, which has the fundamental issues highlighted in our earlier red-yellow-green scorecards and table-of-numbers reporting discussion.

Ron continued, "I need to highlight that what's occurring at Harris relative to this Satellite-level chart doesn't convey that there were no improvements at Harris. During the previous five-year time frame, I'm sure that many external-hospital events occurred, both positive and negative, where some of these occurrences could have impacted EBITDA one way or another. For example, it appears that Harris made a favorable adjustment when a competitor moved into town a couple of years ago, and there was also an economic slowdown. For this time frame, the EBITDA satellite-level reported metric did not go south, which is a good thing.

Janice then stated that the bonuses for leadership, including hers, could take a significant hit if the board of directors and the company that owns Harris started using an IEE satellite-level chart for bonus-payment compensations. Janice continued, "The basis for current bonus payments are enhancing EBITDA, which this chart indicates did not occur."

Ron's replied, "I'm glad that you brought up this valid point. The truth is that there have been no statistically demonstrated improvements to EBITDA in five years. You and others in the organization might not like to hear this, but the current policy at Harris can lead to playing games with the numbers to make things look better than they indeed are. The practice of organizational goal setting with financial compensation linkage is common-place throughout many businesses; however, this policy can provide more fuel to the fire relative to this unfavorable numbers-game-playing issue.

"You and your leadership could stick your heads in the sand and not present an accurate picture of what's happening at Harris Hospital relative EBITDA and other metrics. Or, you could choose to be open kimono with Harris's board of directors and then later to the CEO and board of directors of the company that owns Harris.

"If you want to pursue implementing IEE at Harris, it's essential that there's an agreement to have up-and-down communications in the hospital's organization chart—the good, bad, and ugly. For IEE to be successful, there can be no *shoot the messenger* fear.

"The reason for me highlighting this point is that IEE gives focus to improving organizational processes that benefit the big picture's EBITDA and does not give focus to achieving a next-month goal, which is often arbitrarily set. You could propose an IEE pilot implementation at Harris, which could be leveraged, in time, to other hospitals. However, during any IEE pilot program evaluation, the current system that attempts to manage the Ys of an organization through the setting of specific next-month goals needs termination. A goal for enhancing mean monthly EBITDA is great, which receives focus in IEE's enterprise improvement plan (EIP) for an organization; however, meeting a next reporting time-period goal isn't."

Ron continued by saying, "I've thought about the probable Harris's leadership pushback relative to the potential of not receiving future bonus dollars as in the past, as discussed earlier. My suggestion is to change the current bonus-compensation policy so that efforts from the leadership team and others result in a focused effort to improve the organization's bottom-line through structured process improvement efforts that have linkage to 30,000-foot-level value-chain metrics.

"One potential policy change would be to first to determine over the last couple of years, the ratio of total bonus compensation given to the hospital's EBITDA for the same time frame. There was this distribution of this compensation-ratio-to-EBIDTA-performance even when the statistics indicate that only common-cause variation existed with Harris's EBIDTA, and there were no indications enhancements to the reported numbers.

"This same ratio of past bonus compensation to EBIDTA could then be used for future annual compensation calculations if this satellite-level metric shows no staged degradation during the year. A justification for this policy change is that leadership has been doing something to manage the business at a level of financial performance consistent with that achieved in previous years.

"An adder EBIDTA percentage compensation to this base bonus amount could be included to provide additional bonus dollars if the mean EBIDTA in a satellite-level reporting indicated that enhancement occurred. There could be a linkage for the financial kicker-amount to the magnitude of a mean-staged increase in satellite-level reported mean EBIDTA.

"Another additional bonus option possibility is the monetary gain from a staged improvement in 30,000-foot-level metrics that are part of an organization's EIP. Justification for this bonus amount increase is the occurrence of statistically significant improvement indicators to 30,000-foot-level reports, which are presumed to correlate to EBIDTA. However, no reflection of these improvements may appear in the overall mean EBIDTA because of external outside-of-Harris-control factors such as an economic recession."

Ron elaborated on what was currently happening at Harris, stating that he viewed the explanations that described all the up-and-down chart movements as stories. He said, "The creation of these stories can require much research and consume much effort, but more often than not actually provide no value in determining 'what should' or 'what should-not' be done in the future to enhance future performance. Ron then suggested that there be a redirection of the current effort that compiles these executive reports. Ron's suggestion was incorporating an IEE implementation and giving focus in leadership meetings to process improvement efforts that would enhance 30,000-foot-level metrics, which result in whole-enterprise benefit."

Janice then interjected, saying that she saw the benefit of the EBIDTA satellite-level reporting format.

Ron then responded, saying that it was great to hear that Janice understood and appreciated the benefits of the IEE satellite-level reporting methodology for financial performance metrics.

Ron proceeded by saying that IEE 30,000-foot-level performance metrics provide a means to report a predictive-performance-metric for basically all organizational functions. In Harris's October Financial

Statement Summary, there was an indication that ED visits were down by 1.9% from the budget. Ron then stated that he had created a 30,000-foot-level chart for monthly ED visits over the past five years (See Figure 4.2).

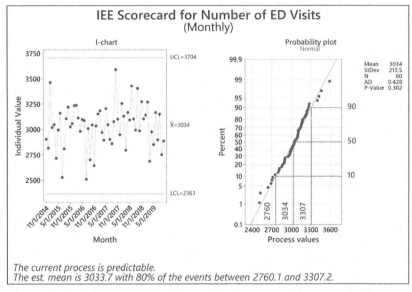

Figure 4.2: 30,000-foot-level Performance Metric Report, Harris Emergency Department Visits during Last Five Years

From this projection of Ron's computer screen, he commented that the individuals chart on the left of this two-chart pair indicates stability for this metric. That is, the individuals chart did not detect any statistical change in the number of monthly emergency department visits over this reporting time frame.

The probability plot on the right side of this two-chart pair provides a graphic description for the number of monthly Harris ED visits that had occurred since the latest region of stability, which in this case was five years. The statement below the report's charting provides a summary of the results from the probability plot, which is that the expected mean number of monthly ED visits was about 3034, with an expected monthly 80%, or four out of five months, variation between 2760 and 3307 ED visits.

Ron continued, "Since the individuals chart indicates stability, the statement below the report's charting is predictive. There's the expectation that these approximate mean and frequency of monthly occurrence reported values would occur down-the-road unless something were to change in Harris's processes, or there was an external event that impacted this hospital metric.

"An example of a within-Harris positive impact to this 30,000-foot-level individuals chart metric could be a process change in the hospital's marketing so that more people who are seeking urgent care select Harris Hospital over other emergency-care facilities in the area. An example of an external-Harris occurrence that could impact this 30,000-foot-level metric negatively is the emergence of more competitors in the region that provide ED offerings."

As he reminisced, Jorge thought about a few of Janice's comments and discussions during the meeting that were most memorable to him:

- "Linking IEE high-level reported process-output scorecards to the process that created them through an IEE value chain makes so much sense. If a current process response has been consistent over time, and its improvement is vital to the business, the organization needs to expend targeted effort for improving the metric's associated process!"
- "Using Enterprise Performance Reporting System (EPRS) software (Reference Appendix B, Web page 14) to provide automatic updating of IEE reported metrics would be invaluable. It'd be priceless to have up-to-date performance metrics and process information in the IEE value chain available to all authorized participants through a simple *click of the mouse.*"
- "EPRS software provides a vehicle for documenting *tribal knowledge* methodologies so that these procedures are readily viewable by everyone and can be improved.
- "Referring to the IEE value chain in monthly leadership and other meetings will reduce the need to spend a lot of time and

resources to create special leadership-monthly-reports. Another benefit of this form of reporting is that there would be transparency. There would be an elimination of any shoot the messenger fear that has filtered bad-news information flow up the chain of command. An IEE system should help us transition to *we're in this together* thinking, which is what I really would like to move toward in our organizational culture."

- "The overall thought process of the 9-step IEE system provides a robust business management framework. Having whole enterprise analytics leading to SMART satellite-level financial goals, then target strategies followed by high-potential 30,000-foot-level performance metrics in areas that need improvement makes so much sense. Giving enhancement focus to specific high-level business metrics that are beneficial to the business as a whole provides an excellent methodology. The IEE system offering is much better than a global statement or a hodgepodge listing of metrics that are to be improved by say 5% this year, as conveyed in a table of numbers posting."

- "I liked how an enterprise improvement plan (EIP) provides a targeted focus on which IEE value chain metrics to improve so that there will be a whole-business benefit. I also thought it was great that as part of this effort, these IEE 30,000-foot-level performance metrics will have an owner who's pushing for the execution of process-improvement activities to enhance their metrics."

- "It's so powerful that a 30,000-foot-level metric chart can show and provide a quantification of the enhancement amount accomplished through process improvement efforts. This methodology offers a vehicle to transition from anecdotal process improvement statements to statistical reporting."

- "The IEE system can provide a how-to approach for implementing the management philosophies of Deming, Crosby, Senge, and others, with quantifiable benefits."

- "Using the IEE system, more productive meetings can now be conducted at the leadership and other levels, where there can be remote access from people working at home or throughout the world, either in real-time or as a recording."

- "Previously, our process improvement projects took forever to complete, if completed at all. With the IEE system, where 30,000-foot-level metric improvement needs *pull* for a project's creation, and there's an owner of the metric, the execution of improvement projects should be much quicker."
- "I did not think it was possible, but I now see how IEE addresses all five of the *Effective Management Attributes* listed on page two of the 'Positive Metrics Poor Business Performance' article."

Janice also commented that she had never seen anything like IEE in her MBA training. MBA students and their current or future organizations, according to her, would benefit a great deal if they were taught and then applied IEE techniques in their future employment.

The next words out of Janice's mouth were: "I'm sold! I'll need to get the okay to conduct a Harris IEE implementation pilot from the hospital's board of directors and the CEO of the company that owns Harris.

"I don't think that this request should be a problem since everyone realizes that there's a need to do things differently to improve Harris Hospital's bottom-line. Ron, what needs to happen next from your end?"

Ron responded, saying that it was great to see that Janice wanted to move forward. Ron also suggested setting up a similar one-on-one conversation c and CEO of the company that owns Harris.

Ron continued by saying, "One more thing is required. This essential element is that Janice, as Harris CEO, agrees to follow the IEE system personally. There cannot be a delegation of IEE's examination of scorecards and process improvement efforts. Also, Janice, as the CEO, you need to agree not only to ask but require, the execution of IEE details from subordinates. I'll assist in how to accomplish this IEE organizational usage and, over-time, buy-in to the concepts throughout your hospital."

Janice gave a thumbs-up gesture with an affirmative response.

An additional requirement, which Janice also agreed to, was that she would solicit the support for an IEE implementation from her leadership team in our-next step meeting in which both Ron and I would participate.

Ron made the point that everything needs to occur quickly. This IEE implementation requires the highest-priority status.

Janice agreed, stating that she would work out the details with Ron on having similar conference calls with the chairman of Harris's board of directors and the CEO of the company that owns Harris. She added the statement, "I want to follow the proverb 'It's better to ask forgiveness than permission' and proceed immediately."

Janice then stated, "Okay, Ron. I'll set up a leadership team meeting next week, where you will introduce IEE to the leadership team."

Ron then said, "Before that meeting, there needs to be a video conference call with you and your IT team. I'd like for this to happen tomorrow to discuss the installation of EPRS software on a dedicated server during the next two days. This installation will allow the server to be accessed remotely by you and your team" (Reference Appendix B, Web page 14).

Janice agreed to set up the IT meeting and to also participate in the discussion conveying to IT that this IEE software installation and other associate implementation details were their number one priority.

Then Ron said that he would need a Harris IEE implementation coordinator for whom the IEE implementation work would be his or her number one priority. He then asked whether I would be this person. Janice agreed by saying, "Yes, Jorge will be the coordinator. His current responsibilities will be reassigned to someone else as soon as possible so that he'll be able to provide the needed IEE implementation focus for success."

Ron continued by noting that he would not be working with Harris to *give fish*, but instead to *teach how to fish*. Because of this, there would need to be some *immediately available on-call* and dedicated resources. For the deployment, the immediately available on-call resources would be IT to resolve any technical server-access and EPRS software installation issues. Another immediately available on-call person was a wizard who could access numbers from Harris databases and put the information on an IEE dedicated server in a format that could be used by the EPRS software to create 30,000-foot-level reports.

The dedicated individuals needed for the IEE implementation would be the people with whom Ron would be working to create the IEE system framework in Harris, which the hospital would continually refine over time. Ron wanted four to six people assigned to this role; however, he stated that there could be more or fewer. He said that it was essential to get people most suited for this role since these people would be an integral part of the backbone to create a successful IEE deployment.

At the end of our meeting the following week, Ron said that he would ask the leadership team to select candidates for this IEE implementation team. Ron added that he would highlight that this IEE implementation team would be doing much more than the execution of process improvement projects.

Ron indicated that there would be a discussion about the characteristics of an ideal candidate in the leadership meeting; however, Ron wanted Janice to sleep on this list of attributes so she could form her opinion about who should be selected.

Ron pointed out that it was a good bet that there would be pushback on the personnel Janice thought were the best fit for the role since these best-fit people would surely be said to be unavailable for various reasons. Janice, as CEO, must take the position to overcome all hindrances so that the chosen people were the best to fulfill the characteristics of a successful IEE implementation specialist team member.

Ron then projected a web page that listed the characteristics of a successful IEE implementation team member, which included becoming an IEE Master Black Belt (IEE MBB) or IEE Black Belt (IEE BB) (See Figure 4.3).

- *Fire in the belly:* They have an unquenchable desire to improve the way an organization does its business.
- *Soft skills:* They have the ability to work effectively with people in teams and other organizations.
- *Project management:* They have the ability to get things done well and on time.
- *System thinker:* They have an appreciation that work is accomplished through processes and that true long-lasting results are made through systematic improvements to these processes.
- *Multi-tasking:* They have no problem managing and scheduling several activities in the same time frame.
- *Unstructured environment management:* They have the ability to work in chaotic environments and create systems within these situations.
- *Big picture thinker:* They focus on aligning their efforts to impact the big picture. They avoid analysis paralysis.
- *Analytical skills:* They have correct and valid reasoning skills and are comfortable using mathematic techniques such as algebra.
- *Organizational navigation skills:* They can work around barriers without invoking higher authority.
- *Critical thinking skills:* They are skillful at conceptualizing, applying, analyzing, synthesizing, and evaluating information from multiple sources.

Figure 4.3: Characteristics of Successful IEE Master Black Belts and IEE Black Belts (Reference Appendix B, Web page 15)

After displaying this table of characteristics, Ron continued explaining the roles for those on the IEE implementation team. Ron said that the kick-off plan for Harris's IEE implementation team was that one person would become an IEE Master Black Belt, while others on the team would become IEE Black Belts. The identified IEE MBB in training would need to fulfill a Harris leadership role for the team and would become an expert in all aspects of implementing the 9-step IEE system. Others on this team as IEE BBs in training would focus on working with the functional business areas on implementing IEE process improvement work, so that identified EIP 30,000-foot-level metrics were enhanced. The on-the-job training for these dedicated IEE resources should take about six months before they receive their IEE Black Belt or IEE Master Black Belt certification.

This IEE belt terminology is similar to a Six Sigma; however, the methodologies that these IEE Master Black Belts and IEE Black Belts would be using, along with later-trained IEE Green Belts (IEE GBs), is different.

As Janice pondered the web page's listing of desired characteristics for IEE implementation team members, she cited all the bulleted items on the web page: fire in the belly desire to help our organization improve; soft skills when working with people; project management ability to get things done; systems thinker, can manage and schedule several activities in the same time frame; can create systems in an unstructured environment; big-picture thinker; analytical skills; organizational navigation skills; critical thinking skills.

"Wow!" Janice then said. "The listed characteristics for a successful IEE implementation team member are very tough criteria to fulfill. However, I do have some people in mind that exemplify many of these characteristics, but they're busy doing other things that are important to Harris."

Ron commented that he would have been surprised if Janice did not make this observation and statement about the availability of the people most suited for filling these positions.

Ron then stated, "In our upcoming leadership meeting, which needs to have a two-hour block of time, others will surely make a similar statement.

"You, as the CEO, need to give thought ahead of our Leadership Meeting to who you believe should fill the crucial IEE deployment team-member positions and the reassignment of the selected personnel's current responsibilities to others. You mustn't make the statement that these people are dedicated resources when, in fact, there has been no reassignment of their responsibilities, and they're not truly dedicated. These people will have much learning and doing to undertake in a brief amount of time."

Janice realized that many of the organization's high performers needed to see a path for upward mobility. And while there were only so many *seats* at the management table, by giving these top performers the kind of responsibility and visibility that an IEE deployment offers, this effort would also serve the purpose of seeing who deserved a more prominent role. It would probably also lessen the risk of attrition. This assignment would be a way to reward these up-and-comers with the CEO-level visibility they want.

In our IT conference call with Janice, there was an initial push back, as expected, by the IT department, who had initially scheduled the install for the following month. However, when Janice asked questions about how long before completing the EPRS software installation, IT realized that this installation was what Janice wanted immediately and that they would need to make it happen.

IT agreed to work with Ron to get this software up and running in two days so that the EPRS software could be used in the following week's leadership meeting to present Harris's EBITDA satellite-level metric and some 30,000-foot-level reports during the session.

In the following week's Harris leadership meeting, every VP was there either physically or through a remote internet connection. In Jorge's dream, he had a perfect recollection of what happened. All the executives physically at the meeting who sat around the long, oval-shaped mahogany table had only a vague idea of the special meeting's purpose. Everyone knew the hospital had to do something to improve its financials. That was no secret.

Jorge knew that several of those in attendance were more than a little nervous. Blame-shifting was occurring in the ranks. Some were wondering if their heads weren't getting a bit too close to the proverbial chopping block.

When everyone was seated, Janice called the meeting to order saying "People," she began. "Let's get right down to it. This hospital is in trouble—the magnitude of the problem could put us all out of a job.

"Some have made suggestions to me on how to fix things at Harris. However, I haven't seen any proposal that addresses the entirety of our issues until now. Last week Jorge suggested a conference call to discuss implementing Integrated Enterprise Excellence (IEE), or I double E for short. I had the proposed conference call with an IEE implementation facilitator.

"Because of the discussion in this conference call, I'm convinced that the implementation of IEE will help Harris address our pressing improvement needs; however, I need your support for this undertaking to be successful."

Janice made a gesture to her left, where Ron, a thin man with glasses, sat. "Ladies and gentlemen," Janice announced, "I want to introduce you to Ron Wilson, a specialist in IEE. IEE is an enhanced business management system that goes beyond Lean Six Sigma and the balanced scorecard. I want your support to implement IEE at Harris Hospital."

The eyes of all the hospital VPs swiveled to Ron. One of the VPs sighed heavily.

"I know what you're thinking," Janice went on, raising her hands in protest to the sigh. "Some of you have heard of, or have experienced, Lean Six Sigma and other process improvement techniques in the past and question their benefits for Harris, and I don't disagree.

"Because of Jorge's introduction, I've had some healthy discussion with Ron about all this. Ron has impressed me with his IEE ideas for Harris."

Jorge noticed that others in the meeting again turned their attention to the stranger in their midst. Because of Janice's introduction, they looked at Ron a little differently. Then, Jorge heard someone, at the end of the table, clear his throat. It was Bill Burman, VP of operations. Janice overheard the throat clearing, too.

Janice then asked, "Got something to say, Bill?"

"No, well, not really. It's just...haven't we gone down this road before, Janice? I mean, what about all our efforts with TQM and other methodologies. These new management initiatives come and go, and I hate to say it, but how much do they fix anything? More often than not, they just take one problem and splinter it into several new problems. Reminds me of that scene in *Fantasia*—you know, with the brooms?"

Bill's comment got a smile from a few people at the table. Some of them were nodding their heads, too. Penny Wilkinson, VP of finance, took up where Bill left off.

"He's right," Penny moaned. "Let's face it. When these things do come along, whom do we put in charge of them? If we're honest, it's the people that we can do without—the most dispensable people in our departments. Am I right?"

There were several more head nods around the room. That was one thing Jorge thought Harris Hospital had going for it—the execs were all about as honest and straightforward as they could be with one another.

"I hear you," Janice said, with not the slightest bit of defensiveness in her tone, "but I'm telling you, this one is different."

There were several more light-hearted moans around the room. They'd all heard *that* before, too.

Janice protested, "Everything you've just brought up is true, but IEE has an answer to it all. I'm telling you, and I don't want to sway your opinion on this one, but I'm excited about this in a way that I haven't been in a long time."

The excitement communicated by their CEO seemed to alleviate some of the VP's skepticism as they turned their attention back to Ron.

Jorge had had several phone conference calls with Ron over the preceding few weeks; however, this was the first time he had seen Ron in a meeting presentation role. The man looked to be in his mid-to-late forties. Maybe it was the shrewdness and self-control in Ron's demeanor. But, the way Ron let Janice introduce him and debate the effectiveness of *another management initiative* with the executive board without appearing the slightest bit ruffled or getting defensive over IEE when it came under attack was significant. Ron seemed very professional. Jorge got the feeling that Ron had been through this a time or two before.

Janice then said, "I'll now turn over the meeting to Ron."

"Hi, everybody," Ron began. "First of all, I'd like to thank you for your time—I know you all have busy schedules."

Polite smiles and nods appeared around the room.

"Okay, then. Well, I think a congratulations start-off is in order. After you implement IEE at Harris hospital, each of you will become even more important than you already are, and I'm confident that your business life will be simpler and more fun. This personal benefit to you will happen while Harris's financial numbers are enhanced."

Jorge noted how Ron's final statement got the attention of everyone in the room.

Ron then said, "Let's get started."

Ron again walked through the IEE one-minute video and "Positive Metrics Poor Business Performance" article, similar to what he had done earlier, first with me and then with Janice.

During the video and article-figure presentation, Janice shared her thoughts. She commented that she would now be looking at performance metrics differently and would be requiring the utilization of IEE metric reporting and other aspects of the business system throughout Harris's enterprise.

Ron deviated from his earlier presentations to Janice and me. What he did differently was:

1. Ron assigned small teams to document on a flip chart what items, if any, of the five *Effective Management Attributes* on page 2 of the "Positive Metrics Poor Business Performance" article they thought were prevalent in Harris. One person from each team then presented their flip chart statements. Those remotely connected to the meeting participated as one group, and they also shared their thoughts. The leadership interaction from this exercise was perfect! The leadership team's consensus was that Harris had issues with all five of the listed Effective Management Attributes.

2. After a general IEE value chain discussion, Ron accessed a dedicated Harris server on his computer. He projected a live IEE value chain on the conference room's screen, using EPRS software. Ron highlighted that the software for this IEE value chain resided on a Harris server that was behind its firewall, where there would be a later inclusion of the hospital's processes

and metrics, which would receive automatic updates. Everyone authorized in Harris would have access to the organization's IEE value chain and more.

3. Ron then *clicked* on the 'Report financials' link, which showed a recent leadership report with an IEE satellite-level reporting, like the one Ron had presented earlier in the meeting with Janice. However, this time, the satellite-level metric was part of Harris's IEE value chain. To say that the leadership team was impressed with the creation of a first-pass IEE organizational *live* value chain, which had automatic updates, in only one week is an understatement!

4. Ron then fielded questions about IEE satellite-level reporting so that everyone understood the report's methodology. He then had the small teams document on a flip chart what additional insight the IEE satellite-level report provided over Harris's traditional reporting. One person from each group presented its flip chart statements. Those connected remotely through the Internet also shared their thoughts. The dialog from these reports was excellent. I was feeling the lights turning on relative to IEE and its benefits. The IEE business management system was not going to be a flavor-of-the-month program at Harris but something long-lasting.

5. Ron next stated that there needed to be agreement on whom to consider for IEE's Implementation dedicated resources and on-demand support.

There was much discussion about the selection of IEE implementation team members who had characteristics consistent with the 'Characteristics of Successful IEE Master Black Belts and the IEE Black Belts' list previously presented to Janice.

Janice shared with the leadership team, the personnel who she thought should fulfill these critical positions. As anticipated, there was much pushback by the VPs for freeing up those individuals who were working on essential business projects but considered by Janice to be the best fit to fulfill the list of desired characteristics for IEE implementation team members.

Janice pointed out that many of the hospital's high performers considered that there was a lack of paths for upward mobility in Harris. Assignments driving IEE would give these people a more in-depth understanding of the operations of the hospital and provide them with visibility at the top levels of the company.

After much discussion, there was consensus about the people thought to be the best match for the positions. There was also agreement who would be the focus IT person for addressing any software issues. A database wizard was also agreed upon who could access Harris's database numbers and put data into an acceptable format for EPRS software to create 30,000-foot-level and satellite-level performance metric reports for Harris's IEE value chain.

Janice told her leadership team that she was reassigning Jorge's past duties so that he could become the full-time IEE implementation coordinator.

Ron then said, "We're making great progress! Let's talk more about the IEE implementation specialist selection process. Each candidate must personally want to pursue this new role, which will be a life-changing event for them. If any candidate isn't interested, then we'll need to move on to someone else who does have an interest."

Ron also stated that he needed to be involved in the interviewing process. Ron could answer any interviewee's questions and would be a fresh set of eyes in the decision-making process of whether the proposed candidate should be a good fit for the position or not.

Jorge could not believe how the participants had experienced a 180-degree turn from their initial apprehension to showing excitement. Jorge could not think of ever experiencing such a change in people's opinions in such a short period. He supposed that Ron's approach for having the leadership team gain a first-hand understanding of IEE through break-out sessions was a real plus. Also, the use of Harris's actual financial reporting data was super.

The team's eyes opened wide when they saw Ron demonstrate how the IEE approach to metrics reporting provided so much more than our current reporting methodology. Plus, there would be an automatic metric updating system for both financial and operational metrics in Harris's IEE value chain. This use of real numbers from Harris to demonstrate IEE could have been the final clincher for the leadership team's thought-change transition.

Ron proceeded to say, "Let's now talk about the next steps. Harris's IEE implementation must have top priority. Everything needs to done expediently. If there's not expediency in the deployment of IEE, there's a tendency for things to drag on, and interest will be lost.

"Now I'm going to discuss the basic plan that I've put together for the next six months. Some minor tweaks are acceptable relative to dates and times for the deployment, but we need to keep on this basic aggressive schedule. I want to highlight that all these activities can occur using both a physical meeting and a remote-access connection format.

WEEK 1

"In the next two days, we need to interview all of our IEE implementation team member candidates. This interview process, either face-to-face or through a remote internet connection, will focus on what we discussed as the essential characteristics for people to have in this position.

"After the finalization of our selection process, I'll facilitate a meeting with Jorge and all selected IEE implementation specialist team members. In this meeting, I'll provide a high-level view of IEE and its benefits to the IEE implementation specialist team candidates. We'll be going through the IEE one-minute video and 'Positive Metrics Poor Business Performance' article, as I did with you.

"Next, during this IEE implementation team meeting and other sessions, we'll create a first pass at the functions and metrics for Harris's IEE value chain.

"Both the IEE implementation team selections and this first pass at IEE value chain information will be completed in time for our next IEE leadership team meeting a week from today. Our IEE implementation team will also participate in this session and future IEE discussion meetings.

"A deputy directors' and managers' IEE awareness meeting will also be conducted, which will be similar to the leadership team presentation that you just saw.

WEEK 2

"During our next leadership meeting, we'll polish what the IEE implementation team did relative to the initiation of the IEE value chain's functions and some of their metrics. For this two-hour face-to-face and remote-connection meeting, I want to include deputy directors and managers.

"Also, the leadership team will identify some metrics that they think are most important to the business and will want to see initially reported in a satellite-level or 30,000-foot-level format.

"After this leadership team meeting, I'll conduct some hands-on IEE implementation Team training on how to create satellite-level and 30,000-foot-level metrics and then put these metrics into Harris's IEE value chain. Also, there'll be an update to Harris's IEE value chain to include all agreed-to functions and their measurements.

"Some of these IEE value chain metrics will just have names; however, other performance metrics that you want to see initially in a report will receive automatic updates for a satellite-level or 30,000-foot-level performance metric reporting format.

"During this week, our IEE implementation team will work with the chosen IT coordinator to establish IEE value chain authorization for all leadership personnel, deputy directors, and managers. After completing this authorization, the leadership team and others will be able to access the Enterprise Performance Reporting System's IEE value chain and other functions 24x7 at any place in the world where remote access to Harris's IEE server is available.

WEEK 3

"Our next meeting will need to be a four-hour session. In this time together, you all will need to bring your notebook computers. This meeting will be a hands-on training event where you'll be *clicking* through live Harris IEE value chain functions and metrics, both as an individual and in teams. As before, this meeting will include people connected remotely.

"We'll discuss the 9-step IEE system and take the first pass at the creation of items for a Harris enterprise improvement plan (EIP). In time, an EIP creation will have the benefit of step 3 in the 9-step roadmap, which is 'Analyze enterprise.' However, I suspect that you have some general awareness of which 30,000-foot-level reported metrics that need improvement so that there would be enterprise as a whole benefit. One needs to consider how this IEE metric-enhancement approach for process improvement is in contrast to common-place strategic efforts that were to improve operational processes with no specific associated measurement enhancement statements. Process improvement efforts without an accompanying targeted metric enhancement objective typically lead to end-of-project anecdotal claims with no metric enhancement demonstration like a 30,000-foot-level reporting offers.

"I'll ask for three 30,000-foot-level metrics considered to be good candidates for process improvement efforts.

"We'll also discuss what current operational procedures you'd like to initially include in your IEE value chain and the names of additional people to provide authorized access to Harris's IEE value chain.

WEEK 4

"During our next one-hour meeting, you'll be shown the IEE value chain updates and other software reports from the week's activities,

"Your IEE implementation team will work during this week-long time frame at refining your IEE value chain, with the inclusion of your first-pass EIP and the functional procedures that you desire to include initially. Also, there'll be an inclusion of the three provided 30,000-foot-level metrics to improve through a listing of process-improvement projects in the EPRS software. With this listing of projects, everyone will be able to see the status of these projects and their metric improvement efforts at any point in time.

"During this week, it'll be determined which IEE Black Belt trainee will be working on each identified 30,000-foot-level improvement project metric to enhance. Also, these IEE implementation team members will begin their training in how to execute IEE improvement projects efficiently and effectively. The IEE implementation team specialists will start the execution of the improvement projects. The IEE improvement project reporting function will be initiated and used in the EPRS software.

"IEE awareness training will start with the identified functions in your IEE value chain by first initiating a general IEE awareness session for the functional leaders in your organization and then individual department training.

"I'll work with the IEE implementation team on how to conduct this training over time. Included in this training will be the solicitation of functional metrics that those involved in operations think are valuable to include and the documentation of current processes where this information is electronically stored. This training will also cover how team members should utilize and benefit from Harris's IEE value chain metric reporting and documented processes.

WEEK 5

"There will be a discussion about Harris's current process for regular leadership meetings and what to do differently to improve reporting so that there's consistency with IEE thinking. There will also be a dialog about how to conduct productive process-improvement-project status meetings.

NEXT SIX MONTHS

"The IEE implementation team will facilitate the refinement of Harris's IEE value chain reporting and its utilization by leadership and operational personnel. The IEE implementation team will also be executing projects that are to improve 30,000-foot-level metrics over time. The IEE implementation team, with my assistance, will train Harris employees and some suppliers in the understanding and use of IEE tools and techniques.

"After six months from an initial IEE kickoff, Harris's leadership team should again meet to discuss what has occurred since the start of IEE, with the inclusion of any lessons learned. There'll also be a discussion of what Harris did with its IEE implementation and the potential leveraging of this IEE effort to other hospitals that are a part of the conglomerate company that owns Harris Hospital. This discussion should also consider the inclusion of suppliers in an expansion of Harris's IEE's value chain.

Penny Wilkinson, VP of finance, then spoke up. "Wow! Is all this possible in six months?"

Ron responded, "Yes, but there's a big *if.* There must be a steadfast commitment to implement the IEE system in Harris, including the selection of the best people to be members of the IEE implementation team and these people being a truly dedicated resource for this undertaking."

Janice followed up by stating, "Yes, my intention and focus are that Harris will implement IEE per Ron's described basic plan. I want to work with Ron to improve my understanding of IEE details, including how to view IEE's system for performance metric reporting. Will this work for you, Ron?"

Ron's response was, "Of course, Janice. An invitation goes out to everyone that I'm available for discussion of any IEE detail, concerns, or other issues."

5 ROLL OUT

A long, steady tone from the pulse monitor sounded in Sandra's room. Jorge bolted upright in his chair, his mind fuzzy from lack of sleep. A spasm caught hold of his back, the result of trying to sleep in such a cramped position in the uncomfortable hospital chair. At Harris, they had small cots so that family members could stay with a loved one in the hospital for an extended period with a little more comfort and dignity in an otherwise trying situation. Because of this change, customer satisfaction went way up. People wrote letters, thanking them: All a direct result of reacting to Voice of the Customer (VOC) feedback.

But these thoughts were far back in his consciousness and fading quickly, mere remnants of the waking IEE dream he'd been in only moments before. He stood stiffly, slightly bent, as Flo rushed into the room, but before she could even make it to Sandra's bedside, the long, unceasing tone of the heart monitor blipped back into a normal rhythm. Jorge's own heart began beating again, too.

"What happened?" Jorge asked Flo as he took his wife's hand and held it, "Is she all right?"

Flo was unperturbed as she examined the readouts of Sandra's different monitors.

"Seems fine now, honey," Flo assured him. "That happens sometimes. Some people have an irregular heartbeat once in a while, and this heart irregularity sets off the machines."

"Are you sure that's what it was?"

"Well, all her readings are now stable and normal. Just to be sure, though, we'll have the doctor come in and check on her when he does his rounds, which shouldn't be long now. What about you—you all right, sugar?"

Jorge nodded, stroked his wife's hand, face filled with worry and relief.

"Can I get you anything?"

"Um…No…" then, gripped by a muscle spasm in his back, he added, "actually, you don't happen to have a cot on hand, do you?"

"A cot? No, we don't, but that sure would be handy around here. That's a pretty good idea."

"Thanks," Jorge said wryly, rubbing his back with one hand.

Flo misconstrued his tone and looked hurt. "I can get you a blanket and pillow," she offered.

"That'd be nice, thank you," Jorge answered her with a warm smile to make amends. He hadn't meant to take his frustrations out on her—having her as a nurse was the best thing he and Sandra had going so far at City Hospital!

A few moments later, Flo came back with a blanket and pillow for Jorge, and he apologized once more to her. He then set himself up again in the hospital chair right next to Sandra's bed. Soon, he began to get sleepy, lulled by the now steady and reassuring rhythm of his wife's heart monitor.

However, even with the blanket and pillow, the chair was still uncomfortable. To make things worse, Jorge was now afraid to let go of Sandra's hand as he tried to get back to sleep. He lay there, one hand under his cheek, the other draped across Sandra's bed. He dreaded the muscle spasms in his back that were sure to seize him the next time he tried to stand up.

"Darn chair," he grumbled to himself, "Got a cot?" "No, but what a good idea!" "Glad I could help you out…hmph."

Uncomfortable as he was, however, he still managed to fall asleep. When he slept, he dreamed again of the IEE implementation at Harris Hospital. It was natural that he would, considering how quality systems, or the lack thereof, had suddenly become very important to him—maybe more important than they had ever been.

Slowly, he drifted back to the never-never land of IEE, his dream picking up when he recalled how Ron's IEE implementation plan had progressed well relative to his initially presented proposal in Harris's Leadership Meeting.

Jorge recollected how Janice called a few series of larger meetings according to Ron's schedule.

The next leadership meeting, after its IEE kick-off session, was now being expanded to others at Harris. This expansion provided both organizational transparency and valuable input for the creation of Harris's IEE value chain. This meeting included Janice, all the VPs, deputy directors, managers, and newly-selected IEE Black Belt candidates. Ron Wilson was there, too. Part of Ron's job was to help Janice and the execs not only to deploy IEE but also to create an organic IEE buy-in throughout the company over time. Many of these meetings and discussions were connected remotely, which was great.

Ron conveyed that those attending this meeting could tell others that Harris was deploying IEE. When informing others about this IEE implementation, an accompanying message should communicate that there would be a general meeting in a few weeks, which would provide more specifics. The particulars included in this meeting would be a refined Harris IEE value chain, and more.

The second expanded IEE information and high-level educational meeting occurred on a Wednesday. This meeting took place in Harris's conference room, referred to as *The Big Room*, where all staff-wide meetings happened. Everyone who was at the previous meeting was there, but also present were several high-performing staff members from nursing, laboratory, x-ray, patient financial management, the emergency department, the operating room, and materials management. Ron was also there, but this time he wasn't the one doing the talking.

It was Janice who got up behind the podium first, "Thank you all for coming or connecting remotely," Janice said into the microphone.

The room quieted down.

"I know there's been a lot of talk in the halls this past couple of weeks, and I'm sorry to have kept you all waiting so long, but we needed to dot some i's and cross some t's. So, the big news is that Harris Hospital is going to implement an Integrated Enterprise Excellence or IEE business management system. Here to explain any questions you might have about IEE, and our IEE deployment is Ron Wilson."

Jorge watched as Ron took the podium, and the rank and file of the staff shifted uncomfortably. Sensing the nature of their discomfort, Ron went into his IEE apologetics, letting them all know that their jobs were safe, but that their roles within the company might be changing.

Ron conducted this meeting differently from previous meetings in that he did not show the IEE one-minute video or talk through the "Positive Metrics Poor Business Performance" article. The reason for this, as Ron explained to me later, was that the new audience in the room probably was not interested or could not relate to an IEE high-level view with its benefits.

In the meeting, Ron immediately used his computer to display on the conference-room screen Harris's IEE value chain, which included all the information that the IEE implementation team had recently added. Ron then asked three people what they did at the hospital and showed them how he could drill-down to their specific IEE value chain functions. He then explained that the IEE implementation team would be working with Harris's functional areas in upcoming weeks to refine or add any metrics that need inclusion in the IEE value chain, along with documented processes that personnel currently were following.

Ron made the statement that IT had given all participants in the room access to this Harris's IEE value chain, which they could view anytime that they wished. Ron then showed them how to access the appropriate Harris server and how to personally sign-in.

Ron then *clicked* to a couple of IEE value chain 30,000-foot-level metrics that the IEE implementation team recently created. He explained the interpretation of outputs from this IEE high-level charting methodology for various types of input data.

With the described 30,000-foot-level metrics reporting approach, there was some initial confusion; however, after answering several questions, Jorge could see light bulbs going on in people's heads. Attendees began understanding the difference between common- and special-cause variation and appreciate how if a statement below the report's charting is stable but not desirable, a process needs enhancement.

There was one particular chart in Ron's 30,000-foot-level performance metric discussion that piqued the attention of everyone in the room. Ron made the statement that a 10% improvement in the output of this performance reported metric occurred five months ago. Jorge indicated that he did not know what happened, but felt confident that something happened during this time frame.

The group that was responsible for this function stated, in amazement, that yes, they had changed a procedure that they thought made things better but did not know how to make an improvement claim, with quantification.

Jorge then drifted off, thinking about what else had happened in Harris's six-month IEE implementation initiation, after the deployment's initial meetings. He recalled how he had been amazed that even though the IEE implementation was aggressive, its execution progressed basically without any major hitch.

He recalled many comments that Harris's employees and Ron had made during the IEE six-month deployment initiation. Numerous observations were from past-employer experiences or self-reflections on how Harris's implementation of IEE had addressed the issues. Jorge's mind went non-linear, revisiting some of the outstanding shared remarks.

JORGE'S FIRST RECOLLECTION

About three weeks after our IEE Deployment initiation, Ron divided those attending a leadership meeting into discussion groups. Each group, whether physically at the meeting or remotely connected, was to provide their thoughts about business goal setting.

The consensus response to Ron's question from the teams was to set time frame goals for every organizational department with some form of bonus incentive to ensure that each department would meet their goals.

Ron then asked, "Do you think that this goal-setting approach will lead to the best behaviors?"

Janice spoke up, saying, "Ron, what the teams described is very similar to what we're now doing at Harris, and it's not working."

Ron's response to Janice was, "Why is that?"

Janice responded, "Now that I think about it, what we're suggesting is management to the Ys, which is what you showed us is *not* the best thing to do."

Ron followed up by saying, "I'd venture to say that more than 90% of organizations presented the question that I asked of these breakout teams would give a similar response. Janice, would you like to hear my thoughts about this?"

Janice responded, "I'm all ears!"

"Leadership needs to *take to heart* that goals are useful for setting the direction. Systems are great for actually making progress. The primary benefit of having a goal is that it tells you what sort of system you need to put in place. However, the system itself provides the means for achieving results. For businesses, IEE, with its enterprise improvement plan (EIP) and other facets, provides a structured system for both the setting and achievement of business goals."

Janice followed up by saying, "I see where you're going, Ron. What you're saying makes sense."

"Next question for the group: what are the characteristics of a good metric?"

Sue then said, "Ron, I suspect we could put something together as a response to your question; however, my bet is you'd say there's a better way. I suggest that to save time and energy, you just tell us what you think."

Everyone in the meeting immediately smiled in agreement with Sue's suggestion.

Ron then said, "Okay, here goes. In my mind:

- A *good metric* provides decision-making insight so that the most appropriate action or non-action occurs.

- A *good metric* is measurable, auditable, sustainable, and consistent.

These metrics need to provide good:

- Business alignment
- Honest assessment
- Consistency
- Repeatability & reproducibility
- Action-ability
- Time-series tracking
- Predictability
- Peer comparability.

Sue responded, "That response is a mouthful to appreciate fully. Your list is rather long. I wonder how many of our metrics fulfill your good-metric description."

Janice then said, "I don't think many, if any, do."

Ron then said, "Harris doesn't have a monopoly on this shortcoming relative to their reported organizational metrics.

"Unlike traditional organizational performance measurement reporting techniques, IEE 30,000-foot-level reporting provides the means for addressing all of these attributes for the creation of operative and reliable, *good metrics* within a business management system."

Sue then said, "You used the phrase 'appropriate action or non-action occurs' in your listing. What do you mean non-action?"

Ron responded, "Good question Sue. I've seen some organizations focus on creating measurements that they want to react to, such as how many problems did we have today and what the issues were. We do need to gain insight from metrics to determine if there is a need for immediate action.

"However, with an IEE value chain, there could be metrics reported today that are just for information and non-actionable but might be important in the future. 30,000-foot-level responses for a non-conformance rate, work in progress (WIP), and lead-time in today's operations may have a predictable, acceptable response level. Hence, at this point-in-time, non-action is appropriate for these metrics; however, a future reprioritization of EIP priorities may result if one or more of these metrics becoming actionable relative to executing process-improvement efforts. Another example of an actionable situation is a special-cause event occurring for one of these metrics, which triggered a causal investigation."

JORGE'S SECOND RECOLLECTION

During a leadership team meeting when discussing our up-to-date IEE value chain metrics, someone stated that he was still having difficulty understanding the difference between common-cause and special-cause variation.

Ron's response was, "I like to use a travel-time commute example to illustrate the different types of actions to consider for common- and special-cause process-output variation.

"For this illustration, someone has been experiencing a typical home-to-work drive time commute of 25 to 35 minutes. The source of this variation in the time to arrive at work is more often than not due to common-cause variation. Common-cause variation for this home-to-work-commute process response could originate from differences between day-of-the-week traffic, traffic-signal delay differences, and precise commute start time.

"If this commuter experienced, instead of a typical 25 to 35-minute commute, a one-hour commute for a specific day, this occurrence could be considered a special-cause event that leads to a causal investigation. Perhaps for this longer-than-normal commute, an accident or inclement weather caused an additional traveling delay. However, there should be no search for causal reasons for individual values in the 25 to 35 minutes common-cause range, since these value differences are the result of typical input noise differences in our overall commute response time.

"Consider now that the commuter wants to reduce her commute time and decides to set a goal where travel time would be no more than 32 minutes. The natural tendency for this situation would be to attempt to understand the cause for any drive commute time that is higher than 32 minutes to take corrective action. However, as previously noted, this should not be done for drive times between 25 and 35 minutes since these values should be considered *noise* to the duration in driving times.

"This commute-time goal setting and reaction to individual drive-time data points beyond a goal is not unlike what often occurs with red-yellow-green scorecards. With red-yellow-green scorecards, there can be a color transition from green to red, where nothing has happened beyond typical process-output variability expectations.

"What frequently happens in red-yellow-green scorecard reporting is the creation of goals that are within the common-cause variation response range of a process. This goal-setting-process leads to the thinking that a process improved or degraded at a color change when the process output response was not fundamentally different from the norm.

"If one wants to reduce the common-cause 25 to 35 minute's response time, the commute-from-home-to-work process needs to be improved. In an attempt to reduce commute time, consider that this driver leaves home 30 minutes earlier than in the past to see if her commute time decreases.

"With this change in the commute-to-work process, the driver noted a reduction in travel time to 18-22 minutes. For this illustration, there was a reduction in both the mean and variation in commute-time duration. This example highlights the reason for separating common-cause and special-cause variation when tracking the output of a response.

"To reiterate, the approach for enhancing a process-output metric can be quite different when addressing common-cause versus special-cause process-response variation situations. Common-cause variation improvement needs should give focus to the execution of process-improvement efforts, which, in this commute-from-home-to-work illustration, was leaving 30 minutes earlier."

JORGE'S THIRD RECOLLECTION

During one of our IEE Specialist coaching events, someone asked Ron about the use of analytics to improve the response of a process.

Ron's response was, "When a 30,000-foot-level process-output-response is stable, one should not attempt to understand and explain all the up-and-down changes from individual datum points in the stable process-output response region.

"Instead, when a stable-process-output-response is undesirable, a more productive endeavor is to execute hypotheses tests that assess theories that team members and other experts have for what process-input levels can impact the output response of the process. Data for these evaluations should be from the most recent region of stability for the process, which might be three days, three weeks, or three years, as identified in the 30,000-foot-level individuals chart or charts.

"This process understanding investigation can identify areas that need improvement. An illustration of this line of thinking is what an organization might do to address the process-output-response-duration of callers' hold time in a company's call center. For an individuals chart in a 30,000-foot-level report, the sources for common-cause input variation would probably include which call center received a call, days of the week, and time of day. For this call-center 30,000-foot-level reporting, a weekly subgrouping interval for an overall call-center-hold-time metric would seem to be most appropriate.

"Hypothesis tests offer the vehicle to statistically assess causal beliefs for the significance of process inputs thought that could affect the response. These investigations aren't unlike a murder mystery that has an uncovering of clues to determine whodunnit. This process-assessment-investigation similarity could uncover evidence that provides valuable insight into improvement opportunities for the process output response."

JORGE'S FOURTH RECOLLECTION

Someone asked Ron to explain EPRS software integration with other enterprise software packages, including working with a supplier.

Ron's response was, "Many ERP and other software packages can be very good at answering all sorts of inquiries. What-if inquiries, such as how often an event occurred when several different factor combinations were present, can be addressed using these software packages. This form of investigation isn't bad but usually doesn't provide structured insight into what we, as an organization, might do to address undesirable issues—from a process-execution point of view?

"This software may also offer scorecard reporting. However, these reports aren't typically from a high-level IEE process-output point of view, and there's usually no structural linkage of the reported metrics to the process that created them.

"Organizations gain much if they first utilize the IEE value chain with its predictive 30,000-foot-level process-output response reporting format and then apply the power of what-if software as part of the 'Analyze enterprise,' step 3 in the 9-step IEE system."

JORGE'S FIFTH RECOLLECTION

In an IEE implementation team meeting, one person asked Ron, "As an employee of three companies in the past ten years, I've been helping companies execute Lean Six Sigma projects. But each company decided to let me go when times became tough financially. Why should this gig be any different?"

Ron's response was, "Over the years, many Lean Six Sigma practitioners have been laid-off from their company or reassigned when financial times became challenging. One might wonder why this occurs when it'd seem that, when an organization's financials have challenges, efforts to improve processes by doing things better should be given even more focus. However, this isn't typically the case.

"For these situations, it's apparent that executives aren't seeing or feeling the benefits of their organization's Lean Six Sigma deployment process improvement work. An IEE implementation overcomes this situation, where a structured enterprise improvement plan (EIP) creation gives focus to improving metrics and their related processes so that the business financials, as a whole, and customers benefit.

"In an IEE deployment, leadership will see and feel the benefits of EIP process improvement efforts that benefit high-level organizational performance metrics, which are in direct alignment to the organization's overall financials. Hence, process-improvement practitioner lay-offs should not occur with an IEE deployment as they have in the past with many organizational process improvement deployments."

JORGE'S SIXTH RECOLLECTION

In a functional team meeting, a manager asked Ron about the past process improvement assistance received by her department. She said, "If I ask Joe or Sarah, both process improvement specialists, for guidance to improve a process, one person provides a Six Sigma tools approach while the other a Lean tools approach. Why does this occur?"

Ron's response was, "In all honesty, the phrase 'if all you have is a hammer, everything looks like a nail' is the way Lean and Six Sigma zealots often approach process improvement. Lean zealots often push for the use of Lean tools in kaizen events where there's a focus on reducing waste with no mention made relative to improving a process-output response. In contrast, Six Sigma zealots may push for utilization of a Six Sigma DMAIC process improvement roadmap and its tools, which are to address an improvement project's problem statement.

"With an IEE approach, the tools and methodology for improvement do not matter. Techniques to make improvements might follow the detailed IEE DMAIC roadmap. The IEE DMAIC roadmap provides a structured integration of Lean and Six Sigma tools so that there is the use of the right tool at the correct time for improving a critical 30,000-foot-level tracked metric.

"In IEE, other alternatives for improving identified EIP 30,000-foot-level metrics are also acceptable. These approaches include the plan-do-check-act (PDCA) cycle, a kaizen event, and 5S workplace organization.

"IEE's process improvement practitioners follow a similar thought process when making process improvements, which is not specific-tool based; hence, there should be more consistency between those undertaking process improvement projects."

Author Note

Over eighty additional 'IEE application stories' are provided in Appendix A.

---

6 DEPLOYMENT

Author Note

First-time readers or listeners of this book can have very different needs. For example, an executive or middle manager may initially desire only a high-level view of IEE, while a practitioner wants the details.

This chapter illustrates the details of an IEE value chain and more. I suggest first reading or listening to the content of this chapter from a high-level viewpoint. This chapter should then be revisited when the time comes for a better understanding the particulars of an IEE implementation.

Jorge woke up with the words "there should be more consistency between those undertaking process improvement projects," still echoing in his mind. He forgot where he was for a moment, then looked to the right and saw Sandra. She looked peaceful, which Jorge took as a reassuring sign. He stood up and stretched, gave her a light kiss on her bandaged cheek.

"You're going to be just fine, kid," he whispered to her.

A grumble from his stomach reminded him that he hadn't eaten since he and Sandra had had breakfast that morning—wait, scratch that, he thought, noticing the wall clock which read past 2 am—make that *yesterday* morning. For Jorge, a man who had always enjoyed a healthy appetite, going this long without a meal was rare.

He checked his cell phone to see if there was a message from Sam, but there was nothing. He became somewhat annoyed, wondering where their son could be at this hour. Of course, it was Saturday night, and Sam was a young man. He was probably out on the town somewhere, enjoying the city's nightlife, blissfully unaware of his mother's accident. No, he reasoned, if the boy hadn't called by now, he wouldn't hear from him until tomorrow morning at the earliest. So, he resigned himself to getting through the night under his own steam.

He stepped outside Sandra's room and tried to spot Nurse Barnes at the nurse's station, but didn't see her anywhere. The halls were brightly lit even though it was so late at night, which somehow unsettled Jorge—reminding him that things weren't normal.

He approached the counter and spoke with the nurse there, a middle-aged man with brown hair, "Excuse me," Jorge asked him, "Did Nurse Barnes sign off for the night? My wife is in room 1272."

"Yes sir, she's gone for the night. I'm Cliff."

"Hi, Cliff. Jorge Santos."

"Good to meet you, Jorge. I'll be taking care of Ms. Santos tonight. I looked in on you earlier, but you were sleeping, so I didn't want to wake you."

"Oh," Jorge said, suddenly feeling a little guilty for falling asleep in such a situation. "Yes, I'm not usually up so late."

"Hey, you've got to rest," the nurse replied. "Have you eaten?"

"No, actually…"

"There's a vending machine down the hall with snacks and things. Complimentary coffee, too."

"Is there a cafeteria?"

"Yes, but it doesn't open till 5 a.m."

"Oh."

"Have a cup of coffee or something. Sandra has had a quiet night since I came on; her signs are strong. I understand there was a brief episode earlier?"

"That's right. Her heart monitor went off for about five seconds. Scared me half to death."

"Well, the doctor came by while you were sleeping and…"

66

"The doctor came by?"

"Yes, we didn't want to wake you."

"But…I was hoping to have a chance to talk with him, hear what he had to say…"

"Don't worry; he said to tell you that she's recovering well. He thinks the episode earlier was nothing to worry about; people have irregular heart patterns all the time—it's just that she happened to be hooked up to a heart monitor when it happened."

What Cliff said made sense, but still, he would have liked to have been able to ask the doctor some questions. Again, he felt guilty for falling asleep.

"It's okay," Cliff offered, seeing the worried expression on Jorge's face. "The specialists will be here this morning, bright and early. They start their rounds at 5:30 am."

That was only a few hours away.

"Thanks," Jorge said, brightened somewhat by the news.

"Don't mention it," Cliff said good-naturedly. "Now, go to eat. If any doctors come by, I promise to send someone down the hall to let you know."

Jorge thanked Cliff again, checked in on Sandra, who was still sleeping peacefully and then went down the hall to find the vending machine. He hoped they had snack cakes or mini-donuts or something. That and a cup of coffee sounded pretty good right then.

He found the vending area, in a well-lit alcove off the main hallway. He peered in through the glass of the vending machine, and there they were—both snack cakes *and* mini-donuts! He poured himself a cup of coffee and then took out his money for the device. The snacks were $2.25 each, but the smallest bill he had was a 5.

"Well," he thought to himself in feigned disappointment, "Guess I better just get both of them—no sense in changing a 5 dollar bill."

He slid the 5 dollar bill into the machine and pushed the button for the snack cakes first. The spindle holding the cakes spun but didn't turn far enough, and the cakes didn't drop.

"Hey!" Jorge said aloud.

He slapped the glass a little, then nudged the machine a bit, hoping to shake the cakes loose from the spindle. They didn't budge. He stared into the vending machine glass at the cakes, defeated, as the acronym KPOV for a key process output variable sprung to mind. It didn't surprise him that a performance measurement term would be so prominent in his thoughts, considering his dream and the situation he and Sandra were in.

He chuckled a little that IEE metrics were even applicable to his experience at a vending machine. But then again, delivery of products from a device is output to a process, isn't it? Indeed, the situation fits perfectly, since KPOVs are the outputs of processes considered necessary, whether they are transactional, manufacturing, or development. These too can be tracked at the 30,000-foot-level, to separate common-cause variation from special cause events, and *pull* for the creation of a process improvement project whenever performance metric enhancements are needed.

Whether Jorge received or didn't receive his snack cakes would be an example of one of the KPOVs a vending company might have. The process that went into getting those snack cakes into the machine at the hospital didn't matter to Jorge, the customer. What mattered was that he receive his purchased snacks once he paid his money. He didn't even much mind having to buy two different products just so that he didn't have to walk around with a pocketful of change. It would have been nothing more than a comforting indulgence in a bad situation. But now, he had to pull out more money and push the snack cake button again, just to make the spindle turn another notch. Hopefully, this action would get him the snack that he had already purchased. This vending-machine interaction was just plain annoying—and expensive. Even though the snack cakes and coffee hit the spot, he doubted that he would return to that vending machine.

Of course, he reflected further as he wandered back to Sandra's room. IEE system techniques also taught that someone had to be careful about how they collected data. How samples are selected is an essential aspect of creating IEE 30,000-foot-level reports. When collecting data, the approach Jorge's team used at Harris Hospital was to select process samples so that short-term variation from the natural variability of input variables resulted in an individuals chart or charts that conveyed these fluctuations as common-cause variations.

To continue with the vending-machine scenario, Jorge imagined that a 30,000-foot-level performance metric report for a vending company might quantify the overall product-dispensing defective rate of all machines in the hospital or even in a broader region. This 30,000-foot-level report might be a daily or weekly plot of the failure rate ratio for all devices. For this type of situation, the centerline of a non-transformed, stable 30,000-foot-level individuals chart provides a process-performance estimate. This approximation is not only for past performance, but future expectations. That is, for a stable process, if 10% of the people on average had a problem in the past when attempting to get a drink from a vending machine, then Jorge would expect a similar percentage of issues in the future unless something were to change. For this 10% problem, the vending company could then determine the cost of doing nothing differently, which should include lost sales.

Collectively, the organization would then look for improvement opportunities using an IEE enterprise improvement plan (EIP) creation approach. If the vending-machine issue ranked high relative to other areas of the business, the vending company would then have reason to pursue this as an IEE performance metric improvement project. An IEE process improvement team could then look at vending machines collectively, using an IEE DMAIC project execution roadmap to determine where the most significant improvement opportunity existed.

Jorge imagined that this investigation might lead to the removal of problematic machines, modifications to the loading procedures for the devices, and/or more convenient change-making machines. He theorized that more convenient change-making tools were a possible solution since a lost sale could occur in a situation in which someone who has a $5 or $10 bill might not want to buy a $1 item and get his change back in quarters and dimes.

Jorge's thoughts floated once again to the IEE implementation at Harris Hospital's emergency department (ED). One 30,000-foot-level metric that they were reporting in their IEE ED value chain function was the patient wait time. Another 30,000-foot-level ED tracked metric was the percentage of erroneous medications. The data to create this 30,000-foot-level report were collected daily and examined over a long period-of-time within Harris's IEE value chain. The manager of the Hospital's emergency department was the person who was responsible for these department performance metrics.

An IEE sampling plan for this ED situation led to a 30,000-foot-level charting approach that considered differences between time-of-day, shifts, and day-of-the-week to be sources of *noise* to the system's metric response. Because of this conclusion, there was a weekly subgrouping for the 30,000-foot-level performance metrics. With this weekly-subgrouping approach to 30,000-foot-level tracking, any differences between time-of-day, shifts, and day-of-the-week would be considered a source of common-cause variation in the metrics' reports.

Results from causal analyses to assess the impact that current process inputs have on 30,000-foot-level metric responses gave insight into making high-impact changes to the system. From this work, both patient wait time and erroneous medication rates dropped significantly within six months.

Jorge made it back to Sandra's room with his coffee and $9.00 in snacks waving to Cliff at the nurses' station as he went by.

"All's quiet," Cliff called softly to him.

"Thanks!" Jorge said, feeling reassured as he re-entered room 1272.

He greeted Sandra with a light kiss between the bandages over her eye, then sat down in the chair next to her bed and turned on the 24-hour TV news channel. The sound came out of the little box speaker on the cord hanging from the side railing of Sandra's bed. The commentators were talking about some court case that Jorge found interesting. They had some legal experts who kept disagreeing with one another. What would the IEE system do with lawyers, he wondered? Jokingly, he answered himself that perhaps they would be labeled as an *incapable* or *unpredictable* process that needed a lot of process improvement work!

He flipped through some of the channels, grinning to himself, but nothing was on. He went back to the news where the legal experts were still bickering. His mind, bored with the proceedings, picked up his thoughts on Harris's IEE value chain satellite-level and 30,000-foot-level reporting where he had left off.

Jorge reflected how Harris's leadership reporting under Janice, Harris's current CEO, was different from our previous CEO, Simon. However, in both CEOs' reporting, there was much time spent talking about the details in the lengthy monthly report. Besides, the time and resources required to compile each of these reports were considerable. Discussion meetings about the numbers in these reports could take hours.

Jorge recollected how Harris's CEO leadership reports looked before the deployment of IEE as if he had seen it yesterday. Discussions from this reporting started with the Hospital's Financial Statement (See Figure 6.1).

FORREST W. BREYFOGLE III

| | | | | HARRIS HOSPITAL FINANCIAL STATEMENT July 2013 | | | | |
This Month	Last Year	Variance	% Var	Description	This Year	Last Year	Varinace	% Var
				Operating Revenue				
3,523,005	3,119,781	403,225	13%	Gross Patient Revenue	14,633,555	13,094,120	1,539,434	12%
1,967,962	1,634,861	333,101	20%	Deducttions from Revenue	7,664,745	7,688,813	(24,068)	0%
1,555,043	1,484,919	70,124	5%	Net Patient Revenue	6,968,809	5,405,307	1,563,502	29%
107,742	59,255	48,487	82%	Other Operating Revenue	5,146,970	147,538	4,999,431	3389%
-	-	-	0%	Indigent Care Support	-	-	-	0%
1,662,785	1,544,174	118,611	8%	Total Operating Revenue	12,115,779	5,552,846	6,562,933	118%
				Operating Expenses				
582,623	547,635	34,988	6%	Salary & Wages	2,324,234	1,303,456	1,020,778	78%
153,484	161,928	(8,444)	-5%	Employee Benefits	658,145	420,415	237,730	57%
936	1,373	(437)	-32%	Legal & Audit	32,859	6,426	26,433	411%
151,790	121,621	30,169	25%	Supplies	481,011	252,347	228,664	91%
38,801	34,937	3,864	11%	Utilities	149,934	96,994	52,940	55%
7,056	5,824	1,232	21%	Telephone	18,505	14,601	3,904	27%
462,336	317,806	144,530	45%	Purchased Services	1,928,236	866,164	1,062,072	123%
204,546	219,670	(15,124)	-7%	Physician Fees	869,934	645,733	224,201	35%
474,275	527,750	(53,475)	-10%	Other Expenses	1,930,398	1,199,680	730,718	61%
(4,416)	12,050	(16,466)	-137%	Insurance	128,816	67,646	61,170	90%
2,071,431	1,950,594	120,837	6%	Total Expenses	8,522,072	4,873,462	3,648,610	75%
(408,646)	(406,420)	(2,226)	1%	EBITDA (Loss) From Operations	3,593,707	679,384	2,914,324	429%
1,714,798	1,409,399	305,399	22%	Indigent Care Support	4,316,035	4,011,113	304,923	8%
38,750	100,959	(62,208)	-62%	340B Program	231,189	230,370	820	0%
44,209	13,195	31,014	235%	Nonoperating revenue	198,342	27,290	171,053	627%
1,389,111	1,117,133	271,978	24%	EBITDA (Loss)	8,339,274	4,948,156	3,391,119	69%

Figure 6.1: Harris Hospital Monthly Financial Statement

This Harris monthly financial statement table report lists the current month and annual monetary quantities along with last year's listed amount, including an accounting-variance and percent-of-accounting-variance calculation between these two values. Operating Revenue included in the table were gross patient revenue and deductions from revenue. Operating Expenses involved in the table were salary & wages, employee benefits, legal & audit, supplies, utilities, telephone, purchased services, physician fees, other expenses, and insurance.

There was also a similar discussion about Harris's Budget Comparison Report (See Figure 6.2).

HARRIS HOSPITAL
BUDGET COMPARISON
July 2013

This Month	Budget	Variance	% Var	Description	This Year	Budget	Varinace	% Var
				Operating Revenue				
3,523,005	2,975,375	547,630	18%	Gross Patient Revenue	14,633,555	12,488,001	2,145,553	17%
1,967,962	1,544,064	423,898	27%	Deducttions from Revenue	7,664,745	7,261,793	402,952	6%
1,555,043	1,431,311	123,732	9%	Net Patient Revenue	6,968,809	5,226,208	1,742,602	33%
107,742	55,803	51,939	93%	Other Operating Revenue	5,146,970	138,945	5,008,025	3604%
-	-	-	0%	Indigent Care Support	-	-	-	0%
1,662,785	1,487,114	175,671	12%	Total Operating Revenue	12,115,779	5,365,153	6,750,627	126%
				Operating Expenses				
582,623	560,088	22,535	4%	Salary & Wages	2,324,234	2,190,086	134,148	6%
153,484	186,390	(32,906)	-18%	Employee Benefits	658,145	795,025	(136,880)	-17%
936	1,255	(319)	-25%	Legal & Audit	32,859	9,652	23,207	240%
151,790	115,312	36,478	32%	Supplies	481,011	393,067	87,944	22%
38,801	37,506	1,295	3%	Utilities	149,934	171,067	(21,134)	-12%
7,056	5,914	1,142	19%	Telephone	18,505	24,359	(5,854)	-24%
462,336	317,791	144,545	45%	Purchased Services	1,928,236	1,422,916	505,320	36%
204,546	221,999	(17,454)	-8%	Physician Fees	869,934	1,072,094	(202,160)	-19%
474,275	529,904	(55,629)	-10%	Other Expenses	1,930,398	1,978,948	(48,550)	-2%
(4,416)	11,462	(15,878)	-139%	Insurance	128,816	105,710	23,107	22%
2,071,431	1,987,622	83,809	4%	Total Expenses	8,522,072	8,162,923	359,148	4%
(408,646)	(500,508)	91,862	-18%	EBITDA (Loss) From Operations	3,593,707	(2,797,771)	6,391,478	-228%
1,714,798	1,158,832	555,966	48%	Indigent Care Support	4,316,035	3,298,003	1,018,033	31%
38,750	77,025	(38,275)	-50%	340B Program	231,189	175,758	55,432	32%
44,209	7,214	36,996	513%	Nonoperating revenue	198,342	14,920	183,422	1229%
1,389,111	742,563	646,548	87%	EBITDA (Loss)	8,339,274	690,910	7,648,364	1107%

Figure 6.2: Harris Budget Comparisons

This Harris Budget Comparison table was similar to the Harris monthly financial statement table reporting except that, instead of comparing a current monthly or monetary value to the previous year, the comparison was to budget values.

When discussing these two reports in meetings, it seemed there was always a story for the up-and-down movements of operating revenue, EBITDA, and expense metrics and why there was a difference when compared to a previous year's measurement or budget.

Jorge reflected how he thought that it was interesting that Harris had no real control over many of the reported listed budget-metrics. Also, most of these metrics were probably only experiencing common-cause variation; however, leaders discussed the ups and downs in these reports as though special-cause events were occurring.

Jorge reflected how this form of reporting was not any different from the news media's reporting a specific reason at the daily close of the stock market for every stock-gyration movement, no matter how large or small. Most of these day-to-day movements were, in reality, the result of noise within the whole business-financial system, where there should be no isolation to a single cause.

Leadership's monthly financial-reporting-package was over 60 pages. The file provided performance metric tables with time-series plots. The first month of the fiscal year was the starting point for each of the reports.

One recollected question from Ron regarding this form of yearly reporting was his inquiry about whether things magically changed between the last month of a fiscal or calendar year and the first month of the following year. From a process point of view, a Harris Hospital answer to this inquiry was *no*. A better practice would be to compile and report calendar or fiscal year data as a string of numbers that bridges years, which IEE satellite-level and 30,000-foot-level metric reporting do.

Using Ron's phrase, Harris's Leadership report discussions had been an attempt to manage the organization through the Ys, which, unlike IEE reporting, does not structurally lead to the identification and execution of process improvement efforts that benefit the business as a whole.

What had been the value of expending all the time and effort having these leadership up-and-down metric-change discussions, which Harris had been doing before the hospital's IEE implementation? None!

Jorge then reflected on IEE and what was done initially at Harris Hospital. First, he reflected again on the 9-step IEE business management system (See Figure 6.3).

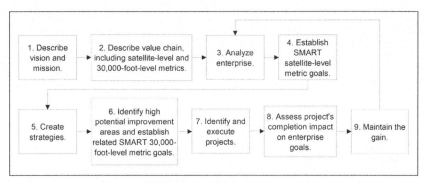

Figure 6.3: 9-step IEE System

Jorge recalled how, in the IEE system, after step one, 'Describe vision and mission,' the IEE value chain in step 2 describes what an organization does and how it measures what is done.

With the IEE system, when an organization wants to improve the bottom-line, a primary business-management focus is first to determine what 30,000-foot-level metrics in the organization's IEE value chain should be enhanced. These metric enhancement efforts would result in an enterprise-as-a-whole benefit after successful completion of the metrics' process improvement work. This whole-enterprise-focus needs to lead not only to *fixes* to run the hospital more efficiently but also to ensure that patients receive the best care promptly. After the creation of a whole enterprise improvement plan (EIP), management then focuses on the timely completion of process improvement efforts that result in the enhancement of the identified 30,000-foot-level metrics.

The structure of Harris's initial IEE value chain (See Figure 6.4) formulated using EPRS software was not much different from the "Positive Metrics Poor Business Performance" article that Ron shared initially with Janice and him.

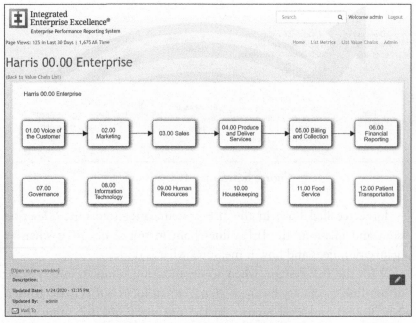

Figure 6.4: Harris Enterprise IEE Value
Chain EPRS Software Report

Jorge recollected how Ron facilitated the creation of Harris's IEE value-chain. Ron solicited inputs from Harris's teams to populate a spreadsheet, including a prefix numbering system for both Harris's functions and its metrics. Ron then used this spreadsheet information as inputs to the EPRS software creation of the hospital's *clickable* IEE value chain.

In a joint leadership and functional managers meeting after about three months from IEE's initiation, Ron gave a live walkthrough of Harris's IEE value chain.

Ron started his portion of this meeting by saying, "Some of you have not seen Harris's IEE value chain; hence, I'll walk you through your hospital's value chain as though you've never seen it before. For those familiar with the value chain, and others too, please ask questions if anything needs clarification or discussion.

"Arrows connect the main functions in the '00.00 Enterprise' IEE-value-chain level of Harris's value chain shown on the screen, which are:

1. Voice of the Customer
2. Marketing
3. Sales
4. Produce and Deliver Services
5. Billing and Collection
6. Financial Reporting

"Listed hospital support functions are:

1. Governance
2. Information Technology
3. Human Resources
4. Housekeeping
5. Food Service
6. Patient Transportation"

Ron then *clicked* on the '06.00 Financial Reporting' function, which led to two flowchart swim lanes.

Ron next said, "The top swim lane has oblong icons to identify satellite-level metrics that the leadership team chose. The bottom swim lane shows the associated processes for collecting this financial data.

"Before proceeding, I want to highlight one thing about satellite-level and 30,000-foot-level reports, which I've discussed with you previously but want to emphasize again. These charts may initially look confusing, but they're easy to understand once you get the hang of it.

"As a refresher, all satellite-level and 30,000-foot-level charts use one or more individuals charts to assess process stability. When a process is considered stable, a predictive statement appears below the chart or charts. There's an inclusion of a probability plot when a satellite-level or 30,000-foot-level plot is a continuous response. This probability plot provides the mathematical means for determining a predictive reported statement. When beginning 30,000-foot-level reporting, don't get stressed out. Quietly breathe deeply and focus on what the predictive statement tells you for a stable process."

Everyone in the room chuckled and took a deep breath.

Ron continued, demonstrating what he was saying with a computer screen projection. "*Clicking on* the 06.00.02 EBITDA link in this '06.00 Financial Reporting' enterprise IEE value chain drill-down leads to Harris's satellite metric EPRS software report" (See Figure 6.5).

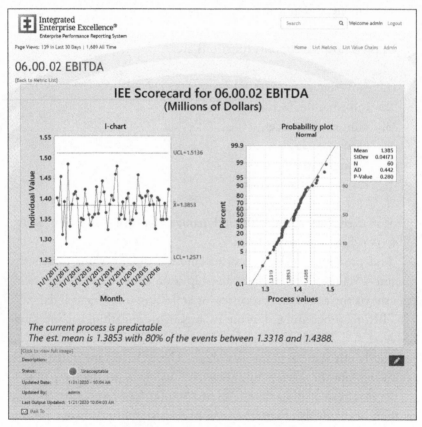

Figure 6.5: Harris EBITDA

"Again, the individuals chart on the left assesses process stability. Since there're no data points beyond the statistically-calculated UCL and LCL lines in this individuals chart, this response is considered stable. Because of this stability determination, there's a prediction estimate below the two-chart pair.

"The determination of this reported futuristic statement is from the included probability plot. Since there're no specifications for this continuous-response metric reporting, there's a reported mean and 80% frequency of occurrence range. In the probability plot, there's a projection of the y-axis values of 10%, 50%, and 90% to the best estimate line and then down to the reported x-axis values, noting that 90% minus 10% equates to the stated 80% in the estimate statement.

"The selection of x-axis time intervals for tracking data in the individuals chart is essential when creating high-level IEE metric reports, where plotted data could extend for years. For satellite-level metrics at Harris, the time-series-tracking interval for EBITDA is monthly; however, for 30,000-foot-level reporting, the tracking-time-interval depends upon the situation.

"You can readily note how the IEE value chain EPRS software satellite-level reporting for EBITDA provides a starkly different perspective for what's occurring financially in the hospital when compared to a table-of-numbers reporting."

Olivia then said, "I appreciate your review. I've seen you describe in another session satellite-level and 30,000-foot-level reporting. However, this is the first time I've seen Harris's IEE value chain, but I think a rolling average over the last three months would be a better reporting approach than a satellite-level report in the value chain."

Samuel then commented, "I'm a newbie too to Harris's IEE value chain. I think that this time-series reporting should start a new sequence at the beginning of every fiscal year instead of satellite-level reporting that bridges years."

Ron then said, "I'm glad you brought up these two measurement reporting suggestions. First, in IEE, we've got a systems-thinking perspective. Because of this, we must present all measurements from a systems-thinking viewpoint. Neither of the common-place reporting methodologies that you suggested provides a system viewpoint for measurements.

"Scorecard and dashboard reporting, including your two-suggested reporting alternatives, give focus to the last measured value. This type of reporting tends to encourage decision making as to whether to take immediate corrective action or not, depending upon the magnitude of the last measured value. Not unlike traditional scorecards and dashboards, both of your suggested reporting formats are consistent with management to the Ys, which all of you've heard from our previous discussions isn't a good thing.

"Your two suggested alternatives for metric reporting offer a slightly different Y-Management approach. The rolling-three-month average method would smooth out data to reduce the risk of overreacting to a single datum value. The start-the-clock-over-at-the-beginning-of-a-new-year approach is in alignment with annual goal-setting thinking. Why else start a new clock?

"With a systems-thinking mindset, it's understood that there typically will be variation, and we do not want to hide it. With IEE, satellite-level, and 30,000-foot-level reporting, system and process measurement variations are front and center.

"An IEE systems-thinking approach needs data presented for both satellite-level land 30,000-foot-level in a format to answer the following three questions:

1. Are there one or more special-cause events that require attention? If so, take appropriate action.
2. Is the common-cause variation response satisfactory? If so, do nothing to improve the process.
3. Is the common-cause variation response unsatisfactory? If so, ensure that appropriate actions are being undertaken or considered to improve one or more metric-associated process."

Janice's follow-up to Ron's response was, "Thanks for that explanation. I never thought about how our current performance metric reports encourage Y-Management thinking with all of its associated issues."

Ron's response was, "Great to hear, Janice. Everyone, please keep your questions coming. My response to your question could also help someone else better understand an important aspect of IEE."

Jorge recollected how both Harris's board of directors and the CEO of the company that owns the hospital were initially hesitant about the IEE system; however, these leaders did change their minds. Now, these leaders feel that, through IEE, they are gaining much insight into not just current performance metrics but also what is being done at Harris so that there will be a long-lasting enhancement to the organization's future financial performance. Now, this leadership is considering implementing IEE in other hospital systems.

Jorge recalled how previously Harris's leadership tried to give an appearance that EBITDA measurements were going north. However, IEE metric reporting and analyses indicated that there was no statistical evidence of improvements in the hospital's satellite-level EBITDA reporting for the last five years.

Ron continued by saying, "Since this financial-metric-response is considered stable, the statement below the report's charting provides a not-only-now but also a future declaration estimate for EBITDA. For Harris, this satellite-level EBITDA mean-monthly estimate was 1.38 million dollars. Another best-estimate expectation was that 80% of monthly EBITDA amounts would be between 1.33 and 1.44 million dollars unless something were to change.

"With IEE thinking, when a satellite-level response has an undesirable stable-response magnitude, things need to be done differently to enhance the overall system of doing work in the hospital's IEE value-chain."

Jorge recollected Ron's insistence that the mean or median monthly EBITDA value be the IEE Step 4 'Establish SMART satellite-level metric goals' metric objective. In the IEE system, there are not any specific end-of-the-month or end-of-the-quarter measurement value goals.

Ron's reiteration of two points related to this critical goal-setting-statement was that first, a company's annual performance is a reflection of the increase in a satellite-level mean or median response, not any individual monthly or quarterly response value. Secondly, an increase in a central tendency for a high-level financial metric response, which is stable, requires the enhancement of 30,000-foot-level metrics and associated processes that are inputs to making this big-picture needle move in an enhanced direction.

IEE systems-thinking and reporting concepts were initially tough for our executive team to grasp and adopt. Still, with Janice's consistent focus on using and implementing the IEE methodology, they finally got it and could see the benefits. Everyone on the leadership team now wants to examine metric reports no other way.

Because Harris's Board of Directors viewed the magnitude of this EBITDA financial metric report as undesirable, this overall metric reporting was assigned the color of red, using EPRS software. Ron emphasized that this red color assignment was *to the metric response as a whole, not to any individual monthly value.*

Ron then said, "Tools in the 'Analyze enterprise,' Step 3, of the 9-step IEE system, provide insight as to where to focus improvement efforts so that both customers and the big-picture-financials benefit. One of the tools included in this analysis is the current magnitude of 30,000-foot-level metrics in the organization's IEE value chain.

"This Harris's IEE value-chain investigation started with examining the first drill-down function on the left side of the enterprise-level of Harris's IEE value chain.

"This '01.00 Voice of the Customer' functional drill-down (See Figure 6.6) has two swim lanes.

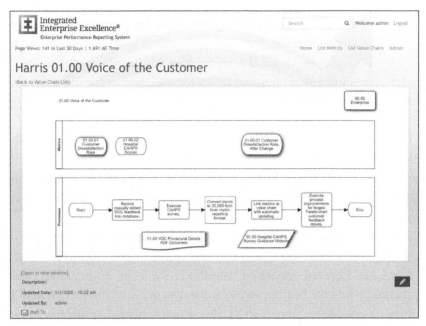

Figure 6.6: Harris 01.00 VOC Enterprise Drill Down

"In the top swim lane of this value-chain image, the text in the oblong symbols contains the hospital's initial functional metrics selection. In contrast, the bottom swim lane includes associated processes, linked-to documents, and web pages for capturing and reporting information.

"The top swim lane listed two Voice of the Customer (VOC) metrics for this IEE value chain function:

1. Customer Dissatisfaction Rate
2. Hospital CAHPS Scores

"The bottom swim lane included process steps for executing this hospital function:

- Record casually stated VOC feedback into a database.
- Execute CAHPS survey.

- Convert inputs to a 30,000-foot-level performance metric reporting format.
- Link metrics to the IEE value chain with automatic updating.
- Execute process improvements for the category having the most Pareto chart customer feedback issues.

"Teams chose to put the details for executing each of these process steps into a linked-to document in this IEE value-chain drill-down, which was titled '01.00 VOC Procedural Details PDF Document'. An additional website link in this IEE value-chain function provided further procedural execution details."

Janice commented, "I like how EPRS software provides an up-to-date IEE value chain that has access through a simple *click of the mouse*. Also, I like how the top swim lane shows the Ys of an organizational function, while the bottom swim lane shows many of the Xs that could impact Y responses. Since Y=f(X), this image could help with executing process improvements and provide a location for documenting process improvements."

Ron responded, "Janice, thank you for highlighting this significant point.

"In the metrics swim lane of this visual, I'll now *click on* '01.00.01 Customer Dissatisfaction Rate,' which leads to this metric's 30,000-foot-level report" (See Figure 6.7).

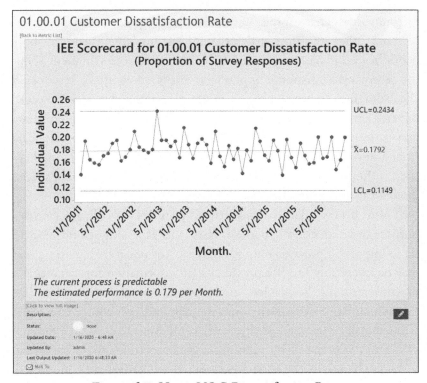

Figure 6.7: Harris VOC Dissatisfaction Rate

"This stable-metric response indicates that Harris's processes are consistent relative to its overall customer-feedback metric. The statement below the charting in this EPRS software 30,000-foot-level report suggests that about 17.9% of Harris's customers are dissatisfied. Since this process-output response is stable, the hospital should expect to continue to receive this approximate amount of negative feedback until establishing enhanced procedures for its hospital services."

Janice said, "From this chart, it appears that from about 2012 to 2013, customer dissatisfaction was getting worse. Also, over the last two years, it appears that this response was cyclic. In addition, it appears that the chart's centerline is the same value as the predicted non-conformance rate statement in the reporting."

Ron's response was, "I understand how it appears that there was a trend a few years back; however, we don't have statistical evidence from the individuals chart in this 30,000-foot-level report that a pattern was present. Other statistical analyses could test out your theory in more depth from different angles. Similarly, relative to your comment about the recent cyclic response appearance, various hypothesis tests could check out any causal theories you might have about this, too. However, patterns often appear in individuals charts by chance. To demonstrate how patterns can look when there is no change, randomly generate data from a normal distribution, and examine the data using an individuals chart. Often what appears in the individuals chart are data trends, even though the data are random occurrences.

"Also, it's essential to avoid analysis paralysis. In IEE, the primary purpose of conducting hypothesis tests is to gain insight into what to do to improve a process's output response, not uncover something that may be interesting but not provide useful information for enhancing a process's response. Yes, Janice, you're correct; for an attribute chart like this, which has no transformation, the reported non-conformance rate estimate will be the same as the chart's centerline.

"From your excellent questions and observations, I am beginning to see a change in the room. By looking at performance metrics in a 30,000-foot-level format, it seems to me that you're gaining much more insight into what might be occurring in processes than by a simple examination of a table of numbers or a red-yellow-green scorecard. Your thoughts?"

Janice then said, "I think that I can speak for the entire room and those with a remote connection when I say that IEE metric reporting and Harris's value chain are giving us an improved vision into what's happening in our organization."

Ron said, "Great! Before we move on, I want to point out a couple of other things in this VOC dissatisfaction report.

"Included in this EPRS software reporting is a VOC feedback statement that indicates 'Customers have been complaining that they've had to spend a lot of time waiting, food service has not been good, and staff has not been friendly.' This EPRS software reported insightful comment could help identify where to focus improvement efforts when developing an enterprise improvement plan (EIP).

"While I'm at it, I want to mention that this EPRS software reporting also includes, like other satellite-level and 30,000-foot-level reports, the option to add related links in the reporting. Another inclusion is the option to send an e-mail to someone about the metric, perhaps highlighting an unusual noted observation in the metric's performance."

Janice then said, "I like this. You indicated several VOC feedback issues. Could these issues be presented in a Pareto chart format in an IEE value chain?"

Ron responded, "Yes, EPRS software offers a Pareto chart option. For this to occur, we'd need to work with your database person to get the data into an appropriate format for this chart's creation."

Janice then said, "Tom, please take this on as an action item to work with Ron so we can see a Pareto chart for VOC issues in our next meeting."

Tom's response was, "Got it. Putting the data into the format that Ron needs should not be a problem."

Janice responded, saying, "Thanks."

Ron then said, "Moving on. The second drill-down function from the left at the enterprise level of the IEE Harris IEE value chain is 'Marketing.' One 30,000-foot-level metric for this function was 'Market Share' (See Figure 6.8).

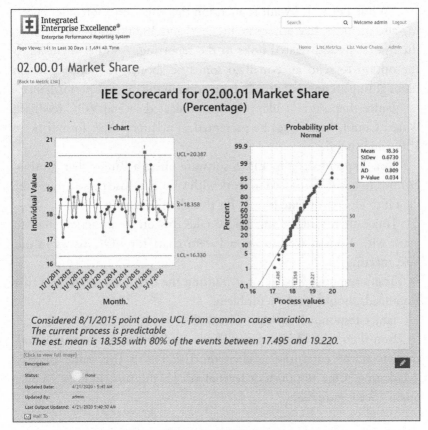

Figure 6.8: Harris Market Share

"From this 30,000-foot-level report, Harris's estimated market share for their hospital's service region has been stable for many years, with an estimated monthly mean of 18.4% and 80% of months reporting amounts between 17.5% and 19.2%.

Samuel then asked, "The proportion of dissatisfied customer's 30,000-foot-level report had only one graphic, while this report has two graphs. You explained this in a previous meeting, but the grey matter between my ears needs a refresh."

Ron's response was, "Glad you asked, Samuel. The proportion of dissatisfied customers is an attribute pass/fail response. Customers were either satisfied or dissatisfied. The calculation of the proportion of dis-

88

satisfied customers for each month is the number of unhappy customers divided by the total customers for that time frame. The chart's non-conformance rate value is an average of these values.

"However, the market-share metric is different. We're considering this response to be a continuous variable, which would result in a similar reporting output format to that of EBITDA."

Samuel responded, "Got it. There's also a footnote stating: 'Considered 8/1/2015 point above UCL from common cause variation'. Please refresh my memory about this, too."

Ron continued, saying, "Good question, nothing wrong with a review. With 30,000-foot-level charting, whenever a point is beyond UCL and LCL individuals chart lines, there's a default statement included in the report stating that the process isn't predictable. EPRS-metrics software offers an option to override this default statement. Since this datum point was so close to the UCL value and there was no causal reason identification, there was the presumption that this point originated from common-cause variability. Because of this conclusion, there was a decision to override the EPRS software default non-predictability statement. There was documentation of this common-cause variability decision in the report's footnote."

Samuel's response was, "Makes sense."

Ron followed up by saying, "Great, let's move on. The fourth drill-down function from the left at the enterprise level of the IEE Harris IEE value chain is '04.00 Produce and Deliver Services' (See Figure 6.9).

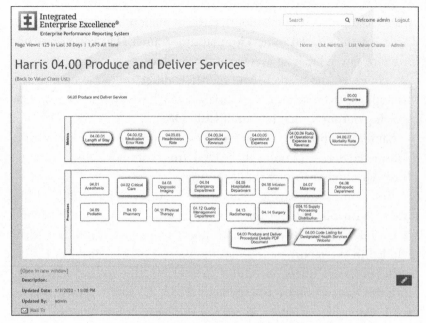

Figure 6.9: Harris Produce and Deliver
Services Enterprise Drill Down

"From this 'Produce and Deliver Services' IEE value-chain function, the top swim lane lists metrics chosen by leadership and this function's management for the performance-measurement tracking of this overall function. These currently reported metrics are:

1. Length of Stay
2. Medication Error Rate
3. Readmission Rate
4. Operational Revenue
5. Operational Expenses
6. The ratio of Operational Expenses to Revenue
7. Mortality Rate"

Janice said, "It looks like everyone did a great job putting together this IEE value-chain structure. I like how there's a listing of our functional areas in the bottom swim lane. Moreover, each of these functional areas has a further drill-down capability for a description of their processes. The numbering system for the 30,000-foot-level metrics and functions makes sense, too."

Ron responded, "Janice, good to hear that you appreciate the work that the IEE implementation team did with both your leadership team and functional departments.

"I'll now *click on* the '04.00.01 Length of Stay' metric, which in this dataset was the length-of-stay duration for one randomly selected patient released each day" (See Figure 6.10).

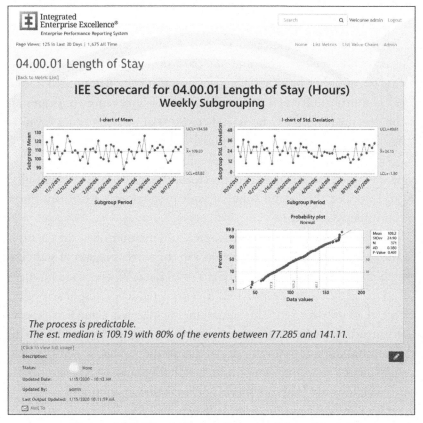

Figure 6.10: Harris Patient Length of Stay (Hours)

Janice then said, "There're two individuals charts for assessing process stability for this metric. Ron, you might have told me before, but I cannot remember the reason."

Ron responded, "The team selected a weekly subgrouping because of the belief that there could be common-cause input differences because of the day-of-the-week, especially weekends. Because of this one-sample-per-day sampling selection, there're seven length-of-stay durations randomly selected for each week, one for each day of the week when the hospital discharged someone.

"One individuals chart tracks the mean of the seven values for a week, while the other individuals chart tracks the standard deviation of the weekly values. This 30,000-foot-level reporting, which is automatically updated daily, indicated process stability, since the individuals' charts of the weekly mean and standard deviation values showed no values beyond the chart's UCL and LCL statistically-determined lines.

"The probability plot in this 30,000-foot-level report indicates an estimated median of 109 hours, where 80% of patients had a hospital length of stay (LOS) between 77 and 141 hours."

Janice asked, "I suspect that the data for creating the probability plot was all of the raw data used to create the individuals chart. Right? Also, I noticed the central value in your prediction is a median, not a mean value. Why is this?"

Ron responded, "Again, Janice, great observations. Yes, the creation of the probability plot uses all raw data in the current region of stability, which, in this situation, is all the chart's raw data. When there's no specification, EPRS software provides a central tendency response option of mean or median. For this situation, we selected a median reporting instead of mean because we believed that the duration of stays in the hospital did not follow a normal distribution. That is, some people could spend a very long time in the hospital because of a severe condition, which would lead to a skewed non-normal distribution.

Did I answer your question, Janice?"

Janice responded, "Yes, the IEE value chain and its 30,000-foot-level reporting were somewhat confusing since it's so different from what I'm used to, but I'm catching on."

Ron's response was, "Great, Janice. I'm now going to *click back* to the '04.00 Produce and Deliver Service' function. In this function, there's a Harris '04.00.06 Ratio of Operational Expenses to Total Revenue' metric (See Figure 6.11). The reason to include this metric is the expectation that a Harris revenue increase would result in an associated increase in operational expenses. However, Harris has the operating capacity to accept additional work with relatively small additional outlay, since fixed costs are about 80% of Harris's expenditures, and the variable costs associated with extra work is the remaining 20%.

"Because of this enterprise assessment, the plan was that there be operational process improvement at the same time. An improved marketing process was adding work. The objective of this dual Marketing and Operational improvement effort was that the operating expense to total revenue ratio wouldn't increase from its estimated current mean-monthly-ratio of 0.59 during this expansion-of-revenue-process-improvement timeframe."

Janice's response was, "I like how you analyzed our Hospital data to determine that Marketing is a bottleneck and also created a metric that'd provide us better insight into the impact of our process improvement effort on the financials."

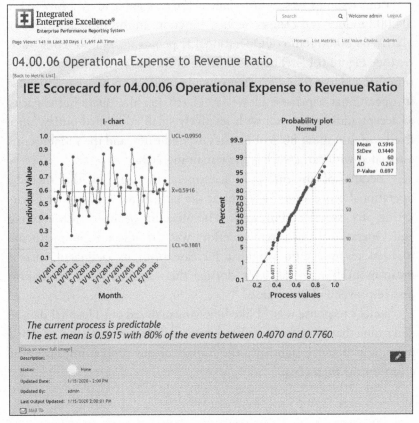

Figure 6.11: Harris Operational Expense to Revenue Ratio

Ron responded, "That's great to hear, Janice.

"The bottom swim-lane of the '4.00 Produce and Deliver Services' IEE value function that we just discussed lists 13 operational medical-specialty hospital and two other operational departments, 'Supply Processing and Distribution,' and 'Quality Management Department.' Two additional links provided in this function's swim lane offer more execution guidance details through a PDF document and web page reference for this Harris Hospital function.

"This '4.00 Produce and Deliver Services' enterprise drill-down figure demonstrates how the IEE value chain structurally displays functional 30,000-foot-level metrics with the processes that created the measurement response.

"In time, Harris's IEE value chain will provide, for each of these functions, their drill-downs with appropriate functional 30,000-foot-level metrics and linkage to the processes that created them, including any procedural documentation and proper web page linkages. For example, a drill-down of the medical-specialty ED department shows procedural details of this hospital function with associated performance metrics (See Figure 6.12).

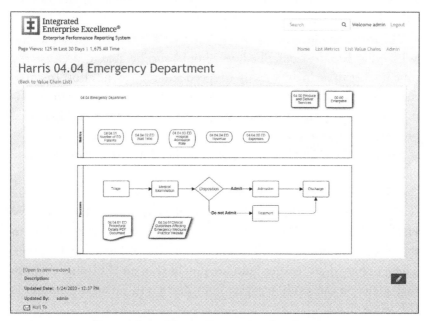

Figure 6.12: Harris Emergency Department

"The metrics listed in the top swim lane of this ED value-chain function graphic are:

1. Number of ED Patients
2. ED Wait Time
3. ED Hospital Admission Rate
4. ED Revenue
5. ED Expenses

The basic functional listed process steps in the bottom swim lane are:

- Triage
- Medical Examination
- Disposition, when admitted or not
- If not admitted, treatment rendered
- Patient discharged from ED

A document and referenced web page in this functional process provide additional process-execution details."

Janice's commented, saying, "I like the IEE value chain structure. With what Ron just described, we should also be able to decrease the time it takes to get new hires up to speed and reduce the effort to cross-train people for other functional areas. I'd think we could also link training videos, too. This IEE value chain usage will save Harris big bucks, plus we'll be able to do a better job!"

Ron replied, "Janice, that's great to hear! Yes, you can also have video links.

"In the top-right corner of the ED value-chain function, there're two *clickable links*. One link provides access to '00.00 Enterprise' of Harris's IEE value chain, while the second link offers return-access to the '04.00 Produce and Deliver Services' IEE-value-chain function. These upper- right- corner links are provided in an IEE value chain so that someone can easily navigate both down and up an organization's IEE value chain.

"Another example of a drill-down in the '04.00 Produce and Deliver Services' visual is the '04.14 Surgery' function (See Figure 6.13).

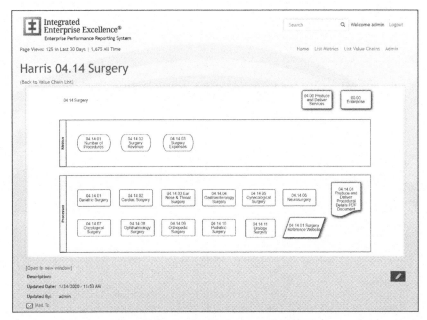

Figure 6.13: Harris Surgery Function
IEE Value Chain Drill Down

"This drill-down shows in the bottom swim lane the eleven surgery procedures offered at Harris, where each of these Harris-offerings will later have an IEE value chain drill-down of its own.

"The three metrics in the top swim lane initially selected for this '04.14 Surgery' function were:

1. Number of Surgery Patients
2. Surgery Revenue
3. Surgery Expenses

In a further Harris IEE Value Chain Enterprise level examination of support functions, it was observed that the magnitude of the '12.00 Patient Transportation' drill-down metric (See Figure 6.14) was more extensive than desired.

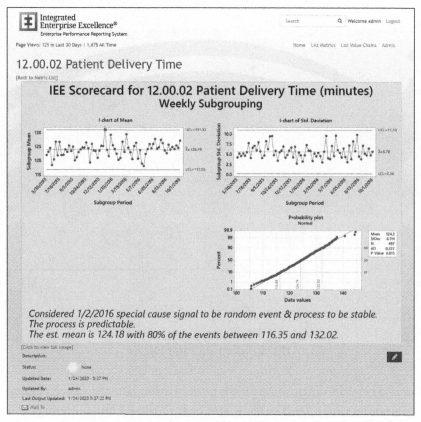

Figure 6.14: Harris Patient Delivery Time

"For Harris's initial creation of this patient-delivery-time metric, one randomly-selected daily patient delivery occurrence was recorded in a database that the EPRS software accessed daily for updating this IEE value chain metric report.

"There was a selection of weekly subgrouping because of the belief that there could be common-cause input differences from the day-of-the-week on the duration of patient delivery times, especially weekends. This 30,000-foot-level reporting assessed process stability by examining the individuals charts of the weekly mean and standard deviation values. For this report, there was one special-cause occurrence in the mean individuals chart."

Ron highlighted that the magnitude of this patient delivery time special-cause-event for the week of January 2, 2016, could be a reason for an investigation. Still, it's a good bet that this event's magnitude, which was barely beyond the chart's UCL line, was a random-chance occurrence. This conclusion isn't unlike the decision described earlier for the 'Market Share' metric. The hospital would achieve more *bang for the buck* by focusing on the magnitude of common-cause variation, not any possible cause for this individuals' chart special-cause-indication occurrence.

Ron proceeded to say, "I want first to expand on an earlier discussed point. If a 30,000-foot-level chart originates from a lot of data, it's a good bet, because of probabilities of the situation, that some datum points will appear beyond the individuals charts' UCL and LCL lines, even when only common-cause variation exists. As previously noted, whenever an individuals EPRS software chart has one or more data points beyond the chart's UCL and LCL lines, a default statement appears in the 30,000-foot-level report that states the process isn't predictable. An owner of a 30,000-foot-level reporting can override this default statement by exercising an EPRS software option. The use of this option results in a prediction statement, where the formulation of this futuristic statement includes data beyond the UCL and LCL reporting lines.

"There was an execution of this EPRS software parameter option for this patient-delivery-time 30,000-foot-level report. A comment entry at the bottom-of-the-chart documented the decision to consider this process predictable.

"The magnitude of the resulting Patient Delivery Time metric's predictive-response from executing this EPRS software parameter option was an estimated mean of 124 minutes with an 80% frequency of occurrence between 116 and 132 minutes. The high magnitude of this patient-delivery-time response is consistent with the received negative VOC comment that customers spent a lot of time waiting."

Janice commented, "I remember seeing this significant amount for a patient delivery time some time ago in an IEE value chain discussion, and I was shocked. With our past reporting system, I never saw this significant process problem with the transfer of patients. I also like the flexibility of EPRS software to override events that, for all practical purposes, should be considered part of an overall common-cause response.

Ron's reply was, "Janice, it's good to hear you say this. I understand that everything said today is not trivial, and the concepts of IEE have a learning curve. But managing a hospital isn't trivial either. The IEE system provides a toolset that'll make the management of your hospital much easier."

Janice responded, "I'm all for that!"

Ron then said, "Let's now switch gears and talk process improvement. As part of implementing step 3 of the IEE 9-step system, the IEE implementation team evaluated all initially-compiled Harris value-chain-metrics. Also, as part of this IEE value-chain step, a theory of constraints (TOC) assessment indicated that about 80% of Harris's expenses were from fixed costs and that the hospital had excess capacity relative to providing its services, as noted previously. Because of this assessment, there was a significant strategic effort given to improve the marketing of the hospital's offerings.

"The operational metrics '04.00.01 Length of Stay' and '04.00.02 Medication Error Rate' were evaluated. Because these current performance metric rates were near the national averages for these measurements, improvement efforts for these metrics *were not* addressed in Harris's EIP first pass (See Figure 6.15).

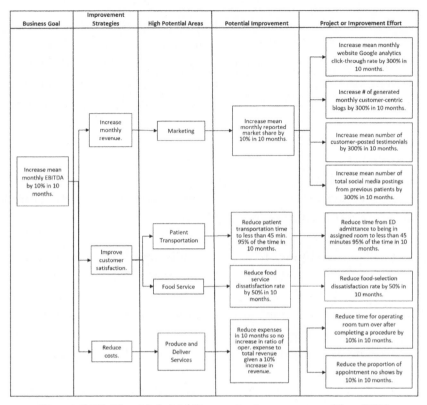

Figure 6.15: Harris's Initial Enterprise Improvement Plan (EIP)

"The five columns in this enterprise improvement plan (EIP) are the specific planned Harris actions for the execution of steps 4, 5, 6, and 7 of the 9-step IEE system roadmap. The satellite-level metric improvement goal in the left column leads to specific process 30,000-foot-level metric goals in the right column, in which the execution of projects is to enhance.

"The first EIP column on the left is 'Business Goal.' Harris's leadership established as 'Increase *mean monthly* EBITDA by 10% in 10 months.'

"The second EIP column from the left is 'Improvement Strategies.' The three items in this column are 'Increase monthly revenue,' 'Improve customer satisfaction,' and 'Reduce costs.'

"The third EIP column from the left is 'high potential areas.' This column listed four targeted functional areas, which were 'Marketing,' 'Patient Transportation,' 'Food Service,' and 'Produce and Deliver Services.' Each of these functional areas has an owner who's responsible for the processes in their area. These functional-area-owners are accountable for their processes' 30,000-foot-level output metrics responses and any enhancements to the processes associated with these performance measurements.

"The fourth EIP column from the left is 'Potential Improvement,' which lists targeted IEE-value-chain metrics and their goals. Listed functional metric-enhancement goals are:

- The 'Marketing' function is to 'increase the mean monthly reported market share by 10% in 10 months.'
- The 'Patient Transportation Function' is to 'reduce patient transportation time to less than 45 minutes, 95% of the time in 10 months.'
- The 'Food Service' function is to 'Reduce food service dissatisfaction rate by 50% in 10 months.'
- The 'Produce and Deliver Services' function is to 'reduce expenses in 10 months, so there's no increase in the ratio of operational expense to total revenue, given a 10% increase in revenue.'

"The right-most EIP column is 'Project or Improvement Effort,' which lists specific projects that are to improve 30,000-foot-level process-output performances in a designated time-frame."

Janice then said, "I like how Harris's EIP compiles everything so that we readily see how our process improvement projects are in alignment with the overall needs of the business."

Ron responded, "Janice, it's good that you appreciate the benefits of IEE's EIP report."

Ron continued, "The setting of organizational goals that include a how-to-achieve improvement system is terrific, but the proof is in the pudding. Organizations need to have, for the timely completion of improvement projects, a method to *git 'er done*.

"The ensuring of timely completion of project tasks needs to initiate with a methodology that provides transparent awareness of what's occurring in a project's execution. Organizations benefit when they have up-to-date project-status tracking so that productive, timely discussions will occur. This dialogue should then lead to the judicious overcoming of any project-completion obstacles or other issues that may be hampering the project's progression. EPRS software offers an option for accomplishing this objective.

"EPRS software can list and track the execution progress of EIP and other projects (See Figure 6.16).

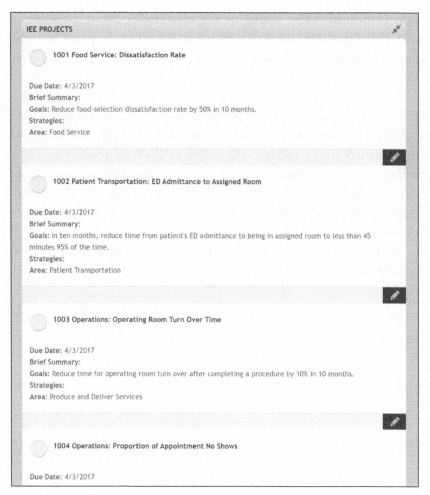

Figure 6.16: Harris EPRS Report of EIP Projects

"This EPRS software project-tracking function provides for each project a due-date, brief-summary, description of goals, project's progression relative to being *'acceptable' or not*, business strategy, and area of the business that the project addresses. There can be linkage to a project's reporting for specific project execution details, along with the minutes from team status meetings and related videos.

"EPRS software content would be available for viewing by anyone authorized at any point in time, 24x7. It's beneficial when project-status presentations use this project information linkage."

Janice again commented, "I appreciate that EPRS software also provides a means where everyone in the organization can readily see the status of our improvement projects. An additional benefit of this inclusion is the dissemination of lessons-learned to others in our organization after a project's completion."

Ron's response was, "Great points, Janice."

Ron then said, "The performance-enhancement results from Harris's IEE projects are to be demonstrated by the staging of the associated project's 30,000-foot-level individuals chart to an enhanced level of performance. I'll now share with you how several business 30,000-foot-level reports appeared when showing their process-output-response enhancement.

"The food service dissatisfaction rate decreased significantly from an approximate 12% mean process response to 6% (See Figure 6.17)."

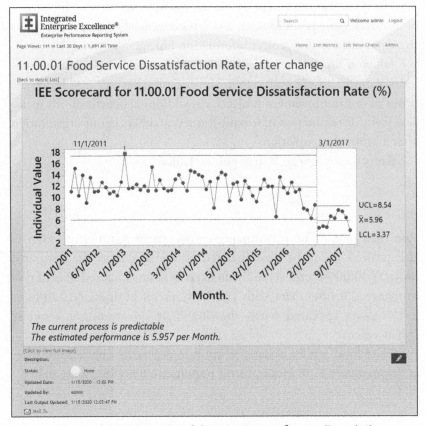

Figure 6.17: Harris Food Service Dissatisfaction Rate (%)

Janice said, "I like 30,000-foot-level charting more and more. It's great that with 30,000-foot-level charting when a beneficial change occurs in a process, there's a staging, which shows the benefit of the process enhancement. No more anecdotal statements about the benefit of a process improvement project at Harris!"

Ron's response was, "I agree. The visual impact from the staging of a 30,000-foot-level chart to the better has to make everyone involved feel better."

Ron continued, "A process improvement project also substantially reduced inpatient transportation time; however, the newly established objective that 95% of patient transportation times should be less than 45 minutes was not entirely achieved (See Figure 6.18).

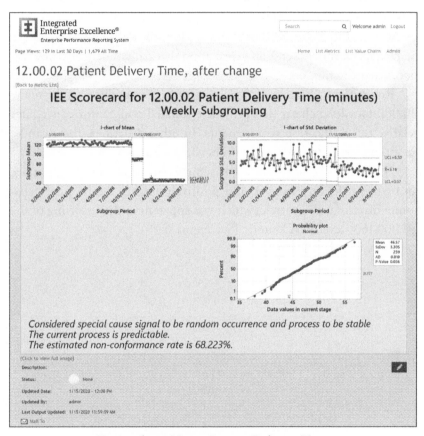

Figure 6.18: Harris Patient Delivery Time
after Process Improvements

"The two mean individuals chart stages in the patient delivery time chart indicate that this 30,000-foot-level metric experienced a substantial amount of process-output-response enhancement *at two points* in time. After process improvement efforts, about 68% of Harris Patient Deliveries were above the maximum criterion of 45 minutes."

Janice said, "This is the first chart that has a specification criterion. If I recall correctly, we did not initially have a specification time goal

when transporting patients. Because there was no specification criterion, a mean and 80% frequency of occurrence range appeared in the
chart as a predictive statement. Now that we've selected a Voice of the
Customer (VOC) maximum duration time, this requires a different use
of the probability plot. This probability plot provides an estimate for the
percentage of times there's an expectation that patient delivery time will
not meet our criterion."

Ron replied, "Exactly, Janice. In manufacturing, there can be many
30,000-foot-level charts that provide estimated non-conformance rates
relative to specification requirements. In other situations, there can be
an estimation of the frequency times when a goal was not achieved.

"Harris's VOC feedback improvements in the areas of food service
and patient delivery time should positively impact the hospital's customer dissatisfaction metric, which was apparent in the reporting of the
30,000-foot-level VOC metric (See Figure 6.19).

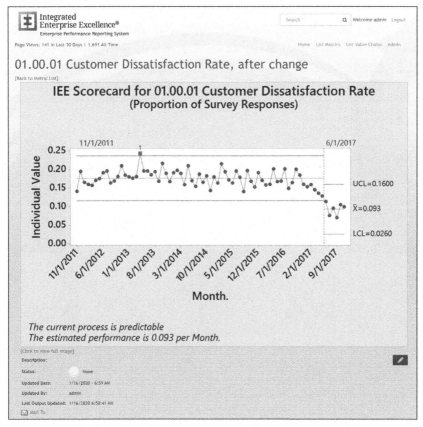

Figure 6.19: Harris Customer Dissatisfaction Rate after Change

"This 'Harris Customer Dissatisfaction Rate' chart indicates a reduction in a monthly mean magnitude response from approximately 18% to 9%."

Janice then said, "This chart looks great in that it shows the benefit of the process improvement project. When we analyze the big picture, we may want to create new projects that give focus on reducing customer dissatisfaction further. When we do the next round on our EIP, we'll consider this when assessing project priorities. Also, I like this, and the other 30,000-foot-level charts, for usage within our IEE value chain as a visual control mechanism for periodic checking to make sure there's no degradation executing our new processes—at no cost."

Ron's response was, "Super comment, Janice.

"Several specific projects to improve the marketing of Harris's medical services resulted in a significant increase in the hospital's market share (See Figure 6.20).

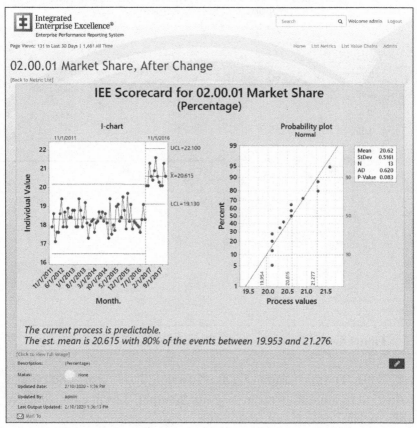

Figure 6.20: Harris Market Share Enhancement

"This 30,000-foot-level Market Share report indicates an approximate mean monthly market share response increase from 18.4 to 20.6 percent.

"Initially, an objective was set for Harris's dual Marketing and Operational improvement effort that the operational expense to total revenue ratio wouldn't increase during this planned expansion-of-revenue timeframe. There was an achievement of this objective since there was no detection of a magnitude increase in the individuals chart in the '04.00.06 Harris Operational Expense to Revenue Ratio' report.

"The bottom-line enhancement from the initial Harris's IEE improvement efforts is that the hospital's EBITDA made a significant enhancement (See Figure 6.21).

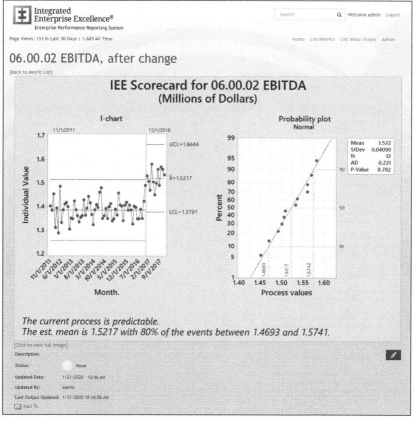

Figure 6.21: Harris EBITDA after change

"This satellite-level metric indicates a Harris Hospital EBITDA mean monthly reported amount enhancement from about 1.38 to 1.52 million of dollars, achieving the ten percent mean monthly enhancement EIP objective in a ten-month timeframe."

Janice, with a smile on her face, said, "This is what it's all about. Harris Hospital has improved customer satisfaction and EBITDA. Great job, team!"

Jorge then recollected how Ron had shown him a graphic that compared the IEE system to what's taught in a typical MBA program, presented in traditional Six Sigma and Lean training, and what's provided in the original balanced scorecard methodology (See Figure 6.22).

Comparison of Systems

SELECTED ATTRIBUTES ++: Attribute included +: Partial/incomplete Inclusion -: Not included	Integrated Enterprise Excellence (IEE)	Typical MBA Program	Traditional Six Sigma	Traditional Lean	Original Balanced Scorecard
Defines process for improvements at operational/project level	++	-	++	++	-
Defines a process for improvements at enterprise level	++	-	+	+	-
Derives improvement projects from enterprise value chain metric performance needs	++	-	-	-	-
Uses DMAIC process to implement process improvements	++	-	++	+	-
Integrates enterprise scorecards, strategic planning, business improvements, and control using 9-step IEE system	++	-	-	-	-
Supports standardized graphical representation of selected data (dashboard)	++	+	-	-	+
Aligns enterprise level business metrics (satellite-level) and operational metrics (30,000-foot-level)	++	-	-	-	-
Includes process for definition of rational metrics that are aligned at operational and enterprise level	++	+	-	-	-
Includes process for distinguishing between "common cause" and "special cause" problems so as to eliminate firefighting	++	-	-	-	-
Uses a traditional approach for business management and/or making process improvements	-	++	++	++	++

Figure 6.22: Comparison of IEE to other Systems

This table highlights many benefits of IEE over other systems. However, as noted in the table, the IEE business management system is different.

Jorge's IEE reverie was interrupted when, on TV, the legal experts took a break for a commercial. Someone was mopping a kitchen floor, very happy about the way it shined after completing the task.

"I didn't even have to scrub that hard!" the person told the camera. "New and Improved Glow really works!"

"New and improved," Jorge mused aloud to Sandra. "Just another way to say, hey, we know our product was junk before, but we made it better now, so try us again! I wonder if they used a design of experiments (DOE) technique approach when developing their product so that its performance didn't depend on the techniques people used to apply the product."

Jorge had watched the cleaning crew at Harris. He had wondered if the product performed consistently no matter if applied to their new or old tile or whether the variation in the amount of product that they mixed with water and variety of product application techniques made a difference. Somehow, he doubted that the *Glow company* was so rigorous in its pursuit of data to qualify its *new and improved* claim.

His wife didn't respond, but he went on talking to her anyway. "At least they're willing to change something that doesn't work. You'd be surprised how many won't. Or maybe not, judging by the way you grip a golf club!"

Jorge always enjoyed chiding his wife about the way she gripped her golf club, stubbornly resisting all efforts of others to correct it—despite the horrible slice it gave her. However, since Sandra couldn't appreciate the humor, it wasn't as fun.

"Have to remember to save that one and use it on her when she gets better," he asserted to himself to keep from becoming depressed by the situation. Then he continued his IEE thoughts—this time to Sandra aloud. He thought it'd be good for her to hear his voice.

"While you've been sleeping, I was recollecting the details of Harris's IEE implementation, but I thought it'd be good for me to review with you some of the basics of the IEE system. Here goes my recollection.

"When a process doesn't have a satisfactory level for its 30,000-foot-level reported response, this metric improvement need *pulls* for a project's creation. One might initially try a couple of things to enhance the measurement's response. However, if these quick-process-improvement attempts result in no 30,000-foot-level individuals chart enhancement, then one needs to use a more structured process-improvement approach, for example, an IEE DMAIC roadmap.

"The IEE DMAIC roadmap leads to the selection of the right tool at the correct time; that selection leads to better process understanding and insight on what to do differently to improve the process. This valuable insight can lead to the identification of process input variables that can affect the 30,000-foot-level response for a process-improvement project.

"See, when there is a control mechanism for important process input variables, error-proofed whenever possible, then one can reduce the variation of the process-output response. Now, I know what you're thinking," Jorge then held his hands up to his peacefully resting wife as though trying to keep her from overwhelming him with questions, "but it's not always as easy as it sounds. Sometimes important input variables to a process are hard to find—actually, finding them is kind of like a murder mystery where the detective tries to determine *whodunnit*. After we determine *whodunnit*, we might need to either control the identified important input variables or redesign the process in some way so that we get the desired 30,000-foot-level response level. See, you didn't know that your husband was a Sherlock Holmes of sorts, did you?"

Jorge was beginning to enjoy this little monologue with his wife. It relieved some tension, at least. Maybe he could talk to her enough about IEE that she'd wake up and tell him to be quiet, as she had done in the past when he got too carried away on the subject. He just wanted to hear her voice—he knew it might be selfish, but he missed talking to her!

"What's that, sweetheart? Do you want an example of a critical process input variable that might affect a process output 30,000-foot-level response? Well, I'm glad you asked. One example, just off the top of my head, is that some medications are unavailable more frequently than other medicines.

"This would be an essential input variable to the 30,000-foot-level turn-around response time for medication. Simple, huh?

"Okay, so, moving right along, after we determine all the important input variables to a 30,000-foot-level metric, the first thing we want to do is try to make the system error-proof to the impact of the input variable. For example, in the 30,000-foot-level 'turn-around time for medication,' which I just mentioned, we always wanted to have medicine in stock when we needed it. Still, we didn't want to have to increase the amount of inventory overall. To resolve the challenge of *you can't have your cake and eat it too*, we worked with our supplier to open an outlet adjacent to the hospital. This way, the supplier acted like our private medication warehouse; only we didn't have to pay a dime! And, incidentally, this little arrangement turned out to help lots of other ailing processes throughout the hospital that we weren't even aware of.

"Anyway, after installing this change, we tracked the availability of medications at the 50-foot-level. We used a frequent sampling plan so that when something changed, we'd know it, and we could stop or adjust the process before it produced excessive non-compliant products—in this case, untimely medicine delivery. So far, things have been great.

"Then there were other times when an examination of the important input variables and the overall process revealed that a process needed changing in certain areas so that it became more robust to input levels that were sometimes high, and other times low. You see, this is not much different from the floor-cleaning process with that new and improved cleaner."

"Um, Jorge?"

Jorge turned towards the door to see who had interrupted his discourse to find nurse Cliff standing in the doorway, looking at him as if to assess his sanity.

"Everything all right?" Cliff asked slowly.

"Sure," Jorge said, flushing a little, "I was just, you know, talking to my wife. Think I read somewhere that if they hear a friendly voice, it helps bring them around again."

Cliff nodded, "Yes, that's true. Usually, though, people talk about more personal matters."

Jorge laughed a little at himself, "I suppose so, but Sandra's used to me talking about this stuff, and she hates patronization. Don't want to get too mushy on her."

"Of course," Jorge added, suddenly wondering just how strange it was that he should be talking aloud to his wife about IEE in the middle of the night, "I guess I might be a little over-tired at this point."

"No," Cliff assured him with a warm smile, "I'm sure you're fine."

Then, in the awkward silence between Cliff and Jorge, a weak voice from the bed said, "Hey, don't you patronize him."

Jorge turned around in shocked surprise, and Cliff walked past him and approached the bed, suddenly all business. Sandra was awake again.

Jorge took her hand; emotions were swelling up inside him. She still seemed groggy, but she was looking right at him through her bandages.

"Well, hello, sleepy-head," he smiled warmly at her. "Good to see you again."

Sandra gave him a feeble smile.

"Hi, Sandra," Cliff said, "How are you feeling?"

She smacked her dry mouth and said, slowly, "You mean aside from my whole body hurting worse than with childbirth? Not bad."

Jorge laughed.

"Well, well, a comedian," Cliff said approvingly. "That's good. You'll need a sense of humor when I ask you to try and sit up for me in a few hours."

Even in her weakened condition, head wrapped in bandages, Sandra was able to send her husband a look that indicated that Cliff was out of his mind.

"Sit up?" she repeated in groggy disbelief.

Jorge sighed, knowing that what Cliff had suggested was the best thing for his wife.

"Sorry, hon," he told her. "It's the way they do it now. Used to be, they wanted you to rest after surgery for days. Now they want you to get up and get moving about eight or so hours after surgery."

Sandra fuzzily protested that was the stupidest, most unnatural thing she'd ever heard. During her slow, deliberate rant, Cliff took some readings off the machines and added them to her chart while Jorge watched.

"Looking good, huh?" Jorge asked Cliff as he wrote, elated that his wife was awake and coherent once more, and showing quite a good deal of vigor, too.

"Not too shabby," Cliff said with guarded optimism. "We still have to see what the neurosurgeon and the pulmonologist/intensivist specialist say in the morning, but she's lucid—that's a good sign. Of course, even if everything checks out tomorrow, she'll still take a while to heal."

Jorge agreed and tried to keep his hopes and expectations under control. Who knew what the doctors would say in the morning? Anything was possible. The agony of limbo set in once again.

After Cliff left the room, Sandra said, "I'm so tired, Jorge, I can barely keep my eyes open. I think I'll rest a little more. I'm going to be fine, though; don't worry. I'm in good hands."

"Sure you are," Jorge agreed, though inside, he winced. "Go ahead and rest a little."

Jorge reached down and stroked her hand. He wanted to touch her face, but the bandages prevented him.

Changing the subject, Sandra asked, "What were you talking to me about before?"

"Oh, nothing. Just some IEE."

"I heard you," she said, her eyes fully closed now.

"You did?"

"Mm-hm. Tell me some more."

"What do you want to know about?"

"Tell me about the tools you use."

"You mean the application of Six Sigma and Lean tools at both the enterprise and process improvement project level?"

"Yes," Sandra said, "those are the ones."

"Well," Jorge said, speculating that his wife was half-humoring him to take his mind off her injuries, and the other half just wanting to hear the sound of his voice. Nevertheless, he obliged her request, "Since you asked... there does happen to be many different tools to pick from. It's interesting. Different tools apply to the collection and analysis of different kinds of data. Of course, with IEE, you've got the 30,000-foot-level report, your dot plot, box plot, scatter plot, regression analyses, analysis of variance (ANOVA), analysis of means, design of experiments, and a variety of Lean tools ...that's just to name a few....Sandra?"

She appeared to be asleep again already. Jorge smiled, and without letting go of her hand, he slowly eased himself down into the chair beside her bed.

"Why did you stop talking?" she said, catching Jorge by surprise and startling him a little.

"I thought you'd fallen asleep!" he said.

"Uh-uh."

"Oh, well, okay. Should I keep talking then?"

"Mm-hm."

"Okay. Why don't I tell you about how the right strategic improvement projects are selected so that the business as a whole has a benefit?"

"Sounds juicy," Sandra replied drowsily.

"All right then, here goes. Once upon a time, as is said, Ron, the consultant, asked us how we thought we ought to decide which projects to run. So, someone suggested that we create a list and then choose projects from the list. A lot of people agreed that it seemed like a good course of action, but I wasn't too sure. When I voiced my hesitation, you'll be proud to hear, Ron asked me why I disagreed."

"Well," I told him, "I just thought that you were supposed to line up your projects as needed in our IEE enterprise improvement plan (EIP) as described in step six of the 9-step IEE system."

"Good, Jorge," Ron told me, "IEE tells us that instead of focusing on subjective ideas, we can work down from the hospital's overall analytically-determined needs. That way, we execute strategic projects that'll have the most impact on helping Harris have healthy financials and high patient satisfaction. We also want to assign ownership of 30,000-foot-level IEE value chain metrics and have people throughout the organization referencing their area of the IEE value chain. Having someone accountable for each functional process and its output metric performance is crucial.

"References to the IEE value chain in meetings for 30,000-foot-level metrics and associated processes can provide much value for enhancing the way things are done and making not only targeted strategic process improvements but local process documentation and enhancements as well."

"Great job, sweetheart," Sandra commented from the depths of her pain medication. "You were always such a good student. Always with the right answers in class."

"Thanks," Jorge beamed. Then, excitedly, he went on, "Later, the wisdom of the organization (WOTO) inputs suggested that there was room to improve and standardize procedures in the operating room (OR), which would help Harris achieve its goal of improving the hospital's bottom line. There was then the addition of this OR improvement project to our EIP.

"For this OR project, we observed the execution of current methods, conducted brainstorming sessions with those who were involved in the implementation of OR processes, and analyzed data. From this work, we decided what to do differently. After implementing a few efficiency-improvement procedures, the OR's 30,000-foot-level metrics improved. After this change, Harris could treat more patients in our OR rooms, which increased Harris's revenue, with the only added cost being that associated with fulfilling the additional patient's OR procedures.

"But let me give you another example. Another goal of Harris's overall effort was increasing customer satisfaction. In that case, listening to the Voice of the Customer (VOC) told us that a big complaint that customers had was spending much time in the waiting room. So, we looked at our data and then tweaked our system to handle this dissatisfaction issue, and dropped the average waiting room time over 20 minutes. Customer satisfaction rose dramatically, and we received many positive comments about the change.

"However, before we made changes to the process, we examined metrics from a 30,000-foot-level IEE value-chain reporting perspective. We found the process output response from a 30,000-foot-level perspective to be predictable, but not providing the needed level of performance. So, with this need in mind, we collected data and tested out generated hypotheses from our wisdom of the organization and VOC inputs, which led to specific change items for the process. That's to say:

we initially decided that it was worthwhile to do about the problem by changing the system, which we did just as IEE preaches.

"Yep, Ron did his job well when he taught us to create performance metric improvement plans that positively impacted the organization's 30,000-foot-level measurements, which were in alignment with business metrics enhancement needs. Harris started tracking the whole organization as a system of processes where there was the consideration that typical day-to-day fluctuations were noise to the system and had a common-cause variation appearance in our process-response tracing. We had high-level operational metrics that covered defects, waste, cycle time, days-sales-outstanding, customer satisfaction, on-time delivery, and inventory. I tell you, we had it all covered. Then, when we needed to decide which projects to run, we let the numbers help us discover where to look using the 9-step IEE system. It was very refreshing to see Janice reference Harris's IEE value chain in her status meetings and other conversations. Many in her leadership team resisted at first but then saw the value of the methodologies and were making reference to the IEE value chain and to the 30,000-foot-level metrics that they were responsible for in their physically-attended or remotely-accessed meetings.

"If our 30,000-foot-level metrics revealed a process that had common cause variation and was consistently missing its specification limits or desired output response level, our IEE Black Belt candidates would label the output performance as *unsatisfactory* in the EPRS software. If we decided to run a project to *improve* the process, our EPRS software would convey to everyone at the hospital, the 30,000-foot-level metric improvement project and the effort the hospital was undertaking to improve it. Then, the *murder mystery* would be on! We'd investigate until we uncovered the key process input variables (KPIVs) that were impacting the key process output variable (KPOV) through our wisdom of the organization discussions and analyses. From the compilation of this information, we'd be able to make WOTO analytically determined changes to the processes that benefit the 30,000-foot-level metrics output response. We then document these new procedures in Harris's IEE value chain.

"Take the medication-error rate example that I was telling you about before. We found from a 30,000-foot-level perspective that the process did not provide what we wanted. Then, we found that a specific type of medication had the highest error rate. So, next, we tracked the error rate for that particular medication at the 20,000-foot-level. Eventually, we closed in on our problematic process input variable, which turned out to be a failure of the RN to interpret the prescription correctly in the electronic record. To fix this issue, we implemented a check-off system where the nurse checked the medication against the prescription order in the electronic-record, which improved the process. A demonstration of the benefit from this change occurred when the 30,000-foot-level individuals chart for this process-output-response changed to a new, enhanced level of performance. A 30,000-foot-level report estimate was a reduction in the frequency of failure from 50 per 1000 patient days to about 11 per 1000.

"As part of our 'Control phase' for the project, we worked to make the prescription entry process error-proof. We also tracked the medication errors weekly at the 30,000-foot-level, which was reported and automatically updated in our EPRS software IEE value chain. There was a responsible manager for this metric who was to keep a close eye on this 30,000-foot-level response level in the IEE value chain. Since there was automatic updating of the metric's reporting in Harris's IEE value chain, everyone authorized had access to this and other organizational metrics. If anyone notices something unusual about this, or another 30,000-foot-level response, an EPRS software e-mail can convey someone's observation and thoughts to the metric owner. …Sandra? You asleep?"

Jorge leaned over her bed from his chair and determined that this time, his wife was asleep.

Jorge's mind drifted. The murder mystery metaphor he'd been using conjured up mental images of Elliot Ness and his famed band of crime fighters, closing in on members of organized crime, digging them out of their shady hideouts. Sandra was out like a light and didn't protest as Jorge indulged himself in the fantasy.

Years ago at Harris, when they had first initiated IEE, many processes were in sore need of improvement. Some might say that they were out of control, but that was not true. The 30,000-foot-level reporting indicated more often not process stability; that is, there were no identified special-cause conditions. However, many of these processes were just not capable of consistently giving Harris desired outputs. Hunting root causes in the processes that affected the 30,000-foot-level IEE value chain reported response using a systematic approach had been exciting. Fixing them had been satisfying, like locking up Public Enemy #1 for good.

Harris's 30,000-foot-level metrics reporting identified one of the hospital's most pressing needs was improving the emergency department. Sixty percent of the hospital's business came from the emergency department, and the ED system was problematic. In this case, the operating room systems, revenue cycle, medication errors, and the supply chain had all been suspect.

Hospital personnel tested these issues against the Voice of the Customer just as Mr. Ness would question someone who might have information about a crime. There were two witnesses: internal customers and external customers.

The internal customers testified that what had them all mucked-up were:

- Delays in admitting patients to nursing units.
- Re-work in physician orders.
- Turf wars.
- Lack of customer orientation.
- A slow admission process.
- Gaps in the scheduling.
- The appearance that there was never enough staff on hand to handle the workload.

Then it was the turn of the second witnesses: the external customers. External customers testified to:

- The need for quick and cost-effective health care solutions.
- Better and timelier information from the caregivers.
- Better customer orientation.

"Yes," Jorge nodded shrewdly to himself in thought, "The case wasn't yet closed on these culprits, but now there was their identification; shutting them down for good was just a matter of time. When an improvement team ran a project to impact these issues, they'd know for sure that they weren't just going to be firefighting, or working a low-priority problem. They'd be working on something that would make a definite impact on the hospital's bottom-line and customer satisfaction.

"TQM, Utilization Review, Scientific Problem-Solving Methodology, benchmarking...left to themselves, did not take the broad-based approach of IEE." Jorge harrumphed at the thought of the inadequacy of these methodologies. He had a recollection of how all those quality improvement efforts that had come and gone. Using them to solve a problem was like Elliot Ness going after Al Capone armed with no more than a cap gun.

7 OWNERSHIP

At 3:30 a.m., when Cliff came into Sandra's room again, Jorge was watching an old Hitchcock thriller, *North by Northwest*, on the hospital TV.

"Hitchcock, huh?" Cliff asked, stopping to watch for a moment on his way to Sandra's bed.

"Yep," Jorge said. "Thought it might take my mind off things. I'm not as much of a fan as Sandra, though. She can watch Hitchcock all day."

"And you can't?"

Jorge shrugged, happy to be talking about something that he and Sandra did together, "Well...sometimes it seems a little hokey. I mean, *The Birds*? Come on."

Cliff laughed, "I like your attitude, Jorge."

"Thanks," Jorge replied, "but I wish I could do more."

"You can," Sandra said, suddenly awake again. "You can get me a drink of water. I'm so thirsty."

Jorge practically jumped; he was so surprised. "Will you quit doing that?" he protested to his wife.

"Doing what?" she protested weakly.

"Waking up all unexpected like that."

"Well, I heard you badmouthing Hitchcock and couldn't let you get away with it."

"She's tough, huh?" Cliff said to Jorge.

"You've no idea," Jorge responded.

"I'm sorry, dear," Sandra said to Jorge, "but could I've something to drink?"

"Better make it ice chips for now," Cliff warned. "Water might make you nauseated right now."

"That's fine," Sandra said. "I'll take anything."

"I'll go get you a cup of ice; be right back," Cliff said, and he left.

"Well, won't be long now until the doctors are here," Jorge told Sandra as they waited, "Soon as they clear you, I'd like to have you transferred to Harris."

Sandra winced as she tried to shift in the bed. "Do you think that's necessary?"

Jorge quickly leaned over her to help adjust and fluff her pillow so that she would be more comfortable. "Well, I'd just feel better at Harris, knowing how smoothly things run there, knowing the doctors and everybody—you know."

He didn't want her to worry about all the things he knew could still go wrong before she checked out of City Hospital, but he couldn't help but worry himself. When a 30,000-foot-level metric response was unsatisfactory, mistakes could occur, and he knew that Sandra might become one of the bad-process-output victims if they waited around too long.

"Well, if you think it's best," Sandra said, trusting her husband's opinion. "Do you think they'll ask me to stand up when we get to Harris?"

"Fraid so."

"Oh, nuts."

A moment passed, and then Cliff returned with the cup of ice and handed it to Jorge. Sandra opened her mouth, and Jorge slipped an ice chip in between the bandages.

"Better?" Cliff asked.

"Mmm," Sandra said.

"Don't give her too many. Three should be plenty for now, if she wants that many. She can have more in a little while, okay?"

"Got it; thanks, Cliff."

"Just hit the button if you need me."

"Will do."

He left the room, and Jorge and Sandra were alone again.

When Sandra finished the first ice chip, she asked, "So, how long did you talk until I fell asleep?"

"A long time. Do you remember what I was talking about?"

"Not really. I just liked listening to your voice."

"Thought so. Want to hear some more of it?"

"How else am I going to fall asleep?"

"I'm flattered."

Sandra closed her eyes. "I'm waiting," she said.

Jorge chuckled. He thought she was just delightful.

"Well, if you'll recall," he began, "I was telling you about how we used various techniques to identify enhancement opportunities that we had for Harris 30,000-foot-level value chain responses. Our process improvement work involved evaluations from VOC feedback, competitive analyses, the wisdom of the organization, and other methodologies in combination, as part of the 'Analyze enterprise' step 3 in the IEE's 9-step system. And as you also recall, I'm sure, in IEE, defining the 30,000-foot-level metric that needs to be improved and baselining its current performance is a first step toward improving the metric's performance."

"Ah, yes, that's right," Sandra said.

"Ron, our IEE consultant, taught us that a traditional Lean Six Sigma approach had problems with project selection in that often projects were selected from people's opinions and resulted in only organizational silo benefits after their completion if completed at all. When traditional Lean Six Sigma projects do get completed, project benefits are often only an anecdotal statement.

"In the IEE system, the focus is to improve performance metrics that benefit the enterprise as a whole. The IEE 9-step system through enterprise analysis identifies areas of the business and 30,000-foot-level metrics that, when improved, will benefit the overall financials and customer satisfaction, as summarized in the organization's EIP."

"So, bet that gets your CEO's attention?"

"Wow, you haven't fallen asleep yet?"

"No. Tell me about one of your projects that benefited Harris."

"So, you *were* listening!"

"It must have soaked into my subconscious. Well, go on. Tell me about your projects."

"One project appeared in on our IEE EIP about three months after IEE's initiation. Emergency department wait-time was the 30,000-foot-level metric that we were to improve. This opportunity was a low-hanging fruit with a big payoff for the hospital. We later moved on to medication error reduction, reduction of accounts receivable, and reduction of inventory."

"How long did they all take?"

"There were varying durations for individual projects; however, the essential overall measure of success is the accomplishments made in one year. We met our initial EIP objectives and more through the execution of many projects. Our satellite-level tracked mean EBITDA was increased by about 10%, and customer satisfaction also was enhanced by approximately 50%.

"What we did to speed the completion of our process improvement projects versus what a traditional Lean Six Sigma program might experience was to follow the 9-step IEE system and the deployment model that Ron led us through. Getting the buy-in of our CEO, Janice, initially and working with her to view performance reports from an IEE satellite-level and 30,000-foot-level, made all the difference in the world. This transition by Janice did not occur over-night. Still, when Janice started *clicking through* our IEE value chain in her physically-attended or remotely-accessed meetings a couple of months after our IEE kickoff, magic started happening. When your CEO starts asking process metric owners to explain their EIP project's 30,000-foot-level reporting using common-cause and special-cause variation terminology, things begin to occur throughout the organization.

"I'm impressed, *Professor*," she said, sarcastically invoking the title his old college friends had given him.

"That's okay, Ms. Santos. I'll let you take the make-up exam later in the semester on all the recent topics that I've covered in my lectures."

"You're too kind."

"Not at all. The systems-thinking message that Janice was sending by her embracing and usage of IEE concepts went through Harris like a wildfire. Janice's transition to systems thinking did not occur overnight, but when the light came on in her head, she became a real IEE disciple.

"Initially, Harris's VPs, directors, managers, and others resisted IEE and its implementation. The consensus was that the IEE system would be a *program of the month* and would go away. However, Janice's visible commitment and personal use of IEE methodologies made a big difference. Janice continually asked for system solutions and threw out some sacred cows, including the meeting of arbitrary monthly goals throughout the hospital. People's opinions about IEE and its benefits changed over time.

"The IEE Harris value chain, with its automatic updated performance metrics, was a significant factor in getting everyone on board. People throughout Harris could look at the IEE value chain from their computer anytime. These folks could see where they fit in the big picture, what processes they were to execute, and the processes that the 30,000-foot-level metrics were to impact.

"With the visibility of processes through the IEE value chain, managers and their teams were taking on local process improvement efforts. When there was an agreement to a process change in a function, there was documentation of the new methodology in the IEE value chain. There was the elimination of much local wasted effort, and the customer benefited too.

"Because of IEE value-chain performance metrics reporting transparency, the hiding of bad things did not occur. Everyone realized that whenever issues occurred, a blame game was not to happen. The general understanding was that we were in it together to make Harris the best it could be. When unexpected issues popped up, there was a resolution to the immediate problem, and thought began on what to do differently to make sure the problem did not reoccur. If an easy procedural change were beneficial to eliminate reoccurrence, this change would be documented in the IEE value chain and be put into place immediately. If a process improvement fix took more thought, there'd be Voice of the Customer (VOC) database documentation of the issue for future evaluation and undertaking.

"It was no secret that before IEE, Janice's job was in jeopardy because of our gloomy financials, poor operational metric performance, and our dismal customer satisfaction feedback. After our IEE implementation, all this turned around. Now she's a super-star in the eyes of our board of directors and the company that owns Harris.

"Janice candidly shares the benefits of IEE to me personally. She says now she sleeps better because of fewer Harris headaches and worries. Also, she now has time for a personal life beyond the hospital's administration and likes her job much more.

"Janice always felt that not-so-good things were happening in the hospital, but not shared with her. The transparency of 30,000-foot-level performance metrics that are automatically updated and aligned with the processes that created them through EPRS software and the IEE value chain flatten all these past concerns.

"Janice loves the monthly leadership reviews that she now receives about improvements to 30,000-foot-level metrics that our EIP has identified. She also thinks it's terrific how EPRS software provides up-to-date EIP project status that was supplied by process-improvement teams, which she can review at any time. Periodically, Janice asks process-improvement-teams questions about their EPRS software posted project summaries and team meeting minutes. When the CEO asks a question about your project and its 30,000-foot-level metric's enhancement, this inquiry provides a high-impact stimulus that gets the project teams pumped up!

"Janice also likes that after a project's completion, she sees a 30,000-foot-level metric response transition to a superior level of performance through the staging of the individuals chart in the reporting. Janice also likes to see the enhancement of a process's cost of doing nothing differently (CODND) numbers because of process changes.

"Janice appreciates the project's CODND spreadsheet summary, which includes all estimated costing impacts—both hard and soft savings. Janice commented that she's grateful that Harris is not going through all the cost-savings benefit investigations in their Lean Six Sigma projects like she knows some CEO friends are doing in their deployments. These CEOs candidly state that they are confident that their organization is putting together questionable cost-saving numbers since he cannot find the claimed savings in the organization's overall financial statements.

"Janice also no longer dreads board of directors meetings. She says now all she has to do is summarize the presentation she received in her monthly EIP progress review meeting. Having to create no special presentations is terrific! Now she only talks to an EPRS software posted presentation that has links to Harris's IEE value chain to describe how things are going from a high-level satellite and 30,000-foot-level perspective, along with actions that are being underway to make things better.

"Janice says that it's great no longer to hear people creating stories when talking to a table of numbers about why this quarter's number is up or down! Janice says her board of directors' meetings are now much shorter and to the point.

"Janice believes that the concepts of IEE provide additional benefits with the management challenges associated with more people working remotely from home or residing at other locations, including our board of directors. With EPRS software, up-to-date metrics and processes are readily accessible by all. Also, the software provides our organizational EIP and the status of all improvement projects. All this readily available, up-to-date information provides a framework for more productive meetings and discussions.

"Janice believes that our hospital could win the Malcolm Baldrige award with minimal effort in a first-time application. She said that all we'd have to do is learn how it'd be best to *fill out* the Baldrige application forms since IEE addresses all seven Baldrige award criteria categories, which are:

- Leadership: How upper management leads the organization and how the organization leads within the community.
- Strategy: How the organization establishes and plans to implement strategic directions.
- Customers: How the organization builds and maintains strong, lasting relationships with customers.
- Measurement, analysis, and knowledge management: How the organization uses data to support key processes and manage performance.

- Workforce: How the organization empowers and involves its workforce.
- Operations: How the organization designs, manages, and improves critical processes.
- Results: How the organization performs in terms of customer satisfaction, finances, human resources, supplier and partner performance, operations, governance, and social responsibility, and how the organization compares to its competitors."

Jorge stopped talking and leaned over Sandra's bed. Her eyes were closed, and she was breathing normally.

"Sandra?" he whispered.

No answer. She had zonked out fast this time! Satisfied that she was asleep, he got up and strolled over to the 12th story hospital window, looking out into the early morning darkness. He clasped his hands behind his back as he watched intermittent bursts of traffic roll down the highway visible in the distance.

"One more hour," he thought.

It seemed like an eternity.

8 PROJECTS

As Jorge looked out the window, he reflected on the 9-step IEE system. The methodology wasn't flashy, but it was imperative in that, among other things, the IEE approach was considered a business management system that structurally linked performance measurements, which were often predictive, with the processes that created them. In his opinion, this linkage has been missing in all past business improvement initiatives. The IEE system, with its 30,000-foot-level metric reporting and automatic EPRS software metric updates, gets organizations out of the firefighting mode.

Jorge thought again of Ron Wilson, who orchestrated the IEE implementation at Harris. Ron wasn't there anymore. True to his word, he had trained himself right out of a job! Ultimately, Jorge reflected, the consultant was only successful at this job when he wasn't needed anymore. That had been a new one on Jorge. Usually, these consultants try to find ways of sticking around as long as they can.

Ron had done his job well; his many years of experience taught Jorge and the others on the IEE team exactly how to interpret collected data not only at the improvement project level but at the business system level as well. For a 30,000-foot-level metric considered predictable, one could estimate an expected non-conformance proportion; in other words, how far out of whack it's likely to be not only now but expectations for future performance, if nothing were to change!

For example, at Harris, one EIP focus area that evolved was insurance claims. The 30,000-foot-level metric in the IEE value chain for the amount of time to receive monetary collections for insurance claims indicated that the process was stable where the median time was approximately 65 days, with 80% of insurance claims taking between 45 and 95 days for collection. Numbers like that helped put things into a perspective that the IEE leadership and process-improvement team could understand. It wasn't subjective, it wasn't padded, and it was something that could be measured objectively.

Once the team found a process that was incapable of providing what the internal or external customer wanted, the team then went on to develop some improvement plans. There was an inclusion of VOC in the development of these approaches.

Ron taught the organization that customers wanted improvements in areas that were critical to four major areas: care, quality, cost, and satisfaction. To help the teams collect and interpret customer feedback, Ron assisted teams in the development of their skills with the tools and integration of tools that were needed to provide a timely completion for enhancing a project's 30,000-foot-level metric. Jorge still recalled Ron's asking the team questions like, "Who's the customer? What does he or she want? Does our process address those needs?"

VOC wasn't all Ron had our IEE improvement teams examine. There were variation considerations, too. IEE 30,000-foot-level metrics separated common-cause from special-cause variation. It's the special causes that typically get all the personal attention—big disasters do not happen often, but when they do, people remember them forever. However, Harris's IEE implementation taught leadership and teams that more gains are achieved by the resolution of common-cause issues so that they do not reoccur, or are less likely to occur again. Special causes were special events that needed individual attention; you might even leave these situations alone. It may not be practical to give focus on adjusting a process towards conditions that exist only once a year. If you do, you might wind up with more problems than you already have. Also, a special cause can be a good thing; for example, a process that changed to an improved response output level.

Next, Ron had Jorge and IEE process improvement teams walk through the steps of the IEE Define, Measure, Analyze, Improve, and Control (DMAIC) project execution roadmap. Where, with this roadmap's execution, there is a focus on what to do to improve a 30,000-foot-level IEE value chain response, so there is a whole-enterprise benefit. Ron kept emphasizing that a team can make process improvements using other techniques besides DMAIC such as Lean, 5S workplace organization, and the plan-do-check-act (PDCA) cycle. The use of a particular process improvement methodology did not matter. What was necessary for improvement projects was the enhancement of its 30,000-foot-level metric in the timeliest fashion with the least effort and expense.

Jorge left his thinking spot at the window of Sandra's room and walked down the hall to use the restroom. He could have used Sandra's room toilet but felt he needed to stretch his legs. Jorge didn't want to wake his wife until Cliff came around again. As he walked, he recalled the time his IEE team members gathered wisdom of the organization information and found some low-hanging fruit—the medication-error rate. There was something they could do quickly to reduce the likelihood of incorrect medication, and it was so obvious, easy, and cheap that they all agreed to the change—which involved simply redesigning the medication order sheet.

It turned out that the change to the order sheet brought the medication-error rate way down. Jorge remembered when he saw a staging of the team's 30,000-foot-level report outs individuals chart to a new, improved level of performance. This new individuals chart's stage provided evidence that they had improved their process where 'Analyze phase' tools provided a statistical significance statement about the change and quantification of expected impact to the 30,000-foot-level process outputs response. A new process performance prediction statement was then determined for that 30,000-foot-level metric, using EPRS software. These numbers indicated that this change was going to make a significant impact on the bottom-line and customer satisfaction, which, more often than not, were interconnected.

Of course, there were other cases where the team needed more information to determine what to do differently—the *murder mysteries*. These investigations included results from evaluating the magnitude of IEE's value chain 30,000-foot-level EPRS software reported metrics, the wisdom of the organization brainstorming session, and the Voice of the Customer inputs. The IEE roadmap for improving led them to inputs in processes that were the culprits.

Ron taught them that it was essential to analyze compiled data in a manner that provided insight not only for project execution but for enterprise-level evaluations as well. Ron taught the folks at Harris the importance of making statistical assessments as to whether or not apparent pictorial-indicated differences were statistically significant or not.

For example, there could be an examination of an issue affecting a unit to determine whether the frequency of a problem occurrence was significantly different, statistically, between the first shift and second shift. If there were a significant difference between work-shifts, IEE thinking would suggest that focus should not be on what the one work shift was doing wrong. Instead, the focus should be on the work shift that was doing things best. The team would then try to determine how to duplicate the best process for the under-performing work shift.

Or, perhaps the issue might not be a shift-wide issue. Maybe the root-cause problem was the hiring of the most appropriate person to do a particular job. That hiring-process issue happened in one situation at Harris, and so Jorge got HR involved to help fix the problem. After someone with the proper qualifications was assigned to the position, the process 30,000-foot-level report for this function in the IEE value chain shifted for the better.

Jorge came back to Sandra's room from the bathroom. She was still sleeping. Jorge was unable to worry any more than he already had. Waiting this long for a specialist wasn't only bad for business; it was dangerous. What if there were a time-sensitive issue that Sandra faced? If the specialists were only available at certain times due to the process within which they worked, Jorge pondered, then could a hospital's process itself be held accountable for negligence if it failed to provide timely care?

Jorge sat back down in the chair by Sandra's bed and, arranging the pillow and blanket Nurse Barnes had given him so long ago, he tried to make himself as comfortable as possible. 4:30 am, the clock on the wall read.

"Won't be long now," thought Jorge. He turned on the TV and checked the news. The same legal experts who had been on hours ago were still debating the same issue. Jorge fell asleep in his chair as though shot with a tranquilizer dart.

In his dream, Jorge was in a meeting with his process improvement team to discuss which 30,000-foot-level responses for the IEE value chain function critical care unit (CCU) were not meeting performance standards. They noted that the 'diagnosis-to-bed' metric's 30,000-foot-level report indicated predictability.

Jorge and his process improvement team then established a numerical goal for the process's output, noting the negative VOC feedback about the time spent waiting. The team and management agreed that an upper non-conformance goal of forty-five minutes was realistic and acceptable from a customer point of view.

When determining what to do differently to reduce diagnosis-to-bed times, the IEE process-improvement team considered the VOC and the wisdom of the organization that it received. From this effort, some ideas emerged, but these possibilities need testing. So, the team decided to consider a design of experiments (DOE) approach to determine if a change provided a statistically significant benefit.

Jorge's dream jumped forward in time as Jorge and his IEE implementation team analyzed the process. Eventually, the team came up with the top process input issues. They were:

- Amount of time it took the nurse to admit a patient to a bed
- Bed not ready
- Length of time taken for the patient's family to arrive and pick-up a discharged patient and the hospital bed *turned over*.

The IEE process improvement team then talked in more informed detail about what to do so that there was a consistent achievement of their 'diagnosis-to-bed' time 30,000-foot-level objective. The group discussed the specifics within the diagnosis-to-bed process. They brainstormed about ways to express a numerical solution to the problem. Ron kept the team on track by not allowing them to focus on red tape or other barriers like outdated laws or insurance regulations that could inhibit the process; those were problems they couldn't fix.

Finally, the team determined some solutions. After examining the workflow using Lean techniques, the team discovered that the current process was experiencing many inherent delays. This insight led to the implementation of some changes. Two of the modifications were:

- Using a separate discharge process for emergency department (ED) patients with less severe conditions
- Creation of a patient waiting area specifically for family members waiting to pick up a discharged patient so that there could be a quicker preparation of beds for new patients.

Also, an examination of workflow processes led to placing needed materials directly in the path of the process, rather than randomly placed in the room. There was a conversion of internal steps to external actions. There was a conversion of several tasks to an ahead-of-time or defer-until-later execution. There was a minimization of handoffs. There was staff training of easily-learned responsibilities so that they could answer questions themselves, rather than having to ask for another staff member or supervisor to intervene. Much of this training had on-demand availability through a simple *click of a mouse* in the Harris IEE value chain.

In Jorge's dream, an IEE process improvement team member at Harris by the name of Larry Hass gave him the same boggled look as he had worn in the conference room with Ron Wilson over two years earlier. Larry then stated, "Do you know what it'll cost to train all those people and implement all these changes? The hospital will never go for it!"

"Sure they will," one of his other team members offered in defense of the team's recommendations. "A few simple steps can make the execution of this new process a way of life at Harris. First, with putting the new training instructions in our IEE value chain, with perhaps a couple of videos, the new approach can be conveyed throughout the organization very quickly. Secondly, the manager of this 30,000-foot-level metric should closely monitor the overall process response, along with any sub-process outputs, noting to his or her employees the importance of executing all the specifics of the newly defined process. Lastly, the manager of the process should make a conscious effort to conduct a Gemba Walk of this specific process, which was a focused 'manage by walking around' activity."

It was that same Larry, who later suggested that they install medication management bedside devices to help eliminate medication errors, a bold suggestion then, but one which they wound up following.

They also set up a pull system for patients transitioning from Triage to the critical care unit. The initial call from Triage, notifying the CCU of an incoming patient, was designed to trigger a chain of events that eventually led to the patient's being transported to CCU by CCU staff. By using a tool to measure demand over time, they found the admission of 50 percent of ED patients within two hours of being seen by a doctor. The CCU was then able to anticipate the demand for a bed, and have one ready as soon as an emergency department patient needed it.

In his dream, Jorge began tossing and turning a little as he remembered what the Harris IEE process improvement team did to extend the time of the much-demanded physician specialists. One thing the team did was to make a process adjustment so that the specialists perform only the tasks that demanded their specific skills. They matched the physicians' schedules with patient needs.

Some other changes to the system had to do with educating patients during waiting times and scheduling routine care at low-demand times.

When Jorge's team members completed the improvement phase for projects, a calculation indicated an approximate average cost of doing nothing differently (CODND) hospital savings of $500,000 per project, in addition to the benefit of improved customer satisfaction. This CODND reporting was helpful to estimate, but a more substantial demonstration of project benefit was from the organization's EIP and how this metric's enhancement was in alignment with making a beneficial shift to the enterprise-as-a-whole financials and improved customer experience.

Everyone on the IEE improvement team felt good. They didn't just tell staff to do their job better; they worked with staff on the usage of tools to make the right things happen. Not only that, but everyone on the team had the sense that running successful projects like these would not be bad for their careers!

It was 5:30 a.m., and the specialists could arrive at any minute. Sandra was awake in her bed and only slightly tired. The sleep had done a world of good for her. She was still banged up and swollen, and even heavily medicated, but to Jorge, her eyes seemed more-alive this morning. He was in the chair next to her, reading her the paper and sipping coffee.

Sandra appreciated the way that he was staying strong for her. Jorge was acting as though she had nothing at all to worry about. She knew he was worried, though. The bags under his eyes told the story.

She interrupted the newspaper article he was reading to her about how the city wanted to raise property taxes again.

"Jorge?"

"Yes, can I get you something?"

"Did you ever finish telling me about your IEE improvement projects and their maintenance of gains from the improvement efforts?"

"Well, no, I didn't. I suppose you want to hear it?"

"Hm-hm."

"You can't go to sleep on me again. The doctors will be here soon."

"No," Sandra said, "I really want to know. What did you do to make sure that the gains your team made weren't lost after you left the emergency department project?"

Jorge shook his head slowly as something occurred to him. "You know something?" he said, "I think somebody's been listening in on the old *Professor* from time to time when he's been holding a class with his friends."

"Whatever do you mean?" Sandra said innocently.

Jorge wagged a finger at her, "Wait a second...I'm on to you now, young lady. You wouldn't have gotten a business degree in college if you didn't like business. You could've gotten an arts degree or something else. Confess. You find this IEE stuff interesting, don't you?"

Sandra managed a feeble smile. "Maybe I overheard a few conversations," she admitted.

"And all this time, you acted like the IEE methodology was the last thing you wanted to hear!"

"I was trying to keep you humble," she said, "but now that I see there's no hope for that, I might as well come clean. I think that business schools should teach the IEE system as a mandatory topic. It seems to me that MBA students could benefit from the methodology!"

"Ha!" Jorge said.

"Well then, *Professor*. Are you going to tell me how you kept those gains or not?"

Jorge was grinning ear to ear. "Well, how about that?" he asked rhetorically. "Sure, sure I'll tell you, as long as we've got a few moments to spare here. I think we'll be lucky if these specialists show up before lunch."

"Jorge, don't be nasty."

"You're right. I'm sorry. So, to answer your question, the IEE system provided several things to do so that Harris did not lose the gains we made and could leverage what we'd learned to other areas of the business. Relative to this leveraging point, we documented everything in our EPRS software project reports so that others might leverage what we did and learned. Next, relative to control, our EPRS software automatic metric updating of 30,000-foot-level reports offered a free high-level means for process control and maintenance of the gain.

"One of the process owner's jobs was keeping her eye on the performance metric reports that she was responsible for, perhaps daily, to make sure that there were no 30,000-foot-level individuals chart degradations of their processes' output responses. Others, including the CEO, Janice, would also have access to the chart's reporting, which allows other sets of eyes for these high-level process-output-response observations, which also provide a means for controlling the gains. Next, we documented the optimum process settings, conditions, and input variables in our IEE value chain process description and documentation. We attempted to error-proof processes whenever possible. For some processes that we knew would drift over time, we created 50-foot-level charts that'd indicate when timely process adjustments were needed."

"So," Sandra said, "how were the managers of the process that you were working on involved in all this process improvement effort?"

140

"You hit upon an essential benefit of the IEE system over a traditional Lean Six Sigma deployment. With a traditional Lean Six Sigma deployment, improvement projects are often executed and then *turned over* to the process owner after the project's completion. With the IEE system, the process owner, who's responsible for improving the 30,000-foot-level metric in the IEE value chain, will be asking, if not demanding, from his or her improvement team timely completion of the project. This high-level of process-owner focus occurs when there's a determination that the metric's enhancement is critical for meeting enterprise-as-a-whole goals, as identified in the organization's EIP.

"With the IEE system, process owners realize that there's a need for a spotlight focus for making timely improvement to the process that enhances their metric. This sense of urgency occurs whenever they're to be presenting a monthly status of their projects and associated 30,000-foot-level metrics to their leadership. Also, the process owner and his or her team need to be actively involved with the enhancement of these process improvement efforts since, as a group, they're most familiar with the process's current execution.

"One benefit of Harris's EPRS software installation is that all the details of project executions are documented in a readily accessible location so that there's a leveraging of lessons learned to other areas of the hospital. With this EPRS software documentation, everyone has access to process documentation and the process-improvement project execution details. This information could be invaluable to other functional areas so that they do not need to reinvent the wheel. For example, many departments might be able to lower their medication inventory after the prescription supply store opened adjacent to the hospital for the emergency department 'inventory reduction' project.

"In a traditional Lean Six Sigma deployment, much time can be spent *negotiating* financial benefits with the financial officers, which might end up being an underlying justification for the continuation of their Lean Six Sigma deployment. However, in the real world, often these financial benefits lead to reported numbers, where for example, there's a 100-million dollar reported savings, but nobody can find the money. In IEE, there's no emphasis on this project-financial-benefit-calculation. Harris's EIP describes the benefits of our IEE projects, where the improvement of operational metrics is in direct alignment to fulfilling the organization's overall financial satellite-level metric objectives and customer needs."

"Also," Jorge finished, "After making a significant improvement to a process, we do not want future process-executions to revert to the old way of doing things. We would like to incorporate mistake-proofing concepts as much as possible in a newly created process; however, that is not often possible. With a traditional Lean Six Sigma deployment, an end-of-project statement might be 'we will check back in a few months to make sure the improvement procedures are being followed.' With an IEE EPRS software system, the 30,000-foot-level metrics related to the project are automatically updated and can be monitored not only by the process owner but by all others who've authorized access to Harris's IEE value chain. This *no-cost-investigation* feature of the IEE EPRS software system offers a high-level control for maintaining the gains from process improvement efforts."

"So, Mr. Kung Fu hotshot," Sandra teased him, which Jorge thought was remarkable considering her condition, "you said you measured the benefits of the projects you ran in the emergency department and aligned this work to the overall needs of the hospital?"

"That's right."

"Well, what were those benefits?"

"Beds were ready much faster, and patients were moved to inpatient beds much more quickly. Speaking of which, and I hate to say it, but those are some cues this hospital could stand to take from Harris. It took forever to get you into a bed after your surgery. And waiting overnight for the specialists to arrive hasn't been any picnic either."

"Well, we do what we can," said a dry, unfamiliar voice from the doorway of Sandra's room.

Jorge turned in surprise to watch two doctors enter, who Jorge could only assume were the long-awaited neurosurgeon and cardiovascular specialist.

After Jorge recovered from his embarrassment, the specialists introduced themselves as Drs. Thompson and Kader. They then proceeded to examine Sandra and ask her several questions. As they examined her, the trauma surgeon, Dr. Miller, and the plastic surgeon, Dr. Monk, also entered the room and made their examinations of Sandra. Jorge found it strange that none of Sandra's physicians had been there for so long, and now they were all there at once. However, the last thing he was going to do was question the efficiency of their system twice in ten minutes—at least, not until Sandra was out of the hospital!

After finishing their examination, the doctors all seemed satisfied that she was on track for a full recovery.

"Thank you," Jorge said as they reported their favorable prognosis to Sandra and him. "I appreciate everything you've done."

"Yes, thank you," Sandra told them.

"Oh, there's no need for that," Dr. Kader said.

"Not at all," Dr. Miller chimed in, "especially not from a bigwig over at Harris Hospital."

"Oh," Dr. Thompson joined in, "so this is *the* Jorge Santos, IEE efficiency guru."

Jorge felt flustered, surrounded as he was by the doctors in their business suits and white lab coats.

"How can you all possibly know who I am?" he asked.

The doctors all chuckled, and Dr. Miller spilled the beans. "My husband is Dr. Miller from Harris Hospital in the emergency department."

"Kareem Miller?"

"Yes. Kareem told me about you back when your IEE team swooped in and reorganized the whole department. He couldn't say enough about how much more smoothly everything ran after you were through."

"Wow," Jorge said, "that's gratifying to hear. Thank you."

"I'm surprised you don't hear it all the time," Dr. Miller said, "and actually, I'd like to thank you. Since then, Kareem's been a lot happier in his job, really doing the things he was trained for and loves, instead of wading through tasks that could be done by somebody else. He's like a different person when he comes home from work now."

"Hey," Dr. Kader piped in, "maybe you could work some of that magic around here."

"I'll second that," Dr. Thompson added.

"Oh no," Sandra said from the bed, "he's got to take care of me first."
They all laughed.

"Well, I guess we can wait a little while," Dr. Monk said, "but as soon as you're done with him, we'd like *Doctor* Santos here to come work with us for a while. Deal?"

Sandra shot Jorge a look as if she knew what was going through his head.

And she did. It was:

"Hmm…first *Professor* Jorge, now *Doctor* Santos. Now that's a title I think I could get used to!"

9 LEVERAGING THE GAINS

Author Note

This chapter makes reference to Jorge's MBA golfing friends. The challenges that these golf buddies had in business and golf were described in *Management 2.0: Discovery of Integrated Enterprise Excellence* (Breyfogle 2020a).

- Hank is one of the four golfing MBA friends. As a VP, he works at Hi-Tech Computers, which had been using, before implementing IEE, Lean to execute kaizen events to reduce organizational waste.
- Zach is one of the four golfing MBA friends. As a VP, he works at Z-Credit Financial, which had been using, before implementing IEE, the balanced scorecard to improve the execution of the organization's strategic statements.
- Wayne is one of the four golfing MBA friends. As a VP, he works at Wonder-Chem, which had been using, before implementing IEE, Lean Six Sigma to execute improvement projects to reduce costs.
- Jorge Santos is one of the four golfing MBA friends. As a VP, he works at Harris Hospital, which discovered and successfully implemented the Integrated Enterprise Excellence (IEE) business management system. Jorge introduced his friends to IEE, which they eventually adopted in their companies.

- Sandra Santos, Jorge's wife, is CEO of a non-profit.
- Georgia, Zack's wife, is a superintendent of a school district
- Ellen, Wayne's wife, is a partner in a consulting company
- Sharon, Hank's wife, is a director in a government agency

Three Month after Sandra's Hospital Discharge

Jorge thought to himself when approaching the golf course in his SUV that today was a gorgeous spring day for playing golf. The winter had put a hamper on playing golf with his MBA friends. It would be enjoyable to see his buddies again, play golf, and catch up.

Jorge was the last one to arrive. He noted how his friends were warming up, giving focus to the weakest aspect of their games, whether that was their driving, short game, or putting. This observation was a stark contrast to his friends' warm-up ritual before they were introduced to IEE concepts a few years back.

Because of Jorge's later than usual arrival time, he did not have time to chat before meeting at the first tee box.

Hank spoke first after everyone had arrived at the first tee, saying, "Jorge, how's Sandra doing after her hospital discharge?"

Jorge responded, "She's doing great! She's back to her old self, fully recovered."

Wayne responded, "Jorge, that's great to hear!"

Zack followed up by saying, "I'm sure that the seriousness of her condition put a frightful scare in you."

Jorge responded, "It sure did!"

Hank then said, "Guess you gained a first-hand perspective of the other side of a hospital's system—being the customer."

Jorge replied, "Hank, I sure did get a first-hand customer view on the receiving end of the processes from a hospital, and the experience was eye-opening. But, the important thing is that Sandra is doing well."

Wayne then said, "Yep, Sandra's full recovery is the most important hospital deliverable."

Jorge thought as he watched everyone tee-off their first shot. All golf balls were in the middle of the fairway and had great lies for second shots. What a difference from a few years back!

It seemed like every golfer in the area decided to take advantage of this beautiful spring day to play a round of golf. When approaching the third tee, it was evident that the wait time before Wayne's tee-off shot was going to be lengthy.

Jorge said, "I heard that other areas of each of your households are experiencing a leveraging of IEE."

Hank was the first to respond, "Yes, my wife, Sharon, is working at the application of IEE techniques in her piece of government. She's a director in the state's department of public safety."

Zack next responded, "My wife, Georgia, has heard much about the benefits of IEE over the last couple of years and now is applying IEE techniques in her schools. She's a superintendent in a school district."

Wayne then added, "My wife, Ellen, is a partner in a consulting firm which has initiated IEE in a variety of organizations."

Jorge then followed up, saying, "Looks like I'll make this unanimous relative to our wives' work with IEE. Sandra has been working with the non-profit organization that she heads up on the application of IEE in that organization."

Hank then said, "Looks like we're up next to tee off. Wayne, you've honors."

Jorge followed up, saying, "I've more to share with you and have some thoughts. Let's discuss at the 19th hole over lunch."

Everyone enjoyed their round of golf. However, things could have been better for Hank and Jorge They received the *honor* of paying the lunch's tab because of Zack's 25-foot, 18th hole birdie putt.

Jorge continued his third-tee discussion saying, "I don't know if you've heard or not, but Janice, Harris's CEO, received earlier last week a Hospital Association Award because of our IEE deployment, which she led."

Jorge heard a united response from his friends of, "Wow!"

Jorge continued, "Yes, the award pumped everyone at Harris. Also, by chance, as part of me being Harris Hospital's Chamber of Commerce representative, I had lunch two days ago with the CEO of the chamber. I told her about the award Janice had received because of her Harris IEE work. I also mentioned how the three of you and your wives were using the same IEE business management approach as Harris in a variety of organizations. She thought this was great and wanted to share these organizational successes with the chamber's membership.

"We discussed how we might do this and came up with something that'd take more time than what a monthly chamber breakfast meeting could handle. What we thought would be great to do is set up a special three-hour luncheon meeting. In this session, in addition to Janice's summary of what Harris did and accomplished, others would explain how they applied IEE techniques in a variety of organizations. If people cannot physically attend the luncheon meeting, we think that they could tune into the meeting remotely. The session could close with a panel question and answer session. What are your thoughts?"

Hank responded, "I think that'd be great! I'm an extrovert in our family, and Sharon is an introvert. You know introverts don't say much, but when you get them talking about their passion, you can't shut them up. Sharon has that talkative-way about her with the mention of IEE."

Wayne then said, "I'm sure that Ellen would give a thumbs up for this idea. She's a great storyteller."

Zack responded, "I'm sure that Georgia would also go for this meeting! She enjoys giving presentations about something she loves, like IEE. She's a member of a Toastmasters group near our home."

Jorge said, "Great to hear! I'll check with Janice to get her thoughts about presenting at the chamber's meeting, which I'm confident *will be a go*, and also check with our chamber's CEO to discuss the next steps."

The chamber of commerce luncheon *was a go* for everyone and decided to open the luncheon session to everyone in the community. The chamber thought that offering the three-hour session to non-members might, in time, increase their membership. For the gathering, non-chamber members would pay more than Chamber members. About 120 signed up for the luncheon and 75 for the on-line presentation.

Everyone who attended the luncheon received a copy of the "Positive Metrics Poor Business Performance" article. Those who were viewing remotely through their computers received a website link to the publication.

The agenda for the session was:

- Chamber CEO: Introductions (5 minutes)
- Jorge, IEE overview: One-minute IEE video and "Positive Metrics Poor Business Performance" article figures discussion (15 minutes)
- Janice: Harris's IEE implementation, including a live EPRS software demo, benefits, and Hospital Association Award (30 minutes)
- Lunch (30 minutes)
- Hank: IEE evolution from Lean at Hi-Tech Computers (5 minutes)
- Wayne: IEE evolution from Lean Six Sigma at Wonder-Chem (5 minutes)
- Zach: IEE evolution from the Balanced Scorecard at Z-Credit Financial (5 minutes)
- Sandra, Jorge's wife, CEO of a non-profit organization: IEE application in non-profits (5 minutes)

- Georgia, Zack's wife, superintendent of a school district: IEE application in elementary and secondary schools (5 minutes)
- Ellen, Wayne's wife, a partner in a consulting company: IEE application in a mining company (5 minutes)
- Sharon, Hank's wife, director in a government agency: IEE application in government (5 minutes)
- All Presenters: Questions and answers panel discussion (45 minutes)

All presentations went well. The session was even on schedule for timely three-hour completion.

Jorge facilitated the question and answer session. Someone moved a microphone around the room so that everyone could hear the inquiries.

Jorge started this portion of the event by saying, "Everyone did a great job presenting their stories about implementing IEE in their organization. Now for your questions. Who will be first?"

Someone in the first row raised his hand. When recognized and given the microphone, he said, "From the 'Positive Metrics Poor Business Performance' article and Janice's presentation, I saw an IEE value chain for a US hospital. I'd like to now see an IEE value chain for other types of organizations."

Jorge responded, "Great inquiry! Who'll give the first response?"

Sandra replied, saying, "I'll start things off. Shown on the screen is the enterprise-level for our non-profit's IEE value chain (See Figure 9.1).

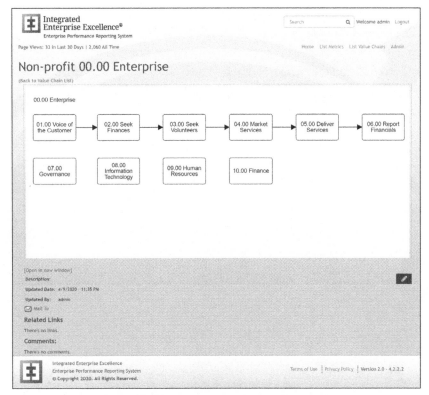

Figure 9.1: IEE Value Chain—Non-profit

"Our non-profit's primary IEE value-chain steps are Voice of the Customer, Seek finances, Seek volunteers, Market services, Deliver services, and Report financials. Our support functions are Governance, Information technology, Human resources, and Finance."

Georgia then said, "Guess I'll go next. Shown on the screen is the enterprise-level of our school district's IEE value chain (See Figure 9.2).

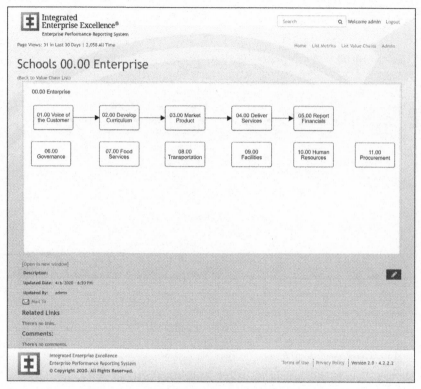

Figure 9.2: IEE Value Chain—School District

"Our school district's primary IEE value-chain steps are Voice of the Customer, Develop curriculum, Market product, Deliver services, and Report financials. Our support functions are Governance, Food services, Transportation, Facilities, Human resources, and Procurement."

Ellen was the next to respond, "Shown on the screen is the enterprise-level of a mining company's IEE value chain (See Figure 9.3).

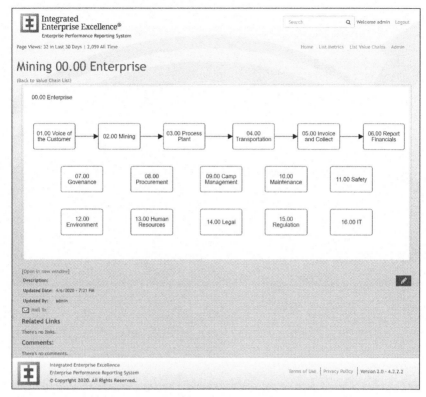

Figure 9.3: IEE Value Chain—Mining Company

"This mining company's primary IEE value chain steps are Voice of the Customer, Mining, Process plant, Transportation, Invoice & collect, and Report financials. Our support functions are Governance, Procurement, Camp management, Maintenance, Safety, Environment, Human resources, Legal, Regulation, and IT."

Sharon then said, "We're in the early planning stages of an IEE deployment. Our current value chain gives focus to one of many agencies in our state (See Figure 9.4).

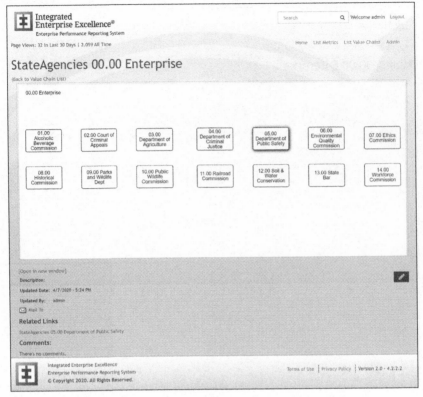

Figure 9.4: IEE Value Chain—Government, State

"The agencies listed in this IEE value chain are Alcoholic Beverage Commission, Court of Criminal Appeals, Department of Agriculture, Department of Criminal Justice, Department of Public Safety, Environmental Quality Commission, Ethics Commission, Historical Commission, Parks & Wildlife Department, Public Wildlife Commission, Railroad Commission, Soil & Water Conservation, State Bar, and Workforce Commission.

"This level of an IEE value chain shows how our agency fits into the state's big picture. There's a shadowing of the agency where I work, 'Department of Public Safety.' *Clicking on* the 'Department of Public Safety' in the IEE value chain leads to components of this agency (See Figure 9.5).

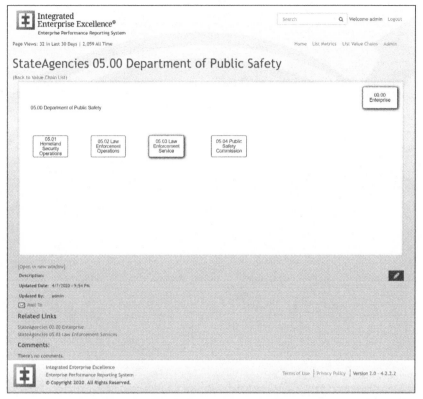

Figure 9.5: IEE Value Chain—Government,
Department of Public Safety

"Shown components for the Department of Public Safety are Homeland Security Operations, Law Enforcement Operations, Law Enforcement Service, and Public Safety Commission.

"For illustrative purposes, a drill-down of 'Law Enforcement Service' would yield eight operational functions (See Figure 9.6).

Figure 9.6: IEE Value Chain—Government,
Law Enforcement Services

"Listed functions under 'Law Enforcement Services' are Infrastructure Operations Division, Drivers License Division, Finance Division, Information Technology Division, Law Enforcement Support Division, Regulatory Services Division, Human Resources Operations, and Cyber Security.

"This value chain drill-down does not show it, but we've report finances in our functional agencies, too. Our state legislature provides monies in a budget that originates from seven goal statements. Each of our departments is to track its monthly financial performance against their specific portion of the budget."

Jorge then said, "Well, that covers the main types of organizations that I can think of. Next question."

Someone in the fourth row then asked, "I noticed that in every presented IEE value chain Voice of the Customer was the first listed function, except for the government's IEE value chain at the enterprise level."

Sharon responded to the inquiry saying, "The next drill-down in our government's IEE value chain, which I did not show, would show a Voice of the Customer entry when executing the work of a function in a state agency."

Georgia followed up by saying, "Voice of the Customer feedback is vital in our schools. We need to get timely feedback about what we're doing right and not so well in our schools to improve. This feedback needs to be more than parents and students filling out a Likert survey questionnaire."

Jorge said, "Great question and responses. I'm in total agreement."

The next question came from someone located in the back of the room. A woman asked, "I was stunned to see money as a driving force in all presented IEE value chains."

Sandra responded, "In a non-profit, people often think we should not be profitable. However, we need to have some monetary gain to keep the lights on. We like how our enterprise improvement plan (EIP) gives focus to both the increase in revenue and management of expenses, while at the same time improving our processes so that we can provide more and better services. We like how our satellite-level metric tracking monitors the monthly performance of financial metrics."

Georgia then commented, "In our school district, we found that IEE's monetary tracking approach is what was needed. Now we give a structured focus to what we can do to provide the most service for the money allotted to our school district. Also, if you recall, there was a 'marketing product' function. One aspect of this drill-down is a process for what to do to receive more funds from government agencies, donations, and grants to enhance our offering. Our EIP summarizes these efforts, which we regularly discuss in our face-to-face and remote meetings."

Janice then said, "Harris Hospital is a for-profit US hospital, which our satellite-level metrics reflect. However, health care in other parts of the world might take a very different perspective and say that money isn't relevant to their health-care operation. I'd challenge this position by saying that there are costs and expenses to all processes. In the health-care industry, we should want to provide, from a process output point of view, the most benefit for our allotted money or budget. The IEE system, with its performance-metric tracking, offers a vehicle that has an alignment to this objective."

Jorge then said, "Another great question and responses from various perspectives. It looks like we've time for one more inquiry."

A man in the middle of the room asked, "It appears that all your organizations are using an EIP to address the identification of 30,000-foot-level metrics to improve through process improvement projects. I'd like to hear about the enhancement of 30,000-foot-level metrics through EIP identified process improvement projects."

Ellen responded, "I've been quiet until now because I think it was most important to illustrate the application of IEE to a variety of organizations besides for-profit companies, but I want to be the first one to field this inquiry. Within the structure of my consulting organization, I was working with a mining company to help them improve their business. Over the years, this company was not successful with its many process-improvement program attempts. They liked the IEE system when our consulting firm presented it to them.

"For this organization, one EIP process improvement effort that we undertook was under the function 'Maintenance.' Every year the mine has an annual preventive maintenance shut-down. This maintenance requires a two-to-three-day temporary addition of many specialists to the company's remote mining camp. There's much to do and orchestrate in a short around-the-clock amount of time. Each hour of lost production is about a one-million-dollar hit to the bottom-line.

"There was one person who led this activity in the mine for many years. From step 3 of the IEE 9-step system, our analysis indicated that we needed to address two items relative to this annual shut down and maintenance. First, we believed there was a significant business risk if this key maintenance-driving person was figuratively '*hit by a bus*.' There was no formal documentation of the planning and execution processes associated with this shutdown and maintenance. Secondly, there was no recording of how long this preventive maintenance operation took over the years and the effectiveness of the procedures over time.

"This high-level critique of the mine's maintenance function led to an EIP project. This improvement project was to document the current methods and record this information along with associated 30,000-foot-level metrics that tracked the quality, cost, and time of the overall maintenance process for the last ten years. When viewing the total plant maintenance procedure from a high-level perspective, we made some changes that reduced maintenance time by about three hours, which was worth approximately three million dollars annually."

Jorge then said, "Ellen, a great illustration of undertaking a process improvement project that a traditional process improvement deployment would probably not have pursued. An organizational EIP often provides a very enlightened viewpoint perspective for the organization as a whole."

Georgia then stated, "In our school district, our enterprise analysis led to an EIP metric for improvement, which was transportation costs. This metric improvement objective led to the re-routing and re-scheduling of buses, which saved much in fuel costs and driver-time expenses. A reallocation of this saved money enhanced our educational offerings."

Sandra was the next to respond, saying, "Our non-profit's EIP led to a staged increase in our satellite-level monthly reported received revenue because of improvements in our donation-request process. Also, we increased our 30,000-foot-level metrics for the number of volunteers and their participation every month through other process improvements."

Sharon's response was, "Our first-pass at an EIP indicated that there was much customer dissatisfaction with the issuance and renewal of driver licenses. Our process improvement efforts led to a reduction in wait times and improved customer satisfaction, plus there was a significant cost saving as well."

Jorge then stated, "Again, great queries and responses! The clock says it's time to close this session. If anyone wants more information about IEE and how their organization might benefit from the techniques, I'm sure that I can speak for everyone on this panel by saying, just ask any one of us."

The CEO of the chamber of commerce then took the stage and said, "I want to thank Jorge for facilitating this meeting, and all presenters for conveying the how-to's of implementing an IEE enhanced business management system. The chamber offers many networking and training events. If your organization isn't a current member, I'd be happy to discuss with you options for bringing your group into our association.

"There's still some food left from our buffet lunch; help yourself to it on the way home or to work."

After the session, all presenters at the meeting went to an early happy hour with the chamber's CEO and her husband.

After everyone was seated, our chamber's CEO said, "I'm so grateful that our community had the chance to see your presentations today. I was amazed by IEE's achievements in a variety of organizations.

"In all types of organizations, complexities are growing. I think that many current management practices have issues managing this growing complexity. From what I saw today, I believe that IEE provides a system to fulfill this growing management complexity need."

Hank then said, "That's great to hear, and I agree! We're so grateful that the chamber sponsored this event.

"I want now to toast Jorge. Raise your glasses. Jorge, thank you for introducing us to the IEE business management system. *Professor,* you've changed our lives!"

10 EPILOG

The previous chapters of this book described the Integrated Enterprise Excellence (IEE) business management and its benefits.

The Appendix of this book offers additional information about IEE and the implementation of its methodologies:

- Appendix A provides over 80 illustrations of the application of IEE techniques.
- Appendix B provides more than 20 website links for further details about the IEE methodology and its use.
- Appendix C provides information about the book's datasets, scorecards, and companies.
- Appendix D describes how-to-implement IEE books and assistance

The book *Management 2.0: Discovery of Integrated Enterprise Excellence* (Breyfogle 2020a) (Reference Appendix B, Web page 20) provides in a novel-book format a:

- Description of how IEE addresses issues that often occur with Lean, the Balanced Scorecard, Lean Six Sigma, and other process-improvement deployments.
- Elaboration on the figures in the article "Positive Metric Performance Poor Business Performance: How does this happen?" (Chapter 7).

- Description of the steps in a *clickable* IEE Define, Measure, Analyze, Improve, and Control (DMAIC) process improvement roadmap (Chapter 9).

Often people do not have time to read a recommended book. For readers and listeners of this book who believe that their organization could benefit from IEE, they might suggest that their manager or others listen to this book when commuting to-and-from work or while exercising. If the book described concepts appear beneficial to this person, he or she could suggest this audiobook to others.

One initial casual book-listening suggestion could lead to an audiobook organizational dissemination of IEE concepts and its benefits. In time, the CEO, or another organization leader, could receive a recommendation that he or she listens to this audiobook. After listening to this book, those organizational leaders who want to investigate IEE further should then be asking for the book-described IEE one-on-one leadership meeting.

For additional thoughts on how to present the IEE business management system to others, see Appendix B, Web page 18.

11 APPENDIX A: APPLICATION OF IEE TECHNIQUES

Jorge shared several Harris IEE implementation recollection thoughts during his wife's Harris Hospital recovery (Reference Chapter 5). Described in this book chapter are more than 80 additional IEE implementation experiences and discussions, which could benefit readers of this book.

11.1 APPLICATION OF IEE TECHNIQUES

Three discussions related to the application of IEE techniques are:

1. Summarizing the 9-step IEE System: Financial Goal Setting and Strategy Creation in For-profit and Non-profit Organizations

A summary of the aspects of the IEE 9-step system with considerations for each step is:

- Step 1: Includes the company's vision, mission, values, and responses to Jim Collins' three-circle questions about a business: What can you be the best in the world at? What drives your economic engine? What are you deeply passionate about? (Collins 2001). High-level statements created in a traditional executive retreat often could be considered an aspect of this first step of the IEE system, which provides direction for the subsequent eight steps.
- Step 2: The organization creates an IEE value chain, which includes its satellite-level and 30,000-foot-level performance

metrics. An IEE value chain describes what an organization does and how it measures what is done. For an organization, an IEE value chain should maintain fundamental consistency over time, independent of leadership, competition, and environmental changes. However, the specifics of what is done in an organization's IEE value chain should be enhanced continuously to make the enterprise, as a whole, better over time. The identification and execution of enterprise-as-a-whole enhancement activities are what the next steps of the IEE 9-step system provide.

- Step 3: In 'Analyze enterprise,' the current state of high-level value-chain metrics are evaluated collectively with other information such as VOC, TOC information, and competitive analyses. This analysis should use statistical techniques, when appropriate, to determine the strengths and shortcomings of an organization for providing direction in the execution of Step 4 through Step 7.

- Step 4: This step of the 9-step system states 'Establish SMART satellite-level metric goals.' In IEE, satellite-level measures are to be financial. This step's objective, as the response to underlying processes, is to have a numerical quantity that is consistent with fulfilling step 1's organizational vision and mission statements and satisfying customer needs. For a for-profit organization, an appropriate financial satellite-level goal might be a mean monthly EBITDA objective. A step 4 goal does not need to be an enhancement to the satellite-level metric's current response level but could be the continuance of the organization's current response level. For government, schools, non-profits, and other similar organizations, EBITDA, or any measure of profit or revenue, may not be an appropriate encompassing measurement to address in this step. For these situations, there is a need for an alternative high-level organizational performance measurement for this step. Non-profits and government agencies might state that money are not relevant to them. However, there is still a necessity for the management of expenses in non-profits, government agencies, and schools, which can address step 4's monetary goal objective. For non-profit organizational situations, a step 4 satellite-level metric goal might be 'mean monthly operating expenses of 33.4 million dollars.' For this situation, the intention would be to enhance organizational processes so that there is an enrichment in the organization's deliverables that is consistent with this step's stated satellite-level metric goal.

- Step 5: The results from Steps 1—4 provide input to strategy creation.

- Step 6: Identify high potential improvement areas and establish 30,000-foot-level performance metric goals. An enterprise improvement plan (EIP) graphic presents the results of this work.

- Step 7: Identify and execute process improvement projects that improve operational 30,000-foot-level metrics and benefit the enterprise as a whole.

- Step 8: Assess how the completion of projects impacts the achievement of step 4's enterprise goal. An EIP is to show the alignment of undertaken projects to the needs of the enterprise and step 4's fulfillment. The staging of a project's 30,000-foot-level to an enhanced level of performance shows the amount of statistical benefit achieved to a metric through a project's execution.

- Step 9: Error-proofing a process is the best means of process control; however, that is not possible for all situations. A high-level metric-tracking control methodology is available by the periodic monitoring of organizational 30,000-foot-level process-output responses to ensure nothing has degraded. EPRS software provides a means for automatic updates for a project's 30,000-foot-level metric in the organization's IEE value chain, which can be monitored periodically for degradation so that there will be timely corrective action when appropriate.

An EIP visually describes the results from steps 4—7 of the IEE system and agreed-to 30,000-foot-level metric process improvement efforts that are in alignment with the achievement of step 4's organizational performance-metric goals. A significant component of this effort should be enhancing the fulfillment of customer deliverables relative to the customer's wants, needs, and desires in the most efficient and effective means possible.

With the focus given to improving organizational IEE value chain metrics, which has owners and is highlighted by an organization's EIP, regularly scheduled leadership meetings discuss the status of process-improvement projects. In these meetings, presentations provide the current state of the identified strategic 30,000-foot-level responses targeted for improvement with the status of their associated process-improvement projects. Such a presentation and discussion lead to a sense of urgency for the timely completion of identified projects and enhancements to associated performance metric responses.

To illustrate the benefit of the IEE approach for focusing on organizational improvement activities over traditional executive retreat strategies, as described earlier, consider this situation. A for-profit company determined, using the 9-step IEE system, that the most critical opportunity for improving its financials, as described in its EIP, is to enhance its organization's processes, so that customer non-conformance rates decline. Such a targeted enterprise-as-a-whole focus to improve both an organization's financials and customer satisfaction would typically never have such a highlighting using a traditional executive-retreat-strategic-creation-statements approach.

2. How Organizations can benefit from IEE

The IEE deployment techniques used at Harris Hospital have applicability to any organization that *does something* to provide a deliverable or service to a customer. Whether documented or not, a process or procedure is used by an organization to accomplish a *do something* task.

For the delivery of *something* to a customer, an accompanying question should address the effectiveness of its conveyance. The measurements for the delivery of something should consider the quality, cost, and time aspects, as perceived by both the final customer and the organization that provides the deliverable.

A *do something* activity and '*how well something was done*' assessment applies to both for-profit and non-profit groups. Both large and small organizations can benefit from IEE techniques. Potential organizational applications are government agencies, schools, healthcare providers, insurance businesses, service establishments, mining companies, software firms, small businesses, and manufacturing.

When applying IEE techniques in a large organization, it is best to start with a subset of the entire enterprise. This starting point needs to be high enough in the organization, where someone is responsible for an enterprise value chain and its deliverables, not unlike Harris's CEO ownership. After the success of IEE in one organization's division or significant component, there can be a leveraging of IEE's implementation success to other areas of the overall entity.

3. How Organizations can benefit from 30,000-foot-level Performance Metric Reporting

Satellite-level and 30,000-foot-level process output response reporting techniques can be applied even if an organization is not undertaking an IEE deployment.

The following process addresses the applicability of IEE high-level performance metric reporting in an organization:

1. Identify several key process output variables (KPOVs) reported in an organization.
2. Record in a spreadsheet historical KPOV values, where date-of-incident and response value appear in occurrence sequence down the spreadsheet.
3. Create a 30,000-foot-level or satellite-level response for each KPOV response using EPRS-metrics software (Reference Appendix B, Web page 13), staging individuals charts when appropriate.

4. Compare the conclusions from the created IEE metric reports to what current KPOV reports convey.
5. IEE EPRS software (Reference Appendix B, Web page 14) can provide automatic updates to these IEE performance metrics reports.

Reference Appendix B, Web page 3 for examples of the conversion of eight traditional scorecards and measurement reporting to 30,000-foot-level reports, with the conversion's benefits. Reference Appendix B, Web page 13 for information about EPRS-metrics software for creating 30,000-foot-level individuals charts.

11.2 OVERCOMING ISSUES WITH EXECUTIVE-RETREAT FORMULATED STATEMENTS

Four discussions related to overcoming issues with executive-retreat formulated strategic statements and goal setting in for-profit and non-profit organizations are:

1. Do you have a Strategy?

The article "Are you sure you have a strategy?" (Hambrick and Fredrickson 2001) describes the shortcomings with developed frameworks for strategic analysis. This article points out that what is often missing is guidance for what constitutes a strategy and what an organization should do to overcome the issue.

"Strategy has become a catchall term used to mean whatever one wants it to mean. Executives now talk about their 'service strategy,' their 'branding strategy,' their 'acquisition strategy,' or whatever kind of strategy that is on their mind at a particular moment. But strategists—whether they are CEOs of established firms, division presidents, or entrepreneurs—must have a strategy, an integrated, overarching concept of how the business will achieve its objectives."

Consider these statements of strategy drawn from actual documents and announcements of several companies:

- "Our strategy is to be the low-cost provider."
- "We're pursuing a global strategy."
- "The company's strategy is to integrate a set of regional acquisitions."
- "Our strategy is to provide unrivaled customer service."
- "Our strategic intent is always to be the first mover."
- "Our strategy is to move from defense to industrial applications."

"What do these declarations have in common? Only that none of them is a strategy. They are strategic threads, mere elements of strategy. But they are no more strategies than Dell Computer's strategy (in the 1990s) can be summed up as selling directly to customers, or than Hannibal's strategy was to use elephants to cross the Alps. And their use reflects an increasingly common syndrome—the catchall fragmentation of strategy" (Hambrick and Fredrickson 2001).

"Executives then communicate these strategic threads to their organizations in the mistaken belief that doing so will help managers make tough choices. But how does knowing that their firm is pursuing an 'acquisition strategy' or a 'first-mover strategy' help the vast majority of managers do their job or set priorities?" (Hambrick and Fredrickson 2001)

Business leaders must have a strategy to meet their objectives. Without a plan, organizations will waste time and resources on piecemeal, disparate activities. Without a plan, mid-level managers will fill the void with their interpretation of what the business should be doing, typically resulting in a disjointed set of activities.

IEE provides the framework for accomplishing Hambrick and Fredrickson's described need for the development and execution of strategies, where targeted strategy creation is step 5 in the 9-step IEE system.

2. Hoshin Kanri and Hoshin Kanri X Matrix

In strategic planning, hoshin kanri is a methodology that is to ensure that a company's strategic goals drive progress and action at every level within that organization. The Hoshin Kanri X Matrix Template, as a single page document, includes goals, strategies, strategic projects (or initiatives), and owners that are to facilitate the execution of hoshin kanri.

Ron highlighted that there is much subjectivity in the creation of a Hoshin Kanri X matrix and is another attempt to manage an organization through the simple setting of lofty desires and Y objectives; that is, in the relationship Y is a function of X or Y=f(X).

The use of hoshin kanri as a methodology for deploying strategic planning statements and goals, which were the result of an annual executive retreat, has fundamental issues. Several *'elephant in the room'* implementation issues exist when creating strategies and goals as basically step 1 in a business management system, which is to be a primary driver of efforts throughout an organization.

First, this common-place business management approach, among other things, often results in strategic statements that are very generic, which can lead to many how-to-implement interpretation differences in an organization. Besides, strategic statements and objectives can change from year to year, resulting in much disruption and confusion.

The IEE business management system addresses these strategic planning issues by creating targeted strategic planning statements in step 5 of the 9-step IEE system and then identifying 30,000-foot-level performance metrics that need enhancement through steps 6 and 7. With the IEE system, strategies are to give focus and be in alignment with improving the financials, which makes more sense than creating strategies that provide concentration instead of organizational vision and mission.

In the 9-step IEE system, vision and mission statements are the focus of step 1. All other steps in this IEE system are to be in alignment with this organizational basic directional compass. Step 2 involves the *creation of an IEE value chain*, which describes what an organization does and reports organizational, functional performance metrics from a process-output-response point of view.

For a given organization, an IEE value chain should maintain fundamental continuity over time. From this value chain, in the 9-step IEE system, targeted strategies, which have alignment with the financials and customer needs, are created in step 5. These strategies then lead to specific actions in steps 6—7 that give a primary focus to the improvement of 30,000-foot-level IEE-value-chain metrics.

With the IEE system, EIP identified 30,000-foot-level metric improvement needs *pull* for the execution of structured process improvement efforts. The method used to enhance an underlying metric's process can follow an IEE DMAIC roadmap, kaizen event, or any other process-improvement methodology. The urgency to improve EIP identified metrics should occur since IEE value chain owners of these metrics will be periodically reporting to leadership the status of their metric-improvement efforts.

With the 9-step IEE system, strategy creation and operational-metric goal-setting activities occur in steps 5 and 6. This IEE business management system sequence for creating strategies and performance measurement goals is after, and in alignment with, what the organization does and how it measures what is done; that is, the organization's IEE value chain in step 2.

In addition to providing a system for continual improvement so that there is a positive impact on an enterprise's bottom-line, execution of the IEE system can lead to significant breakthrough implementations that are very positive to the organization and its customers.

3. Executive-retreat Created Strategic Statements Issues and Resolution

Corporate executives often attend an annual two-day retreat with a primary purpose of creating a strategic plan to later convey to their organization for implementation.

Relative to the creation of this organizational strategic plan, a consultant friend of Ron's claimed that he could expedite the two-day executive strategic statement creation process. The consultant's methodology to achieve this time reduction assertion was to list 20 commonly-used strategic statements from which leadership agrees to five statements for use in their organization.

Ron agrees with this consultant's observation that often the wording of executive-retreat- created strategic statements, from a variety of industries, are very similar. When reflecting on this observation, Ron's inquiry is whether the wording of many executive-retreat-created strategic directives is really:

- Actionable throughout an organization?
- Subject to much how-to-achieve interpretation?
- Something tough to complete because of the time it takes for employees to finish their regular assignments and resolve crises that often occur?

IEE addresses this issue by creating strategic statements in step 5 of the 9-step IEE system, which leads to specific improvement efforts via an EIP that benefit the overall organizational financials and customers.

4. Strategy Creation as Step 5 in an IEE 9-step System

In an IEE leadership training session, an executive commented to Ron that their organization recently formulated, in an executive retreat, their organization's new strategic statements. When creating these strategic statements, there was a focus on the achievement of the organization's vision and mission.

In IEE, organizational vision and mission is step 1 of the 9-step system. The execution of steps 2—9 has alignment with the organization's step 1 directional statements. However, in the IEE system, targeted strategies are created in step 5 and are to be aligned with the financials, step 4, and customer needs.

At the time of this executive comment, Ron asked what made more sense so that the business as a whole would benefit? Jorge would vote for creating strategies that were to improve the financials and fulfillment of customer needs.

Ron then continued, stating that in IEE, vision and mission are step 1, before describing what the organization does and how it measures what is done in step 2. Also, an IEE approach for strategic planning is to lead to targeted operational 30,000-foot-level performance metric improvement efforts in steps 5 and 6 through an EIP.

An IEE approach might result in targeted efforts to reduce non-conformance rates, which would provide the most benefit to the financials. Ron stated that he had never seen a 'reduce-non-conformance rates' statement originate from a traditional retreat-developed-strategic-statements approach.

11.3 30,000-FOOT-LEVEL PERFORMANCE METRIC REPORTING

Seven discussions related to 30,000-foot-level performance metric reporting are:

1. Traditional Scorecard Reports: Why 30,000-foot-level Performance Metric Reporting is Different and Better

Traditional scorecard reports give focus to the achievement of measurable goals at some point in time, where these metric objectives are often arbitrarily set.

In IEE, this form of management is called Y-management. The practice of Y-goal-setting management does not structurally give focus to addressing the reality that a Y-process-response is the result of the Xs executed in the processes; that is, $Y=f(X)$. The achievement of long-lasting Y-enhancements is through improving the processes' Xs.

Y-Management can lead to very unfavorable, if not destructive, organizational behaviors, including playing games with the numbers to achieve a next reporting period Y-response goal and making things appear better than they are.

Performance metrics typically have over-time variation, which could be large or small. Traditional scorecard reports do not typically include this variation in their reporting, for example, in red-yellow-green scorecards or table-of-numbers reporting. The exclusion of process-response variation in performance metric reporting is a big deal!

The achievement of long-lasting Y-response improvements is through the enhancement of the processes that deliver the Y-response; that is, the Xs. Because of the $Y=f(X)$ relationship, it is better to provide a process-output reporting that includes measurement variation.

The inclusion of variation in performance-metric reporting can provide a more accurate representation for current and future expectations from the process-output response, with the understanding that, if this response-statement is undesirable, there is a need for enhancing the process; that is, the Xs.

The 30,000-foot-level performance metric reporting methodology fulfills the requirement for inclusion of process variation in reported statements. Besides, 30,000-foot-level reports can often provide a futuristic statement that, when unacceptable, *pulls for the creation* of a process improvement project.

2. Traditional Lean Six Sigma Process-output Response Reports: Why 30,000-foot-level Performance Metric Reporting is Different and Better

In Lean Six Sigma (LSS), the time-series, process-output tracking methodology typically utilized is a statistical process control (SPC) control chart. In an LSS project and elsewhere, when a control chart has not identified any out-of-control condition, a process capability statement can be determined, which states how the process is performing relative to customer specifications.

For a continuous process output response, process capability indices describe how a process is performing relative to specifications, for example, Cp, Cpk, Pp, and Ppk. For a process response that has an attribute pass/fail response, an estimated non-conformance rate determined from the control chart's centerline describes process capability. Control charts and process capability reporting are two separate analyses and reports.

Traditional control charts used to assess whether a process has any out-of-control signals are dependent upon the selection process of samples from an operation. For example, someone may choose to select five daily samples and then create an and R control chart, while someone else may decide to randomly select only one daily sample and then create an XmR control chart. The reporting differences between these two charting options, relative to the identification of special-cause incidents, can be considerable because of the mathematics associated with calculating UCL and LCL values for each of the two situations (Reference Appendix B, Web page 11).

The reason for this difference is that an individuals chart creates upper and lower control limits as a function of variation between sub-groups. This UCL and LCL limit calculation input is different for and R charts, p-charts, and u-charts. For these three control charting methodologies, the variability between adjacent time-series intervals has no impact upon the calculation of UCL and LCL control chart limits.

The purpose of determining UCL and LCL control-chart plotting values is the separation of special-cause events from common-cause variation. For deciding which charting methodology to use, the question one needs to reflect upon is whether there should be consideration of the differences between adjacent time-series process response values as a source from common- or special-cause variation. A response to this question can differ depending upon whether the control chart is tracking an X-process-input response or a Y-process-output response.

Consider the tracking of hold time in a company's call center for determining the most appropriate Y-process-output charting approach when deciding whether differing process response values are originating from common- or special-cause variation. For this situation, the question to address is: Should any difference between hold times as a function of time-of-day or day-of-week have consideration that these up-and-down values originated from common-cause or special-cause variation?

Since there will always be multiple times in a day and several days in a week, any variation from these weekly time sources should be considered a source of common-cause Y-response variation. For this 30,000-foot-level process-response perspective, an individuals chart of both a calculated mean and standard deviation of weekly hold time values would be most appropriate for determining whether special-cause occurrences were identified or not. When there are no identified special-cause conditions in these two individuals charts, the process response is considered stable and predictable.

Any important time-of-day and day-of-week determined differences should be addressed as X-input differences and managed accordingly to improve an overall Y-process-output hold-time response. An example of this X-management is adding more attendants during analytically-determined times-of-day or day-of-week where call-in demand is the highest.

In IEE, 30,000-foot-level reporting always utilizes the mathematics of an individuals chart to determine process stability for both continuous and attribute data. When not following this charting practice, many false special-cause signals can appear in a chart and then wrongfully reacted to because of common-cause time-of-day and/or day-of-week variations.

When a process is considered stable, the next question to address is how well the process is performing relative to customer specifications for a process response. A traditional Lean Six Sigma approach for providing a process-capability statement has many issues that a 30,000-foot-level report overcomes (Reference Appendix B, Web page 11).

In 30,000-foot-level performance metric reporting, both process stability and capability information are reported—in one chart!

3. No Specification Requirement with 30,000-foot-level Reporting

In traditional Lean Six Sigma training, typically, there is a specification requirement for improvement project metrics. The reason for this specification-need is that an associated process capability statement requires one or more tolerance limits in its calculation.

However, often there are no real specifications for a process output response. Two examples where there are no actual specifications are work in progress (WIP) and monthly-reported business profit. For WIP, a lower monthly value is better, as long as there are no work-flow disruptions, while higher monthly amounts are more desirable for organizational profit.

Traditionally in Six Sigma, a target or objective needs to be assigned and considered a specification if no true-customer-requirement specification exists. However, this specification-fabrication approach leads to subjectivity and questionable value for determining a process capability statement.

In the IEE satellite-level and 30,000-foot-level reporting, there is *no requirement* for a specification. For the described WIP and organization profit reporting situations, where no specification exists, a 30,000-foot-level report would provide for a stable process, both a predicted mean or median value and an 80% frequency of occurrence estimate.

A process improvement project for this type of 30,000-foot-level reporting could give focus on creating a positive shift in the reported mean or median value and/or reduction in the spread of the 80% frequency of occurrence value.

For an organization undertaking IEE strategic metric improvements, an EIP reflects those 30,000-foot-level metrics that should be enhanced for improving an enterprise's mean monthly profit, for example, whether the process-output response has a specification or not.

4. 30,000-foot-level Performance Metric Reporting with and without a Specification

The 30,000-foot-level reporting process includes both a process stability assessment and a capability statement assessment in one chart. With this high-level process-output metric reporting, a stable process provides a prediction statement below the report's charting. This form of process output metric-response reporting provides much value not only for the Lean Six Sigma process metric-improvement projects but also for functional metrics reporting throughout the business.

The two steps to create a 30,000-foot-level report are simple. Step one assesses whether a process response is stable, from a high-level point of view. Step two provides a process capability/performance prediction-estimation statement when the process is considered stable. A 30,000-foot-level report can give a prediction statement even when there is no process-output specification.

For illustration:

- When a specification exists, an example statement is: The process is stable with an estimated 0.13 non-conformance rate.

- When a specification does not exist, an example statement is: The process is stable with an estimated monthly mean WIP cost of $95,500, where there is an expectation that 80% of months will have an approximate WIP cost between $85,500 and $105,500.

5. Red-yellow-green Scorecard Issue and Resolution

At a conference, Ron gave a presentation. Surprise, surprise! He presented red-yellow-green scorecards as a methodology that can lead to wasteful firefighting of common-cause variation as though it were special-cause.

One person in the audience made the statement that he was responsible for one of the metrics in a company scorecard. His metric's color changed to red. In the next reported time-period, the color changed to green, but he had not done anything to improve the metric's underlying process.

This person then asked Ron what he should do. Ron's response, with a playful smile, was, "Take credit, of course ... However, start working immediately on determining what to do to improve the process. The reason for this process-investigation effort suggestion is that it would be a good bet that the metric color will change back to red at some point in time down the road.

"Before undertaking this process-enhancement effort, one should plot and evaluate the performance metric response over time using a 30,000-foot-level reporting metric format. Often, when evaluating a process response from this high-level point of view, the process will be considered stable. If so, one can then determine from the 30,000-foot-level reporting an expectation for the percentage rate frequency of future non-specification-conforming events—if the current state of the process remains unchanged.

"One should then present this 30,000-foot-level report to management, asking if this metric is important enough, to the business as a whole, for the expenditure of the time and effort needed to make enhancements to the metric's associated process or processes. In an IEE deployment, the organization would include this 30,000-foot-level improvement effort in the organization's EIP."

6. Balance Scorecard Deployment Issue and Resolution

A friend of Ron's told him about a how-to-implement-the-balanced scorecard response that she received when working for a previous employer. The organization where this friend was employed subscribed to the services of a large global research and advisory firm that provided information, advice, and tools for businesses. Since the friend was having difficulty understanding how to implement the balanced scorecard, she decided to take advantage of the opportunity to get a clarification statement from someone in this well-respected research and advisory company.

The response that she received was that the people who developed the balanced scorecard don't even use it because it is so complicated. Ron was surprised by the candid response that his friend received from this technology-resource company. However, he did not disagree with the statement given to his friend.

Ron then stated that there is even more to the story. The balanced scorecard and its organizational use have evolved over the years. Wikipedia recently noted that the balanced scorecard is a strategy performance management tool, a semi-standard structured report that managers can use to keep track of the execution of activities by the staff within their control and to monitor the consequences arising from these actions.

This Wikipedia internet posting also referenced a recent survey where 62% of respondents reported using the balanced scorecard for strategy implementation management, while 48% used the approach for operational management.

In 1992, Kaplan and Norton introduced the balanced scorecard in a *Harvard Business Review* article (Kaplan and Norton 1992). Initially, the balanced scorecard was to address the execution of vision and strategies activities with a balance of four quadrants that were 'financials,' 'customer,' 'learning and growth,' and 'internal business processes.'

In addition to implementation complexities, as noted by the research-firm consultant, there seem to be other issues with the balanced scorecard. Inconsistencies now apparently exist in how organizations implement the methodology when compared to its initiation. Has the balanced scorecard phrase become nothing more than a buzzword? There is probably not a universal agreed-to response to this question. Still, there is a need for organizations structurally to address a balance of organizational measurements with the creation of strategies and execution of process improvement efforts that will benefit the business as a whole.

The 9-step IEE system structurally addresses all of the original quadrants in the original balanced scorecard article with a natural, not forced, organizational-scorecard balance. Besides, IEE provides both the creation and execution of targeted strategies so that essential performance metrics to the business are improved, from both an enterprise financials and customer benefits perspective.

7. Y-response Reactive Management Issues and Resolution

One comment that Ron periodically receives from practitioners is that 30,000-foot-level reporting is too complicated for leadership to understand and use. Ron responds that he will not disagree that this high-level charting methodology output initially looks intimidating and perhaps confusing. However, Ron suggests that the interpretation of this reporting methodology is actuality, a lot easier to understand and use than other scorecard formats.

The people who have a leadership role in companies are smart folks, or they would not be in a high-level position. Ron believes that what first needs to be addressed, before getting into the details of a report's interpretation, is having a systems-thinking discussion.

Management often gives focus to what is happening *today* and what to do to resolve any currently-identified issues. This reactive-to-the-Ys of an organization management style is inconsistent with a basic systems thinking model.

Surely any immediate business crisis needs to be addressed; however, an IEE systems-thinking approach gives focus to the implementation of long-lasting improvements so that frequently occurring types-of-issues do not keep reoccurring. In IEE, there is a fundamental belief that, until there is statistical evidence to indicate otherwise, process outputs, in general, are considered stable.

Reacting to process up-and-down output responses can lead to much firefighting common-cause variation as though it were a special-cause event. The reaction an organization should take to address common-cause variation issues is different from special-cause occurrences.

When a process is experiencing common-cause variation, and the response is not satisfactory, process improvement is needed to enhance the process-output response. If a process experiences a special-cause event, then a reaction to this specific event can be appropriate.

When management manages the Ys, more often than not, common-cause variation is being reacted to as though it were a special cause. This type of reaction can be costly and frustrating, since problems frequently keep popping up again and again, resulting in wasteful and perhaps even destructive behaviors in an organization. To overcome this issue, leadership needs first to internalize a systems-thinking model of high-level process-output-response common- and special-cause variation.

Once there is an achievement of this common- and special-cause variation understanding, the next step is more comfortable, which is a discussion about how 30,000-foot-level reports address both special- and common-cause variation in their reporting.

This conversation would discuss the value and understanding of, when a process is stable, there is a reporting of an easy-to-understand 30,000-foot-level prediction statement below the report's charts. When a common-cause variation statement is considered undesirable, there is a need for process improvement efforts to enhance this high-level process-output metric response. When there is effective process enhancement, the individuals chart in the 30,000-foot-level report will transition to an improved level of performance. The 30,000-foot-level report would then provide, when process-stability exists, a new-process prediction statement.

11.4 BUSINESS LEADERSHIP PERFORMANCE METRICS, REPORTING, AND GOAL SETTING

Eight discussions related to business leadership performance metrics and goal setting are:

1. Red-yellow-green Goal Setting and Tracking Issues and Resolution

Inappropriate goal setting can lead to unintended consequences (Reference Appendix B, Web pages 4, 5, and 10). Given a business-management, goal-setting focus, the phrase 'Tell me how you will measure me, and then I will tell you how I will behave' can lead to a meet-the-numbers-or-else culture. There can be an amplification of a measurement-driven behavior when financial incentives are attached to metric goals achievement.

Goal setting without a plan for creating a system that supports the achievement of business goals can result in much playing games with numbers, including the setting of goals that are easy to achieve, so that stoplight scorecard metric colors are green. An illustration of this point is Alan Mulally's experience as the new Ford CEO hired to address the financial issues that the company had been experiencing.

In Mulally's leadership meetings, all reported red-yellow-green (RYG) scorecard metrics from his team were green, indicating everything was okay. Mulally stated in a meeting that Ford was having severe financial issues. Aren't there any problems? Reported scorecards continued to be green in reoccurring meetings. Mulally continued to reiterate his problem-inquiry statement.

Finally, one person in a meeting drummed up the courage to report a metric color that was not green. Everyone in the room thought the person would endure severe consequences from this reporting or be fired since that is what would have occurred with the previous CEO;

however, no employee-firing occurred. Mulally complimented the person and then said, "What can *we* do to resolve this issue?"

Other leaders in the room were stunned by Mulally's response but were still fearful of being candid in their performance-metric reporting. Finally, more honest reporting became commonplace. Alan Mulally did much to turn things around at Ford. Unlike most company new CEO hires that are to address company financial issues, Mulally's hiring resulted in positive change to the Ford company. However, when reflecting on his leadership scorecard reporting approach, one could make several inquiries.

First, how were the RYG scorecard colored goals determined for each manager? It appeared that each manager decided the metrics' goals for his or her leadership meeting report. This goal then triggered a color for specific periods, which depended upon the measurement response value.

In general, when green colored measurements transition to a red color, a trigger occurs for the tracked metric. The conclusion from this color transition is that a problem occurred during the time interval since the last metric reporting. The context from this belief would lead one to approach the color-transition issue as an action for what to do to change the color back to green before the next reporting cycle.

This action is in contrast to the consideration that perhaps a significant amount of process-improvement effort is needed to address an underlying issue with the current process that impacts the metric's response. With this line of thinking, which RYG scorecards do not encourage, a process change is needed so that red for any specific time interval will be very unlikely to occur in the future.

Secondly, if one were to report organizational performance metrics using a 30,000-foot-level format, the expectation is that most red signals would arise from the variation in common-cause responses. For example, there might be a 0.15 likelihood of any particular time-series-reported metric being red. For any given metric-improvement situation, a large amount of effort might need to occur to make a statistically significant difference to a process-output response.

In any organizational leadership setting, the reported level of many metrics can exhibit common-cause variation, where reported values are not desirable. If this occurs, one might ask the question: Where should one start working on making process and other enhancements so that there is benefit in the whole enterprise? Answering this question involves the transition from organizational silo thinking to systems thinking. An IEE's EIP provides a systems-thinking methodology for determining where to focus process improvement efforts so that the big-picture benefits.

Lastly, the determination of which metrics to track is an important consideration. Often performance metrics are selected in organizational silos where there can be little if any direct connection with the big-picture financials and customer needs. Without a direct link, there can be an expenditure of much effort to improve a process that offers little overall enterprise benefit.

The IEE system, with its 30,000-foot-level reporting, IEE value chain, EIP, and process improvement methodology, flattens all these issues. Besides, the IEE system provides, with its EPRS software, automatic reporting transparency that encourages everyone in an organization to move toward the achievement of the 3 Rs of business; that is, everyone doing the Right things and doing them Right at the Right time. A 3 Rs' direction encourages organizational trust and avoids teams' hiding things.

This line of thinking discourages unethical behaviors and assesses potential risks so that there are appropriate actions taken in a timely fashion, which includes a redirection of business focus because of technology changes. This thought process also includes not creating and incentivizing metrics that lead to deceitful, if not unethical behaviors, such as Wells Fargo's creation of fake accounts so that a customer cross-selling metric objective would be achieved (Wolff-Mann 2019).

2. Business Goal Setting and Tracking Issues

Things were not going well in a high-tech company. A newly hired CEO was to turn things around. The board of directors believed that good companies double their revenue in five years; hence, the board of directors set a 2X five-year revenue growth goal for the CEO. The Board did not consider when setting this objective whether a doubling growth goal was a reasonable objective for the company's industry and the type of products that they produced.

Attainment of increased revenue goals over time set by the board of directors was an essential objective to the CEO because of linkage to his financial bonuses. The CEO and his team did not know how to increase revenue by a factor of two in five years with their current product offerings. Hence, in an attempt to achieve the rate of top-line growth goal set for the CEO, the company acquired several companies.

These company purchases increased overall revenue in the short term, so the CEO received bonuses; however, the purchased companies, among other things, did not fit into the core competencies of the company and its culture. Because of this incompatibility, the company's overall profit took a significant negative hit.

This year-over-year poor company financial performance eventually resulted in this CEO being replaced by another CEO, who was a financial-accounting person and did not have any high-tech skills relative to the products that the company offered.

This newly-hired CEO stated that he would not pursue acquiring other companies for sales growth as the past CEO had done since many company purchases proved to be damaging to the business as a whole. However, not unlike the previous CEO, this new CEO continued to set arbitrary monthly product-shipment goals that tended to increase over time whenever there was an achievement of a monthly goal.

This new company leader believed that simply setting aggressive product-shipment goals would result in business success, which was similar to the previous CEO's thinking.

This common-place practice for leadership goal-setting may sound reasonable; however, what was happening internally in the organization to meet the monthly sales goals was the robbing from Peter to pay Paul. That is, there was a movement of future orders into the current month for the achievement of a goal, at a tremendous overall organizational expense.

Both the last CEO and new CEO did not appreciate that the financials are the result of the integration of many processes. If there is a desire to improve a financial response, there is a need to improve the enterprise's underlying operations. The setting of specific arbitrary goals for the next month, such as the number of products shipped, can lead to very unfavorable, if not destructive, behaviors, above all, when there is financial incentive linkage to the achievement of these goals.

It seemed that everyone in the trenches knew that corporate's monthly goal-setting practices were leading to harmful behaviors in the company. However, because of an apparent *shoot the messenger* cultural fear, no one dared describe to the CEOs and board of directors what was truly happening in the organization as a result of their arbitrarily setting of meet-the-numbers-or-else monthly goals.

In contrast, the 9-step IEE Business Management System offers leadership an alternative to attempting to manage the Ys of an organization by setting a next-month or quarterly goal, which can lead to harmful behaviors.

With a meet-the-numbers Y-management approach, goals are often arbitrarily set without a structured linkage of process improvement efforts to the enhancement of the Y responses. Y-management can lead to much waste in the utilization of resources in attempting to describe what happened last month. Y-management can lead to the unfavorable practice of playing-games-with-the-numbers to make things look better than they are.

With the IEE system, there is the use of analytics to determine what metrics in an organizational IEE value chain to focus on improving so that the enterprise, as a whole, experiences a benefit. With the IEE system, there is no claim of improvement to a metric until there is a demonstrated statistical enhancement of the metric's response. In IEE, an indicator of enrichment takes place when an EIP-identified 30,000-foot-level individuals chart transitions statistically to an enhanced level of performance.

An organizational EIP summarizes the results of this analytical work, showing the alignment of 30,000-foot-level metrics improvement efforts with the enhancement of an organization's *mean* satellite-level financial parameter. Rather than giving focus to achievement of a next-month number, an IEE enterprise goal might be to increase *mean* monthly EBITA and/or year-over-year reported revenue growth (monthly-reported-estimate) by a realistic percentage amount.

In IEE, leadership meetings can be more effective when giving focus to the status of EIP execution efforts that should benefit the enterprise as a whole when completed. In an IEE leadership meeting, EPRS software can provide an up-to-date IEE value-chain with linkage to a 30,000-foot-level report for each metric that is to be improved. In this meeting, EPRS software can also provide up-to-date status for each 30,000-foot-level metric improvement project.

In an IEE leadership meeting, productive EIP conversations include:

1. Identification of resource allocation or other roadblocks that need a resolution for the timely completion of identified 30,000-foot-level metric projects.
2. Identification of a 30,000-foot-level operational metric to add to the organization's EIP effort.
3. Identification of a *sacred cow* policy that, when changed, could provide a very significant benefit to the bottom-line of the business.

3. Effective and Consistent Business Leadership Reporting

There can be much inconsistency in the reporting at CEO monthly leadership and board of directors' meetings. Why does this occur? It seems like there should be consistency. An IEE approach not only provides a consistent basic meeting-reporting approach but also delivers a methodology that leads to better organizational actions relative to these reports.

The IEE system can provide a high-level view of what is happening in a business. Organizations can use IEE to evaluate the key financial metrics and relevant process responses that are vital to business performance. This view helps process owners determine specific actions to improve these process responses, thus improving the organization's financial picture over time.

However, over the years, Jorge had observed the expenditure of many efforts to creating statements that justify a table of numbers or a stoplight scorecard value. These justify-measurement-value stories often provide no real beneficial value relative to incorporating process enhancement so that the big-picture benefits.

Shouldn't consistency in reporting that leads to the most appropriate actions be an integral aspect of MBA instruction, which most of these leaders have encountered during their training?

Jorge likes how the IEE system that Harris is now using provides a more consistent and productive approach for leadership meetings. In these IEE meetings, there is a focus on targeted IEE value chain metrics to improve that are consistent with our EIP so that the enterprise as a whole will benefit from process-improvement efforts.

4. Inclusion of Variation in Scorecard Reports

One cannot overemphasize that traditional scorecard reporting, such as a table of numbers and red-yellow-green scorecards, doesn't structurally address process variation. Process variation is an important consideration when determining the most appropriate action or non-action to take for a particular reported measurement-response situation.

A 30,000-foot-level report alternative includes process-output-variation in its reporting, where an improvement to a stable process-metric output could be from a mean response shift, or a reduction in process-output-response variation, or both.

Reference Appendix B, Web page 3 provides eight examples that illustrate the conversion of actual company scorecards to 30,000-foot-level reports. Shown is how this IEE high-level reporting format provides substantially more information as to how a process is genuinely performing and what to do differently to improve a process-output response. This web page uses actual company scorecards to demonstrate the benefit of 30,000-foot-level reporting over table-of-numbers, red-yellow-green scorecards, and other scorecard reports.

5. Scorecard Evaluation Issues and Resolution

There can be much difference in how leadership reports, examines and reacts to the organization's financial and key performance indicator (KPI) reported numbers. For this evaluation, leadership and a company's board of directors might study current monthly financial figures with a comparison to last month's amount, a rolling average value from several months, a year-to-date number and/or a number from the same month from a previous year.

These traditional approaches for evaluation are not assessing organizational performance metrics from a systems-thinking viewpoint. The IEE system offers both systems thinking and a consistent approach to the assessment of performance metrics and execution of improvement efforts that will benefit the enterprise as a whole.

6. Year-over-year Monitoring of KPIs

If a current monthly scorecard reported metric response is better than a previously reported value, even by only a small amount, a statement might be made that implies something changed in the process. A lengthy *what happened* explanation may then describe what caused the change. With an IEE system evaluation, these differences maybe, perhaps more often than not, the result of common-cause variation, which a 30,000-foot-level tracking could uncover.

For illustration, consider three key performance indicators, which were discussed every month by Harris leadership. From an IEE high-level tracking point of view, the use of data from the last four years could provide a much different perspective that offers more process insight than a traditional table-of-numbers report. In all three Harris performance 30,000-foot-level metrics reports, a majority of up-and-down excursions were from common-cause-process-output-response variation.

Consider that in this IEE metric assessment illustration, two of the processes had been stable over the last four years, while the third process experienced a 10% performance degradation, five months ago.

For the process response that experienced a decline, one might meet with the team responsible for this business area and inquire about the cause of this decline. The team's response might indicate that there was a supplier change, and they thought that something happened with the new supplier, but they were not sure. Since there were many fires-to-fight, the team said that there was no time for further investigation.

Now with the 30,000-foot-level quantification of this degradation and a quick cost of doing nothing differently (CODND) financial impact calculation, an estimated $10,000 monthly expense to the company led to an organizational refocus. Because of this financial-impact understanding, the organization provided the team with the time and resources needed to undertake a root-cause analysis and report their findings in a meeting the following week.

For the other two reports that did not indicate any high-level response level change over the years, there might have been many expensive firefighting activities. These fires-to-fight efforts may not have resulted in any long-lasting benefits and proved to be a waste of time and resources.

7. Plan-do-check-act (PDCA) Cycle for Enterprise as a Whole

Plan-do-check-act (PDCA) offers a systematic way to improve continually. PDCA is also known as Plan-do-study-act (PDSA), the Deming wheel, and Shewhart cycle. In the 9-step IEE system, steps 5—8 include the selection, execution, and quantification of improvements to 30,000-foot-level value chain metrics that are in step 2 of the IEE roadmap.

In the 9-step IEE system, step 9, 'Maintain the gain,' of this business management system loops back to step 3. This looping to an earlier IEE roadmap step is analogous to plan-do-check-act (PDCA) cycle thinking for the *business as a whole*.

8. Goal Setting that Leads to the Wrong Behaviors

A friend of Ron's provided the following story, which highlights motivation and reward systems going awry.

Delivering medications to the right patients at the right time has been a manual process for a long time in a hospital, where the current process experienced a significant error rate.

Many of these errors had gone unnoticed. Also, nurses had a higher level of confidence in the delivery of medication accuracy than the results deserved. That is, while nurses would admit that sometimes a patient missed a medication, in reality, many patients were getting meds late, or the wrong meds. As technology became available, some hospitals tried to add tools to ensure the accuracy and timeliness of medication deliveries.

How the system was to work: Nurses were given mobile devices that ran the hospital EMR (Electronic Medical Records) software, which included a bar-code scanner. To administer medications, the nurse would bring the mobile device to the patient's room, scan the patient's wrist band bar-code, and then deliver the drug. The software would track that the right patient got the right med at the right time. There was a 15-minute plus-or-minus window around the medication scheduled time. For example, on-time delivery was the consideration of a 3:00 PM scheduled med when administered between 2:45 and 3:15.

What really happened in the hospital is that the mobile device was clumsy to use and required the nurses to enter their passwords often. Besides, the nurses were overworked and had trouble delivering medication on time. The nurses' supervisors were disappointed in the late medication deliveries and were pressuring the nurses to work faster.

Because of this management push to make the patients' on-time delivery metrics look better, the nurses took a photo of each patient's wrist band bar-code. They printed out the images, putting these pictures near the medication cart.

When medications were to be delivered, the nurses scanned the photo at the right time but put the medicines in their pocket and administered the drugs the old-fashioned way. Nurses attempted to remember when to give the right medications to each patient as they got to each room.

This illustration is an example not of bad nurses, but of management that saw a late medication delivery measurement and didn't dig into the root cause for actual process resolution. Instead, management just started 'yelling' at nurses to do better.

An IEE system implementation with its performance measurements and improvements gives focus to what could be done differently in the process so that both quality and timely delivery occur. This approach is in contrast to 'a yelling at nurses' attitude. This IEE process-improvement evaluation assessment can also address items outside the immediate delivery area.

One example of this beyond-the-immediate-area for making process improvement is the HR process of hiring the best people for specific tasks. Another possibility, if appropriate, is receiving an okay from physicians to make minor adjustments to medication delivery times so that the nurses' delivery of medications workflow would be more efficient, which a specialized delivery-of-products software might provide.

11.5 BENEFITS OF IEE VALUE CHAIN

Seven discussions related to benefits of IEE value chain are:

1. Creation of Performance Tracking Metrics from a Big-picture Perspective

An IEE value chain describes what an enterprise does and how it measures what is done in its organizational functions. A managerial IEE value chain framework should be consistent with leadership changes, where there is a refinement of its metrics and processes over time.

The top-down approach for initially creating an organizational IEE value chain provides an agreed-to holistic approach that can be long-lasting. Rather than having a helter-skelter plan for metric selection, an IEE approach for value chain metrics is selecting for each function appropriate parameters that address quality, cost, and time, along with any process efficiency, productivity, and customer satisfaction considerations.

Many of an organization's current reported functional metrics may have been easy to collect but are not insightful, useful, or actionable. Organizations benefit when they redirect the reporting of irrelevant measurements to the creation of metrics that are informative and lead to the most appropriate action or non-action behavior, understanding that there may be a need to create new functional process-output measurements.

For these new metrics, there may be a need to determine how to collect appropriate data and report the information in a 30,000-foot-level performance metric reporting format. In particular, work may be necessary to estimate cost metrics for the various functions, which can prove to be very valuable in making future business improvement decisions.

2. Availability of Non-silo Documentation of Processes

Having processes and associated documentation included in the IEE value chain provides a means to link processes together, which may have been documented previously as silo activities.

An IEE value chain can also provide an easy-access repository for process procedures and related documentation. This readily-available information is beneficial to ensure that everyone is consistently reading from the same sheet of music when executing day-to-day work. Also, the training of new employees can be more consistent and productive when there is a reference to the IEE value chain's instructional videos and documentation during indoctrination.

3. Expedient Creation of a Clickable IEE Value Chain

In Harris's first four-hour IEE implementation leadership, director, and manager training session after initiating IEE, everyone enjoyed how they, using their computers, could *click through* the IEE value chain. They were impressed how, in such a short amount of time, so many

30,000-foot-level metric reports had automatic updates in their measurement display.

4. Linkage of Organizational Metrics with their Processes

Leadership and others throughout the organization thought a Harris's IEE value chain that provides a structural linkage of high-level process output response to the processes that created them made so much sense. They liked the IEE thinking that when a stable process output was undesirable, there was a need for a targeted process enhancement effort if the organization wanted to improve the metric.

They also liked how a demonstration that a process was enhanced was through the staging of a 30,000-foot-level metric individuals chart or charts to an improved level of performance.

This IEE value-chain function made so much sense to everyone.

5. IEE Value Chain Organizational Access

Everyone liked how the entire chain structure was created so quickly and then would have refinement over time.

Having a discussion on what operational procedures to initially include in Harris's IEE value chain and the names of additional people to give initial access to Harris's IEE value chain sped up the value of the IEE implementation process and organizational buy-in.

6. IEE Value Chain Data

When building an organization's IEE value chain, invariably, a statement will be made that there are no data available to create several 30,000-foot-level reports.

A response to this declaration is the famous Chinese proverb that says: 'The best time to plant a tree was 20 years ago. The second-best time is now.' Similar to the tree-planting analogy, if the data to create a 30,000-foot-level metric are not currently available, effort should be expended to starting appropriate data collection as soon as possible.

As part of a 30,000-foot-level IEE value reporting, it is also vital to address the straightforward data formatting requirements for EPRS software automatic reporting.

7. IEE Value Chain Metrics and Processes: A Software Development Illustration

The IEE value chain creation often highlights how there has not been a reporting of essential metrics to an organization in the past. One illustration of this is what occurred in a company that developed software products for the defense industry.

In this company's IEE value chain, a value stream map of its development process had several phase-gates. In this organization, software-development project managers gave focus to the completion of tasks and the achievement of these phase-gates within its product's project management effort.

The expectation was that the development of a software product relative to quality, cost, and time would be dependent upon project-manager differences, including past experiences and general knowledge. Because of this belief, there was the desire to view the development value stream from a process response point of view, which would consider project managers and their differences to be a source of common-cause process input variation.

For each phase-gate and overall product-development response, there was a need for one or more quality, cost, and time measurement. The reason for this data desire is that these data responses might provide valuable insight into what could be done differently in the development process. This insight could lead to future software products having an enhanced development process that leads to software created in less time and with fewer bugs.

It was interesting that the company had much product development data but not the desired phase-gate information thought to be the most important for collection and analyses.

A representative data sample of the desired phase-gate metrics from past products was then estimated. A 30,000-foot-level tracking of these metrics provided much insight, including what to do to enhance the overall development process. The company had been using Agile and Scrum techniques in its software development process; however, issues and inconsistencies with the implementation of these commonly used techniques were uncovered.

Wikipedia states that Agile software development is to comprise various approaches to software development under which requirements and solutions evolve through the collaborative effort of self-organizing and cross-functional teams and their customer(s)/end user(s). Agile is to advocate adaptive planning, evolutionary development, early delivery, and continual improvement, encouraging rapid and flexible response to change.

Wikipedia also states that Scrum is an Agile process framework for managing complex knowledge work, with an initial emphasis on software development. However, it has been used in other fields and is slowly starting to be explored for other complex work, research, and advanced technologies. It is designed for teams of ten or fewer members who break their work into goals for completion in time-boxed iterations. These reiterations, called sprints, no longer than one month and most commonly two weeks, then track progress and re-plan in 15-minute time-boxed daily meetings, called daily scrums.

Organizations benefit when there is an agreed-to process for implementing Agile and Scrum with documentation in an IEE value chain, where there is a tracking of the execution of the Agile and Scrum process using appropriate and agreed-to 30,000-foot-level metrics.

Organizations benefit when they incorporate a data collection system to capture and include appropriate phase-gate measurements in the organization's IEE value chain, along with documentation of the Agile and Scrum implementation process.

11.6 BENEFITS OF IEE DATA ANALYSES

Four discussions related to benefits of IEE data analyses are:

1. Data Analyses for determining where to focus Improvement Efforts for 30,000-foot-level Performance Metrics

At both the enterprise level and improvement-project level, the enhancement of a 30,000-foot-level performance-metric response might lead to the search for a singular quick-fix solution. This approach to current organizational process output response improvement could result in much-wasted resources and possible misdirection.

When attempting to understand the inputs that affect a process-output response, organizations benefit when they initially solicit a well-diverse knowledgeable team's response to what to do differently to improve a process-output-response. From a generated list of brainstorming items, there may be some easy-to-implement items that are considered no-brainer-process-improvement considerations. It is okay to *'just do it'* relative to implementing these changes in a process. After a *just do it*, process change implementation, the associated 30,000-foot-level individuals chart or charts should have a statistically-staged, enhanced response level near the time the change was incorporated. However, if the 30,000-foot-level chart did not indicate a process-output response enhancement, benefits from the process change could be questionable.

Organizations can gain much from a statistical analysis of factors that might impact the output response of a process. A generated brainstormed list of believed inputs that could affect a process output response can be the factors and combinations assessed in statistical hypothesis tests. Tools such as analysis of variance (ANOVA), analysis of means (ANOM), regression analysis, and general linear model (GLM) can provide beneficial statistically-significant insights to those inputs that affect a process response.

The understanding of which inputs affect a process output response can provide insight as to what to do to improve a process output response. Consider that when analyzing the length of time to complete a transaction, an analysis of a brainstorming list of process inputs that could impact the output of a process resulted in the detection of two statistical significance factors. The first factor was that the mean transactional fulfillment time from site two of six fulfillment centers was statistically less than the mean of all sites. The second factor was that site five had the longest statistically-significant time.

In this data evaluation illustration, there was also an uncovering that a statistical difference in execution time occurred because of the type of transaction. From this information, an IEE process improvement team could examine what was happening differently, from a process execution point of view, at sites numbered two and five. This difference in process-execution times could lead to the development of a best-practice methodology for leveraging across locations with documentation in an EPRS software IEE value chain for future reference. A team can also gain process improvement knowledge with an understanding of the reason for the difference in execution times between the types of transactions.

To improve a 30,000-foot-level performance metric response, sometimes process inputs need to be evaluated beyond or at a different magnitude from current input levels. A DOE statistical assessment of multiple factors at two-levels can address this assessment need in one experiment.

An IEE approach for executing a DOE can lead to the efficient identification of two-factor interactions that prove invaluable for determining what to do to resolve a problem or make a process enhancement. An example DOE that addresses what to do differently to reduce the time it takes to receive payment for a product or service could identify an interaction. An assessment of this interaction might lead to implementing a process change, such as sending a reminder e-mail message to historically slow-invoice-payer companies but not to prompt payer organizations.

2. Process Improvement and Organizational Bottlenecks

Someone during Harris's IEE implementation stated that a past employer had been using Lean to reduce organizational waste; however, from a financial perspective, things were not going well in the company, and there was employee termination for many.

From a new perspective, after experiencing the IEE methodology, Jorge reflected on what might have been done differently in this person's previous company to improve its financials. Jorge began thinking that the organization's Lean waste reduction efforts may not have been giving focus to areas of the business that would provide the most benefit to the big-picture.

During this pondering, Jorge recollected a statement made in Harris's IEE implementation, which suggested a self-reflection question for consideration. This inquiry was whether an organization could supply a product if there were a large-purchase-volume customer desire to order twice the amount of product than they currently ordered. Jorge's conjecture was that leadership for this company's situation would have been a resounding yes!

This consideration investigation is a theory of constraints (TOC) inquiry. TOC is one of the suggested IEE methodologies in step number 3, 'Analyze enterprise,' of the 9-step IEE business management system.

The unquestionable positive response that Jorge believed to be true of the situation would indicate that the sales and marketing processes were the bottleneck or constraint for the organization's financials.

From a big-picture perspective, the company's real problem was its financials. The company's Lean efforts gave focus on the reduction of operational waste. Reducing operational waste is not a bad thing to do; however, since operations were not the organization's bottleneck, this reduction-of-organizational-waste effort was not significantly impacting the organization's financials. Ron refers to the ineffective direction of improvement efforts *as answering the wrong question to perhaps the third decimal place.*

If this company had conducted an IEE enterprise analysis and created an EIP, Jorge felt confident that it would have been evident that there should be a redirection to a big-picture process improvement effort to marketing and sales. The organization might also give additional focus to the development of new products.

In IEE, one or more baseline measurements would be created and reported for each organizational, functional area, where there would be focused process improvement efforts to enhance the metrics that benefit the enterprise, as a whole, the most.

The company's Lean efforts focused on the reduction of waste in operations, not what to do to increase the volume of products sold. As a side note, Jorge also observed how companies sometimes attempt to undertake only a TOC deployment. Jorge now believes that TOC concepts are useful but should be implemented not as a program but instead as a methodology within step 3 of the 9-step IEE implementation system.

3. Benefiting from IEE DOE

A manufacturing facility had been undertaking Lean kaizen process improvement events for seven years. Ron's assignment was to provide additional process-improvement assistance. An initial analysis uncovered a significant manufacturing extrusion die breakage problem.

Further studies indicated that the die breakage issue was particularly bad for one manufactured item, where die-breakage cost exceeded total revenue from the product. To Ron, it was surprising that the company's previous Lean work had not uncovered this issue.

A fractional factorial DOE was conducted, which considered many factors in the experiment. The DOE quickly uncovered the root cause for the extrusion process issue and what to do to resolve the problem.

A pilot test indicated that a simple process change resolved the die breakage issue not only for the product that had the most significant die-breakage problem but for all products that the facility manufactured.

4. Inappropriate Action from Inconsistent Data Measurements

There can be considerable inconsistencies from the measurement system when determining a datum value. A significant measurement inaccuracy can lead to inappropriate action.

A measurement system study on a quantification test for the level of cyanuric acid in a swimming pool illustrates how between-individuals measurement differences can affect an actual reported value from which a decision occurs.

An internet inquiry resulted in the statement: the ideal range for cyanuric acid is 30—50 parts-per-million (PPM) in a swimming pool, where the concentration should not exceed 100 PPM.

Ron collected a sample of pool water that he took to four pool supply stores for a no-charge test. The PPM test responses provided by four testers from a portion of the drawn pool water sample were 0, 30, 40, and 70.

The reactive response of a pool owner who had taken a sample to the store that provided a 0 PPM for adjusting his pool's chemistry would be completely different than if he had received a response of 70.

If a pool owner were willing to invest the time, she could collect a large sample of water from her pool and have multiple stores provide a test-response datum point for a portion of this collected water. The pool owner could then average the values to obtain a better estimate for the correct cyanuric acid pool value. However, most pool owners would not undertake such an effort.

Although the cyanuric acid quantification test for a swimming pool is very subjective, it is unavoidable, and something that a pool owner, or whoever is responsible for managing this pool's chemistry, has to deal with until there is an improved measurement system.

The accuracy of some reported measurements in both business and someone's personal life can also have similar issues.

On a personal level, consider that you or a loved one has a medical condition and seeks the advice of a physician. If a physician suggests something dramatic such as major surgery, it is understandable that it would be a good idea to solicit one or more additional physician opinions before going under the knife.

These illustrations highlight the importance of creating an effective, accurate, and consistent procedure for the collection and measurement of data inputs to 30,000-foot-level reports in an organization's IEE value chain.

11.7 IEE ORGANIZATIONAL VOC FEEDBACK

Three discussions related to IEE organizational Voice of the Customer (VOC) feedback are:

1. More than Likert Scale Question Responses for VOC Feedback

Organizations need to incorporate a Voice of the Customer system that provides focus on how to receive both timely and relevant information that is actionable or non-actionable. A floss-picks quality issue that Ron encountered illustrates how organizational VOC feedback needs to be more than Likert scale 1-5 unsatisfactory-to-satisfactory rating evaluation responses for a variety of customer questions.

Ron said he purchased a package of floss picks from a large retail pharmacy store chain near his home. The first floss string from the product's bag broke immediately.

Ron said that he had never before experienced this type of problem with previously purchased floss picks; hence, there was a quality problem with his new-brand purchase.

Ron returned the floss pick package to the store where he bought the item and received a refund. Ron then told the clerk that he wanted to officially document this product's quality issue to the pharmacy-store purchasing department. The suggestion that Ron wanted to make to *corporate* would be that future purchases of this floss-pick product should address the product-quality issue that he experienced before making any future orders.

The clerk told Ron that he had no way to create such a customer feedback statement to corporate. Ron then asked to speak to the store manager. When speaking with the store manager, Ron received the same response as the clerk had given him relative to not being able to provide corporate feedback about this product's poor quality.

Later, it occurred to Ron that the store had an on-line survey option for customers to provide feedback if completed in 72 hours of purchase; however, the time when Ron discovered the defective product issue was beyond the 72-hour window.

Ron then decided that he wanted to improve his understanding of what this company did relative to the collection of customer feedback. Because of this desire, Ron returned to the store and bought another package of floss picks. Ron did not see the brand which had the quality issue that he had purchased sometime before, which was good.

Upon returning home, Ron immediately tested the newly-purchased floss-pick product. Ron said that it was good to see that the floss string did not break. Ron then proceeded to fill out the company's online survey form, using the link printed on the purchase receipt.

The company indicated on the receipt that there would be an entry, for those filling out the survey, in a monthly drawing for a chance to win a few thousand dollars. The company presumed that this monetary-possibility enticement would lead to more survey responses.

Ron thought that the 29 screens that he saw when responding to the survey asked too many questions, but, in general, the questions and suggested responses were okay, except for the survey response to the follow-up question 'What is the primary type of problem you experienced?'

Ron's response to this question was 'Issue with product quality.' In Ron's mind, the survey should have then asked for a description of the encountered problem, but the study did not make this inquiry.

Ron had four conclusion items from this walk-through of this company's VOC feedback system. First, a longer time should be allowed for feedback, since 72 hours may not be long enough for someone to discover a defective purchased product.

Secondly, if clerks or managers get one-on-one feedback relative to a customer suggestion, they should be able to document the customer feedback into a system so that the customer does not need to complete a lengthy survey.

Thirdly, when the customer experienced a product quality issue, the feedback system should allow timely entry of information about the problem.

Finally, Ron was not sure what this company did with the collected data from their survey. This type of study would have bias and not reflect the opinions of a truly random sample of customers that enter the store. However, the company could still benefit from this survey when there is automatic data entry that EPRS software could use to convey collective VOC feedback as part of an IEE value chain's Voice of the Customer functional.

2. Organizations Need to Capture and React to Candid VOC Feedback

Ron provided a couple of additional examples about how organizations often state that they are receptive to VOC inputs, but their actions do not reflect this openness.

The first illustration is about what happened to a friend whose husband was in an assisted living facility. I will refer to her as Sally. Sally volunteered to collect candid feedback from the people who were paying for their loved ones to stay in the facility and then summarize what the facilities' customers thought to do differently to improve the facility.

However, when Sally presented the summary of process improvement opportunities, the facility's management became very defensive and made excuses about the presented issues. Accusations were then made to Sally by the assisted-living management that she was undermining their customers' opinion of the facility, which could result in people leaving their assisted-living facility.

Because of fear of a threatened lawsuit, Sally transferred her husband to another facility and is much happier with the new facility. Many customers from the former facility have contacted Sally about her husband's departure. Conversations from these discussions resulted in many residents from the previous facility moving their loved ones to the new facility where Sally's husband now resides. By not being receptive to the acceptance of well-intended VOC feedback, the former facility surely experienced a significant impact on their bottom-line financials.

The second illustration that Ron mentioned was the feedback that he gave to a hospital after having surgery. Ron said he was pleasantly surprised to meet and have a great conversation with the CEO of the facility while walking the hospital halls to get exercise after surgery.

Ron gained much respect for this CEO, who, in Ron's eyes, was displaying *management by walking around*, which is a good thing. After returning home, Ron gave much thought and time to the creation of a three-page letter that he sent to the facility's CEO.

The document that Ron compiled described some practices that he had noted, which put the hospital at a very high risk of patient injury and possible lawsuits. Also, the letter included some patient annoyance items that he believed would improve the facility's VOC patient feedback. However, Ron was disappointed when the hospital's response to his letter appeared to provide only lip service relative to the issues that Ron had pointed out. To Ron, it seemed that the hospital's response only addressed the minimal required government mandated customer-complaint feedback requirements.

VOC feedback to an organization needs to be more than filling out a Likert scale 1-5 unsatisfactory to a satisfactory range for many customer questionnaire inquiries. Timely day-to-day feedback can provide more insight into what an organization needs to do to improve so that not only its customer's experience is enhanced, but there is also a reduction in potential organizational lawsuits and other risks.

IEE provides the structure for receiving and then making appropriate process adjustments to address VOC feedback (Reference Appendix B, Web page 7).

3. Customer Interaction and Future Growth

Three CEO perspectives relative to their customers are:

- Henry Ford is quoted as saying, "If I had asked people what they wanted, they would have said faster horses."
- Lou Gerstner, who is credited with orchestrating IBM's historic turnaround in the 1990s, made the statement that "Everything starts with the customer."
- Steve Jobs at Apple stated, "It's really hard to design products by focus groups. A lot of times, people don't know what they want until you show it to them." When Steve Jobs returned to Apple in the 1990s, he stated that you need to start with the customer experience and work backward to the technology.

From these perspectives, one conclusion is that customers don't know what they don't know; hence, customers may not be able to ask for innovative changes from what they have experienced in the past. Because of this, organizations need to have a system that provides:

- More information than responses to Likert survey questions
- More than a customer inquiry that asks for wants, needs, and desires

Organizations cannot do everything trying to provide customer delight. Organizations need to be selective and targeted in what they undertake for their customers.

There can be much gain from first-hand customer observations and general awareness to shifting attitudes from a '*read between the lines*' perspective. For those who agree with the organizational need for this type of customer interaction and involvement, merely talking about what past organization leaders have done is not enough.

Organizations benefit when they have open discussions to uncover how to better understand what their organization should do, from a process execution point of view, to reveal what to do in the future for customers. There should be documentation in an organization's IEE value chain about the decided-upon customer interaction process, along with a high-level metric tracking that monitors activity occurrence, execution effectiveness, and reaction to uncovered findings.

This execution of an effective customer interaction process can lead to both tangible and intangible benefits that drive future growth and profitability.

11.8 LEAN SIX SIGMA'S BACKGROUND AND IEE ENHANCEMENTS

One discussion related to Lean Six Sigma's background and IEE enhancements is:

Motorola initiated the concept of Six Sigma in the 1980s and used its Motorola University Division to spread the word about Six Sigma company-wide, throughout the world. A Motorola executive told Ron that the company's Six Sigma initiative created a culture of quality that permeated throughout the organization and led to a period of unprecedented growth and sales. The crowning achievement for Motorola was attaining the Malcolm Baldrige National Quality Award in 1988.

Then, in the mid-1990s, Jack Welsh, CEO of General Electric, initiated the implementation of Six Sigma at GE where quality improvement efforts gave focus to the execution of projects that were to address problem statements and provide cost-savings benefit.

The GE, Six Sigma deployment, was different from the way Six Sigma had been used and deployed in Motorola. The GE, Six Sigma approach, made use of both statistical and non-statistical tools by trained practitioners. They were to improve processes utilizing a Define, Measure, Analyze, Improve, and Control (DMAIC) roadmap.

Practitioners were taught and then applied Six Sigma techniques to address the problem statements in a project charter. Title references for these practitioners were Green Belts, Black Belts, and Master Black Belts. The progression from Green Belt to Black Belt and then Master Black Belt described the skill set of tool usage and the type of projects and roles that these belts had in the organization relative to making process improvements. When Six Sigma belts satisfactorily completed one or more improvement projects, as part of their training and development, they could become *certified* for a belt level.

A Six Sigma deployment was to have a sponsoring executive and several champions who led Six Sigma activities. Six Sigma champions were to be high-level managers. They worked with the Six Sigma deployment executive to choose improvement projects that Black or Green Belts candidates were to undertake during and after their training.

In a company, the measurement of success for a Lean Six Sigma deployment, in general, was the amount of money saved through the completion of improvement projects. Many companies, both large and small, followed GE's basic model by implementing various versions of Six Sigma. Around the turn of the century, Lean tools were added to the Six Sigma toolset to become the program called Lean Six Sigma (LSS).

GE's Lean Six Sigma deployment methodology looks like it would be a good thing to do in companies; however, the actual implementation of a Lean Six Sigma program has issues.

One issue, relative to these Lean-Six-Sigma-execution difficulties, is that with the program, there tends to be the creation of a *push* or *hunt for projects to undertake* approach, where LSS projects are created from people's opinions, rather than from structured data analysis. One illustration of this occurrence is that there can be much scurrying around to find a project for someone to work on when attending an upcoming Green Belt training session.

Also, with traditional Lean Six Sigma, reported project cost savings are often the primary driver for deployment. A financial project-savings focus for a Lean Six Sigma deployment can lead to playing games with the numbers, among other things, to make this process-improvement undertaking appear to be more valuable than it is to an organization. Also, a traditional Lean Six Sigma deployment can create projects that, when completed, if the projects get completed at all, do not truly benefit the business as a whole.

A basic traditional Lean Six Sigma deployment comparison to an IEE implementation would highlight some very beneficial IEE differences. A significant focus in IEE is to improve 30,000-foot-level performance value-chain metrics that, when enhanced through a process improvement effort, will directly impact the enterprise financials and/or customer experience, as shown in a company's IEE EIP.

On reflection, most organizations need to improve to survive. The 9-steps of IEE take the concepts of Lean Six Sigma to its next level by addressing the shortcomings of a traditional Lean Six Sigma deployment and enhancing its positive attributes.

11.9 BENEFITS OF IEE OVER A TRADITIONAL LEAN AND SIX SIGMA DEPLOYMENT

Ten discussions related to benefits of IEE over a traditional Lean and Six Sigma deployment methodology are:

1. Project Benefits need to be more than Anecdotal Statements

Lean and Six Sigma conference case-study presentations typically seem to provide only end-of-project anecdotal process improvement statements. More often than not, it looks as if these process improvement project reports and performances of a company's deployment do not show an enhancement to process-output responses.

With an IEE approach for process improvement, there is a demonstration of the benefit of a process improvement undertaking when the project's individuals chart in its 30,000-foot-level report has a staged transition to an enhanced level of performance.

Also, with an IEE improvement project reporting, an EIP inclusion shows how the enhancement of the project's 30,000-foot-level reporting benefits the business as a whole.

2. DMAIC Training that follows Books' Roadmap and is Substantive

The content of many Lean Six Sigma training offerings has declined over the years. At GE and in other organizations in the 1990s, Black Belt training consisted of four week-long sessions of training over four months, while a Green Belt offering was two-week-long sessions over two months.

After week one of this belt training, attendees typically would provide a report of their process-improvement project's progress that followed a Define, Measure, Analyze, Improve, and Control (DMAIC) project execution roadmap, where the class instructor gave feedback to this reporting.

Currently, the duration and content of both on-line and public classroom Lean Six Sigma belt training offerings can be much less than it was in the 1990s.

It also seems that now those who are interested in attending various public Lean Six Sigma training offerings are more interested in getting *certified* than learning how to benefit from the techniques. Individuals whose primary focus is to get a Lean Six Sigma certification item to put in their resume often seek the most effortless approach to get this so-called *certification stamp on their forehead.*

In a conversation with a friend who had taken IEE training, Ron noted that his friend indicated she was having difficulty interviewing people for a Black Belt position. She said that the individuals she spoke with who stated that they had belt certification often could not answer fundamental questions about the execution of a DMAIC project.

She mentioned one interview conversation in particular where the interviewee had attended on-line training from an on-line provider that was very popular. For belt certification with this training organization, there was no real project completion required for certification.

Another point that Ron made was that he has noted that most Lean Six Sigma training offerings only provide a copy of the presented information for future reference. This training and accompanying documentation may discuss the use of various Lean Six Sigma tools. However, this information typically provides little focus to the finer points of how to link all the described tools together so that a critical business process output metric response is improved, with a demonstrated and quantified organizational bottom-line benefit.

In the IEE system, Lean and Six Sigma tools training for both practitioners and leadership are available with the inclusion of books that provide all the details of executing improvement projects that benefit the enterprise as a whole. These books can be referenced for the correct application details of the methodologies long after training.

3. CODND and COPQ Calculations

There is a suggested project financial calculation difference between a traditional Lean Six Sigma deployment and the IEE methodology. A common Lean Six Sigma approach gives focus on determining the cost of poor quality (COPQ). However, not all processes have a specification from which there can be a COPQ calculation.

For example, a work in progress (WIP) measurement does not have any actual specifications. An IEE approach addresses this issue effectively through the use of a cost of doing nothing differently (CODND) calculation. A CODND method can determine the value of a process improvement project where the difference between an after process change CODND value is subtracted from a before amount to determine the monetary value of a project's execution.

4. Reporting Financial Benefits from Lean Six Sigma Deployment

Ron attended a professional organizational meeting some time ago. The person who was in charge of the company's Lean Six Sigma program gave the presentation.

In his appearance, the presenter stated that his company was saving well over a billion dollars annually through Lean Six Sigma projects. Ron questioned in his mind how this amount of reported savings could be valid.

One reason for Ron's opinion was that the company's stock prices were now in a steep decline. Secondly, Ron knew people in the company who had previously told him that the reported financial saving from their Lean Six Sigma project benefits was not valid and did not truly impact the company's bottom line.

When a Lean Six Sigma deployment gives focus to savings, guess what will happen in many organizations? Yes, people will often do whatever it takes to make the numbers look good to keep the program alive. However, a Lean Six Sigma deployment that presents a façade will not be long-lasting.

Not long after the presentation describing how this company was saving billions annually, the company abandoned its Lean Six Sigma program—leadership did not see the benefit of continuing the program.

An IEE approach addresses this traditional Lean Six Sigma deployment short-coming by giving focus to the improvement of 30,000-foot-level IEE value chain metrics that benefit the business as a whole, as identified in the organization's EIP.

In IEE, each of the EIP highlighted metrics that are to be improved has an owner. The person who has this measurement ownership should be working with a team to complete the metric's improvement project effort promptly.

In an IEE implementation, the metric owner regularly reports to leadership the status of his or her 30,000-foot-level owned metric, which is to have enhancement through the executing of a project. Because of this metric-improvement visibility, the metric owner will be anxious to see the targeted 30,000-foot-level individuals chart transitioning to a superior response level with a desirable reported predicted statement below the report's charting—through timely completion of the process-improvement project.

Quantification of the monetary value for an individual completed project is the difference in CODND before and after project completion. However, the real business value of an IEE project would be a quantification of the project's impact on the bottom-line, as determined from a financial EIP benefit analysis.

5. Selection of Lean Six Sigma Training Projects

With current Lean Six Sigma deployments in companies, there can be significant inconsistencies between what organizations do relative to LSS project selection and execution.

Unlike many online Lean Six Sigma training offerings, company deployments typically require execution of an improvement project before certifying someone as a Lean Six Sigma Green or Black Belt. This practice is good since Lean Six Sigma students need to experience the real-world challenges of pulling together a team to make process improvement happen.

However, what often occurs is a scurry of activity a week or so before belt training, trying to identify a project for each workshop attendee. The official Lean Six Sigma deployment statement may be that projects are selected so that there is an alignment to strategies; however, in reality, this alignment often is questionable.

Another issue is that students will work on their Lean Six Sigma project between class sessions, which often does not happen because of other work priorities for the students. Also, after the course's ending, a project's completion can take a very long time, even years, if at all. The Lean Six Sigma projects that do get completed are often the result of the pure perseverance of the training attendee, who wishes to get a Lean Six Sigma certification stamped on his forehead, so to speak, for his resume.

Why does this non-timely-project-completion occur, if the completion of Lean Six Sigma projects is so financially valuable to a company? Ron's opinion, when responding to this question, is that, with a traditional Lean Six Sigma deployment, there often is little, if any, focus given to improving a specific metric that is to improve the organization's overall financials.

What is needed for an active, long-lasting process-improvement deployment is a system where process owners are asking, or preferably demanding, timely completion of a project so that their 30,000-foot-level metric in the company's IEE value chain transitions to an enhanced level of performance.

For strategic identified metrics to improve though the completion of process-improvement projects, these process owners need to have a sense of urgency for improvement project completion. There is an achievement of this desire when process owners understand that they will be reporting to executive leadership the status of their 30,000-foot-level metric's enhancement and associated process-improvement activities in monthly or quarterly meetings.

In an IEE implementation, there is a structural integration of process improvement efforts within an overall business management system and enhancement of the organization's bottom-line and customer value. This approach is quite different from a traditional Lean Six Sigma deployment, which often, in the end, might simply be considered an expensive training exercise.

6. Calculating the Financial Benefits from Projects

Ron was conducting remote coaching for a Lean Six Sigma project in a specialty chemical company, where the organization was not undertaking an IEE approach for its process-improvement-effort deployment.

In a coaching session, Ron inquired about the expected financial benefits of the project upon its completion. The response given to Ron was three thousand dollars annually. Ron then stated that this is not very much money.

The coached person's response to Ron was that the project was worth much more. She then described the situation to Ron.

The project's purpose was to increase the daily volume of a produced chemical, where this product is a component of all other products delivered by her facility. The shortage of her product was affecting deliveries of all the specialty chemicals produced by her facility.

Ron then stated, and she agreed that the product volume produced by her department was a bottleneck for the entire facility. Ron continued by saying that the project value of three thousand dollars did not reflect the project's real value.

Ron then asked why this perhaps huge, under-valued-project statement was being made. The response given to Ron was that their company's Lean Six Sigma program focuses on savings and not revenue enhancements, which is not uncommon in traditional Lean Six Sigma deployments. This financial-project-benefit issue would not occur in an IEE implementation since the primary focus is to improve a metric that benefits the business as a whole, as described in an EIP.

For this particular situation, the 30,000-foot-level metric to increase could be the overall quantity of product produced weekly. In IEE, the cost of doing nothing differently (CODND) value change from the completion of this project would then be the value from all additional facility shipments because of the increased availability of this project's component product in the other product's production processes.

When reporting a value for an enterprise improvement effort, this reporting should encourage systems thinking and the continuation of the identification and execution of projects that provide the most benefit to the organization as a whole. An IEE cost of doing nothing differently (CODND) reporting addresses this need by providing an estimate for both cost savings and revenue enhancements.

7. Sample Collection for Hypothesis Testing

In Six Sigma training, alpha and beta hypothesis test risks are to be discussed, along with associated sample size calculations. Because of its novelty and often confusing aspects of the topic to a trainee, there can be much training time expended introducing the hypothesis testing topic and associated sample size calculations.

Lean Six Sigma trainees must understand hypothesis testing, but a simplistic usage of a traditional hypothesis sample size calculation and its resulting test evaluation considerations can have issues.

For purposes of illustration, consider an example of a hypothesis test for the non-conformance rate of a vendor-supplied part. A hypothesis test is to provide a bridge from sampled data information to a population statement. A null hypothesis test for a vendor-supplied component might be that there is a non-conformance rate of 0.01, while an associated alternative hypothesis is that there is a non-conformance rate that is greater than 0.01.

Upon completion of a hypothesis test, the testing conclusion is whether to *reject the null hypothesis* or *fail to reject the null hypothesis*. When making either of these two decisions from a population's sample, there is a risk of being wrong.

A beta risk of being in error is associated with a '*fail to reject the null hypothesis*' decision. In contrast, an alpha risk is related to a '*reject the null hypothesis*' decision. Before beginning an experiment, the sample size can be calculated for a chosen acceptable alpha and beta levels of risk for the test.

For many situations, the resulting sample size from this determination is large. In an attempt to collect a sufficient number of samples for evaluating a vendor-supplied product, one might diligently gather the specified number of samples from the only lot of supplier product that is available. However, it is vital when conducting hypothesis tests that there be a random sample of the population of interest.

When samples are from only a single lot, the population under consideration is a single-lot assessment, not product characteristics from multiple lots, which would more accurately represent the population of interest.

With 30,000-foot-level reporting of a product non-conformance rate or a critical product measurement, the y-axis in an individuals chart would be a lot-characteristic response, and the x-axis would be lots, reported in a time-series sequence. The over-time multiple-lot data from a 30,000-foot-level individuals chart could be considered a random production sample from the supplier's process.

When this vendor-sampled process indicates stability, the statement below the 30,000-foot-level charting would be a best-estimate for the performance of the vendor process over time. This statement with the individuals chart over-time response presentation can provide a more accurate representation for the vendor's product performance, not only now but in the future. This reporting can be more valuable to determine how a process-output response is performing than collecting a much larger number of samples from a single lot.

8. Hard and Soft Savings Project Benefit Calculations

Often there is much discussion in an organization's Lean Six Sigma deployment about the quantification of savings from an improvement project. This discussion can include much dispute relative to a project's potential *hard savings* and *soft savings*.

The following is an illustrative example of a project's hard saving. Because of a project's process improvement work, the amount of employee hands-on work effort was reduced by one headcount. When one person is 'let go' from the company, the amount saved by the company because of the employee's salary and benefits reduction is considered hard savings. In contrast, if there were a transfer of someone to another job, the project's savings would be typically regarded as soft, since there would not be a reduction in the company's payroll and employee benefit payments.

When creating a company Lean Six Sigma deployment, the specifics of hard and soft savings are often fiercely debated. An IEE implementation approach flattens this hard- and soft-savings discussion.

IEE focuses on determining what 30,000-foot-level metric needs improvement so that the enterprise, as a whole, benefits, as identified in an EIP. For this situation, the measurement to improve could be the cost of an operation process. The reduction of operational cost might include process changes that result in, among other things, a reduction in the number of reworks and an improved workflow so that there is a need for fewer people in the process's execution.

Data from a before and after staged 30,000-foot-level individual's chart reporting could provide a value-of-improvement-project determination. If someone wants to quantify the value for a specific project, what an IEE implementation system suggests is creating a spreadsheet that assesses the cost of doing nothing differently before and after the change.

With an IEE approach, this cost of doing nothing differently (CODND) spreadsheet should detail everything. This spreadsheet should include associated travel expenses and other indirect expenses, including people's time spent undertaking fixing-the-process-problem issues, as opposed to using their time doing something else that would provide value to the company.

Hard- and soft-savings-type notes should be included in the spreadsheet so that someone could easily view a project's value from different perspectives. However, this calculation is not inherently necessary in IEE since the primary focus is to improve 30,000-foot-level metric responses that are beneficial to the business as a whole, as shown in an EIP.

This IEE EIP focus is in contrast to a traditional Lean Six Sigma focus of reporting the amount of saving from projects, which can waste much time have many soft-savings and hard-savings project discussions.

9. 5S and Organizational Improvement

Some companies decide to start their process improvement journey with 5S workplace organization. For this undertaking, there may be a direction that functional areas implement 5S components; that is, Sort, Set in order, Shine, Standardize, and Sustain in their immediate area. This effort would include, among other things, the cleaning up of operational areas and positioning of tools so that there is more expedient execution of tasks.

From 5S workplace organization, there should be increased standardization and waste reduction, which is good at the local-process level; however, typically, it is often a tough stretch to quantify the value of 5S efforts in the financials and at the customer level, strategically.

In the IEE implementation initiation and execution approach, 5S is a process improvement alternative, which makes more sense than only 5S executions in isolation. In IEE, 5S is considered one possible technique for making improvements that enhance a 30,000-foot-level metric response.

At the enterprise level, the organization can undertake both strategic and local process improvement efforts. For both situations, in IEE, the documentation of current and improved processes is to reside in the organization's IEE value chain, where process information and associated metrics can readily be accessed.

In IEE, local process improvement efforts, which could be 5S events, would occur as part of a business process improvement event (BPIE). Strategically-identified 30,000-foot-level metrics that are to be improved may use the 5S workplace organization method when executing the 'Improve phase' of the IEE DMAIC roadmap.

10. Achievement of Organizational Control 'C' in DMAIC

In Lean Six Sigma training, there is a stated emphasis on the importance of the 'Control phase' or *C* as part of the Define, Measure, Analyze, Improve, and Control (DMAIC) improvement project execution roadmap.

The reason for this DMAIC 'Control phase' after a project's completion is that processes tend to revert to past practices when the spotlight of process improvement efforts redirects to other business areas.

Ron agrees that defining how to maintain the gain through the DMAIC control step is vital at a project's completion. However, in practice, what Ron has observed is that, in most Lean Six Sigma project reports, a 'Control phase' statement is: there are to be periodic checks to see if people are continuing to execute the new process.

A control mechanism that is needed, whenever possible, is a poka-yoke or mistake-proofing enhancement to processes. Mistake-proofing by design examples include the various interlocks that are now available on automobiles. As-soon-as-possible identification of an issue is a second alternative to poka-yoke.

However, often it is not possible to make a process mistake-proof and to promptly identify when a process change has occurred. A periodic check to see if people are correctly performing new tasks does not provide timely feedback. It is also not a realistic future expectation for this type of inspection to occur as a regular process control mechanism.

In IEE, a 30,000-foot-level process-output response may not provide an alternative optimum timely feedback mechanism for control. However, through automatic EPRS software IEE value chain metrics updates, this alternative offers a no-cost visual control mechanism. Besides, there is a direct linkage in the value chain to the enhanced process change and associated documentation, which resulted from the executed process improvement activities.

With IEE EPRS software, corrective action should be undertaken, as a means for process control for a completed project, whenever the project's enhanced 30,000-foot-level value-chain metric degrades from its post-project improvement level.

11.10 IEE IMPLEMENTATION OF BUSINESS MANAGEMENT APPROACHES

Twelve discussions related to an IEE approach for implementing commonly-described business management methodologies and philosophies:

1. Management and Leadership

Peter Drucker, the father of management theory, stated, "Management is doing things right; leadership is doing the right thing." (Drucker 2001)
  Drucker's leadership and management concepts include:

- Make sure your objectives and your team's objectives are in alignment with the company's overall mission. Start with a straightforward answer to the question, "What business are we in?" This statement is consistent with Step 1 of the IEE 9-step system.
- Maintain a clear list of priorities--never more than a few, and always tackle one at a time--as well as *stop doing* and *never start* lists. This statement is consistent with IEE's EIP.
- Favor the future over the past, and focus on opportunities, not problems. This statement is consistent with an IEE's EIP.
- Routinely demonstrate that "leadership is not characterized by the stars on your shoulder. An executive leads by example." This Drucker-described principle is consistent with CEO Janice Davis' leading Harris Hospital's IEE deployment, by example.

IEE provides a systematic 9-step system for addressing all of Drucker's management theory principles.

2. Deming's Management Philosophy

Ron indicated that he had experienced organizations that have stated that their company embraced Deming's concepts at its founding; however, over the years, leadership lost its way with following Deming's 14 points and his management philosophy. These organizations typically state that attempts to reinitiate Deming's concepts have not gone well.
  Ron agrees with most of Deming's philosophies; however, the statements alone do not provide how-to- implement details. IEE provides a structured, long-lasting approach to implement Deming's philosophy.

3. Goal Setting and their Achievement

A Lloyd Nelson quote in Deming's book, *Out of the Crisis* (Deming 1986) is: "If you can improve productivity, or sales, or quality, or anything else, by (e.g.,) five percent next year without a rational plan for improvement, then why were you not doing it last year'?"

This quote highlights an issue with a standard business management practice that IEE resolves. With an IEE implementation, there is an understanding that for improvement of a high-level stable process output response, there is an enhancement needed in the execution of its associated process. With an IEE approach, the setting of performance improvement goals is consistent with a 30,000-foot-level output format, so that metrics' enhancements would benefit the whole business, as highlighted in an EIP through the execution of process improvement projects.

4. In Search of Excellence

In the book, *In Search of Excellence* (Peters and Waterman 1982), Tom Peters and Robert Waterman developed, from the research of sixty-two companies over a twenty-five-year review, eight principles that make big business excellent. These eight principles are 1. A Bias for action; 2. Close to the customer; 3. Autonomy and entrepreneurship; 4. Productivity through people; 5. Hands-on, value-driven; 6. Stick to the knitting; 7. Simple form, lean staff; 8. Simultaneous loose-tight properties.

Many of the *excellent companies* identified in the 1982 published book are now either non-existent or are having difficulties. One might conclude that each of these recognized companies did not have a system for the long-lasting integration of the identified eight book-described principles through changes in leadership and the environment in their industry.

IEE provides a method for having a collective, long-lasting fulfillment of these eight In-Search-of-Excellence principles and more.

5. Business Process Reengineering

In the 1990s, Michael Hammer's Business Process Reengineering (BPR) methodology was popular. BPR is the act of recreating a core business process to improve product output, quality, or reducing costs. BPR analyzes the company's workflows to find processes that are sub-par or inefficient, and figures out ways to get rid of or change them.

IEE provides a systematic approach for implementing BPR, and more.

6. Business Risk Management

Business Risk Management is the process of identifying possible risks, problems, or disasters before they happen. A Business Risk Management system is to allow leadership to set up procedures to avoid the risk, minimize its impact, or, at the very least, help cope with its implications.

IEE provides a systematic approach for the inclusion of business risk management within its overall business management structure (Reference Appendix B, Web page 8).

7. Creating a Learning-Systems-Thinking Environment

Peter Senge, in his *The Fifth Discipline* book (Senge 1990), describes how one person is no longer sufficient for a company to rely on. Senge's writing discusses the importance of creating an organizational-learning systems-thinking environment.

The most important life lessons that someone will learn are from their wrong decisions. We need to learn from our mistakes so that we do not run the risk of repeating them. We must develop wisdom and sense to make the right decisions and choices. Similarly, organizations need to learn from their mistakes.

IEE provides an organizational framework for implementing the concepts described in Senge's book. An illustration of organizational learning in IEE is how step 9 of the 9-step system loops back to step 3.

8. Creating Leaders and a System that is Level 5

Jim Collins' book, *Good to Great*, (Collins 2001) describes Level 5 Leaders as those who display a potent mixture of personal humility and indomitable will. Level 5 Leaders are incredibly ambitious, but their ambition is first and foremost for the cause, for the organization and its purpose, not for themselves.

IEE provides a means to create not only Level 5 leaders but also a Level 5 system that offers a culture that is long-lasting and works effectively even when Good-to-Great organizational Level 5 leaders leave an organization. The IEE system can be the vehicle to implement Jim Collin's Level 5 philosophy.

9. Jim Collins' 5 Creep Stages toward Company Doom

How the Mighty Fall by Jim Collins (Collins 2009) provides 5 silent creep stages toward the doom of companies, where stage 4 is *grasping for salvation*. In business, the *denial of risk and peril* in stage 3 typically will lead to stage 4.

In a grasp for salvation, organizations often attempt to resolve the company's major down-fall problems by hiring a new CEO; however, this resolution strategy is rarely effective and can accelerate the downward spiral of a company.

Just consider how difficult it is to hire rank-and-file and other employees that are a good match for a particular position and the associated costs when things do not work out well for a new hire.

Now consider that a newly-hired CEO is not a good match. A lack-of-hiring-fit could even lead to the bankruptcy of a company. A study indicates that nearly 50% of executive new hires fail within 18 months (Sullivan 2017).

Ron said that he had had a conversation with a past IEE-trained student who never could upsell IEE in his hospital's organization. This past-student stated that his hospital had its third CEO in a couple of years, and in this same time frame, there was a continuing downward spiral for the facility. This past-trained IEE student no longer is an employee of the hospital as its process-improvement leader because of these management changes.

Before hiring a new CEO that is to make things better, organizations should consider what Toyota does when changing people in leadership positions. Toyota is well-known for its Toyota Production System (TPS). However, perhaps Toyota's general policy for filling leadership vacancies through internal company promotions, instead of outside hiring, is an often overlooked significant policy that has fueled the company's success.

For an organization that does not have a long-lasting Toyota-like culture, it can be much simpler, less expensive, and more effective for the board of directors to do something different than hire a new CEO from outside the company. This CEO replacement alternative would be to select a well-respected internal person who is a systems thinker and has leadership skills to take over the CEO leadership position. This systems-thinking person could receive coaching on how to implement the IEE system and deploy the methodology throughout the organization.

The IEE business management system can both cut an organization's downward spiral before stage 3 issues become prevalent and be a business resolution for pursuit even if stage 4 organizational problems are currently present.

10. Objectives and Key Results (OKR)

Objectives and key results (OKR) methodology is a framework for defining and tracking objectives and their outcomes (Grove 1983). An EIP can be used to determine what OKRs for an organization to undertake so that the big-picture benefits. The success of OKR undertakings could be tracked and reported at the 30,000-foot-level.

11. Leadership Change in an IEE System

A situation that Ron has seen many times over the years is that when there is an assignment of a new organizational leader or manager to a functional area or organization, one of the first statements made by the *troops* is: "We need to see what this new leader wants." This simple wait-and-see thinking is inconsistent with established systems-thinking and -learning organizations, where no one person is sufficient for a company to rely on (Senge 1990).

When organizations incorporate an IEE system as the underlying architecture for a system- thinking and -learning organization, there is flexibility for organizing differing thoughts in an organization's decision-making process.

With new leadership from outside a current organization function that has incorporated an IEE system, an initial review of the organization's IEE value chain and EIP would undoubtedly be appropriate.

A new set of eyes looking at an existing EIP might provide valuable future specific directional thoughts that could be incorporated, while at the same time still residing within the organization's basic IEE framework.

12. Total Quality Management (TQM) Deployment and IEE

Ron believed that TQM methodologies were sound, but in most organizations, TQM, as a program, was not long-lasting. Ron believes that one reason for this short-lived tenure is that the Quality Department typically facilitated the program's organizational implementation. The work that Quality Departments do is good; however, in some companies, the quality organization can be hardline concerning how the quality function views problems.

In some businesses, the Quality Department is considered by others as having no concern for overall business issues, with its total focus placed on quality. As a result, the Quality Department may have a hard time getting operations managers to cooperate and allow their people to join Quality Improvement Teams.

Ron remembered one meeting in particular. During this gathering, the TQM program leaders demanded more top-management support and financial resources to address a long-range improvement, while ignoring the hard business reality that the funding they were requesting would severely impact production operations.

Because of this TQM implementation observation, Ron believes that the Quality Department should *not* sponsor an IEE deployment.

11.11 IEE ADDRESSING BUSINESS CULTURE AND RISKS

Six discussions related to IEE's addressing business culture and risks are:

1. Creation of a Lean Culture Issues and Resolution

There is much talk about the need to create a Lean culture. However, what does the nature of this culture genuinely mean? What would a Lean culture look like? An internet search defines Lean as "the elimination of waste and the providing of customer value." Also, commonly stated is that, without top-down leadership commitment, the general perception is that shifting to a Lean culture is a trend or the *flavor of the month*. One might also see from an internet search that for success, everyone in the company must become committed to a Lean culture.

It is clear that the reduction of waste is a good thing, but getting one's arms around how to establish this type of philosophy throughout an organization is a challenge.

To address another question of whether the creation of a Lean culture is enough for a business to succeed reminded Ron of a conversation that he had had at a quality-practitioner conference. An acquaintance that Ron had known for many years told him between-session presentations that at his company, much was done to *lean-out* the company's operations as part of creating a Lean culture.

Ron's response to him was that he thought that he, Ron's acquaintance, was involved in a lay-off by the company. The friend affirmed that that was so. Ron then followed-up, asking, "Didn't a competitor purchase your company at a bargain price since its financials had significant issues?"

Ron's friend responded that this statement was correct, but that much had been done in the company's Lean work to remove waste. Ron's response to him was then an inquiry as to whether he thought that all his Lean work had any real company benefit. It would seem like the business financials were not positively impacted enough by this Lean work to avoid a *fire sale* of the company to a competitor. Ron received no response to his question.

Ron then reflected on how an EIP in the IEE system could flatten the issue that this company had with its Lean implementation. EIP strategic focus is on the execution of process improvement efforts that enhance 30,000-foot-level performance metrics through the use of Lean and other process improvement tools. IEE provides a system for leaning out an organization that is also financially beneficial to the business as a whole.

2. IEE Alignment and Implementation of TPS Principles

The Toyota Production System (TPS) is an often suggested benchmark that companies should model; however, this is easier said than done. TPS is an integrated socio-technical system that comprises a management philosophy and uses practices that Toyota has implemented and refined over decades in its company.

TPS organizes manufacturing and logistics, including interaction with suppliers and customers. TPS's six principles are:

1. Continuous improvement
2. Respect for people
3. Long-term philosophy
4. The right process will produce the right results
5. Value is added to the organization by developing your people and partners
6. Continuously solving root problems drives organizational learning

The IEE methodology is in alignment with TPS's principles and also provides a structured approach using IEE for moving toward implementing many aspects of TPS in a company, and more.

3. Corporate Policies and Process Improvement

Ron described a situation where his organization was helping an organization's VP of Operations address issues that the VP's company was experiencing with vendor quality and supply of parts.

An analysis of the company's situation indicated that, before the end of every quarter, product sales and shipment demands increased dramatically. This end-of-quarterly spike resulted in the placement of a considerable fulfillment demand on manufacturing and its supply chain.

This short-term-quarterly-burden-increase resulted in much additional expense from the manufacturing department because of overtime and expedited supplier shipments. The extended hours in manufacturing also resulted in more defective units because of employee fatigue.

Additional investigation indicated that the policy for the financial compensation of the company's sales force to meet arbitrarily-set goals was encouraging this quarterly spike issue. It became apparent that to truly resolve many of the problems that the VP of Operations was having, the product sales compensation policy needed to be changed.

The VP of Operations agreed with the analysis and conclusion that was made relative to the sales force and its bonus incentive. Still, he was not willing to escalate this sacred cow company policy issue to his peers and CEO because of feared personal reactions.

Over the years, Ron has noted more and more that, for organizations to have long-lasting business enhancements, some corporate policies need to be changed. This business-improvement need is the reason that, for a successful IEE implementation, an organization's CEO or President must be the driver. He or she, as the leader of an organization, needs to be willing to address changing policies head-on, if that is the need to provide bottom-line value to the organization.

4. KPI Goal Setting with Financial Compensation

Ron's reflection on the quote, "Tell me how you will measure me, and then I will tell you how I will behave," led to him recalling a three-hour keynote presentation that he gave to all plant managers of a coop organization.

For this presentation, Ron evaluated one facility's raw data for a critical key performance indicator (KPI) measurement regularly reported to the coop's leadership. In a presented 30,000-foot-level report of this KPI's data, Ron showed how it appeared that only one process enhancement was made that affected this metric in the last six years. The 30,000-foot-level reporting indicated that an improvement enhancement occurred in September about two years earlier.

The plant manager of the facility that owned this data was surprised by what the metric stated and was not sure what happened during the specific process-change time frame but did provide speculation.

Ron then noted that the general manager of all individual site managers in the room had no engagement with his presentation and his organization's 30,000-foot-level metric's analysis conclusion. This general manager had been texting during Ron's presentation.

The general manager left the room to take a phone call. When the GM was not in the room, one plant manager stated that if their coop-company adopted what Ron suggested, there would be a negative impact on all site managers' compensation.

Ron then stated that he was not suggesting that the overall compensation of manufacturing site managers take a financial hit. However, Ron indicated that what he was saying was that the current policy governing this and probably other similar manufacturing output metrics was not leading to the most beneficial activities for the coop as a whole. The same bonus amounts could be provided, for example, by a different approach, which leads to more organization-as-a-whole-financial benefits.

The current reporting methodology for these metrics seemed to be very wasteful and could lead to playing games with the numbers and possibly very destructive behaviors. The overall IEE system could address this, and perhaps many more, performance measurement goal setting and improvement issues in their coop-company.

Ron then suggested that the coop's plant managers approach their general manager. When meeting with the GM, a candid discussion could state how the current-plant-manager-compensation policy is not encouraging the best behaviors and how this policy should be changed so that more advantageous actions occur in the coop, through implementing IEE concepts

The plant managers realized how an IEE system implementation could benefit their facility. Ron's suggestion made sense to the plant managers; however, there was no pursuit of Ron's proposal. Perhaps the plant managers did not want to *rock the boat* or could not answer the personal question: what's in it for me?

5. Management and a Sense of Urgency

With the current competitive environment, there is a natural sense of urgency for the completion of tasks in a timely fashion. Addressing this organizational need through intimidation to meet Y-set goals is not a good approach to motivate people to do the right things promptly.

Intrinsic motivation, meaning the person is genuinely on-board and willing to demonstrate pride in his work or accomplishments. For any program of improvement to be effective, this sense of intrinsic motivation would come from a cultural shift caused by the transformation of individuals.

Motivation by punishment and denigration needs to be replaced by motivation through effective leadership. A CEO-orchestrated IEE deployment provides the means to achieve this objective.

6. Outsourcing and Risks

Ron provided another thought about the quote, 'Tell me how you will measure me, and then I will tell you how I will behave,' relative to the avoidance of risk of doing something that looks good in the short-term but could have severe, long-term consequences.

One example of this behavior is soliciting and then assisting an off-shore vendor for the production of a company's high-tech product. The reason for making this outsourcing decision is typically to save money so that the short-term financials are enhanced. A similar illustration is outsourcing the manufacturing of high-tech equipment that produces a product which the company sells.

Both these strategies could benefit the financials in the short term, which might even provide attractive short-term executive bonuses. But, in the long-term, these actions could significantly shorten a competitor's learning curve for making a knockoff of one or more of the company's products, which down-the-road would negatively impact product sales and profitability.

Outsourcing a low-tech developed product can offer much financial benefit; however, when sensitive technology is involved, the long-term implication of outsourcing decisions should be considered. For the situations where intellectual property of a product's manufacturing or other details are valuable, the company should pursue an alternative to outsourcing.

For this situation, a full-court press on undertaking IEE process improvement efforts should be a primary consideration to reduce costs and other related parameters for the product's or equipment's financials. This internal process improvement effort is a more desirable undertaking to pursue than outsourcing so that there could be an enhancement of short-term benefits without the potential cost associated with long-term negative implications.

11.12 GENERAL APPLICATION OF IEE 30,000-FOOT-LEVEL METRIC REPORTING

Five discussions related to the application of 30,000-foot-level metric reporting to both business and personal metrics are:

1. Improvement of Expense and Value from Vendor Audits

Ron described a reoccurring reported underground-water contamination issue and what to do differently using a 30,000-foot-level reporting methodology. Ron highlighted that the described techniques for this water-purity issue are also applicable in manufacturing and transactional environments.

A local newspaper article stated that a periodic test of groundwater for a community's drinking water did not meet a purity-level requirement—again. Over several years, periodic government-agency-scheduled testing at this location indicated an unacceptable level of impurities in some tests.

There was the establishment of an action plan to resolve any non-conformance underground-water issues whenever observed. Testing that followed a non-compliant action plan implementation typically indicated that the water-purity level was in compliance, and there was a 'resolution' to the non-conformance sample. However, an unacceptable level of water impurities had been reoccurring in later testing.

To Ron, this underground-water evaluation was no different from what Deming and others have said about trying to inspect quality into a product. Testing an underground-water impurity level is not unlike testing a produced product's quality-level response.

The question is: what could be done differently for this and other similar business and government response situations? For addressing this do-different query, the samples of water taken over time would be considered samples from a ground-water-creation process.

The next consideration was whether it would be best to present results as an attribute pass/fail or a continuous response. The newspaper article gave the water impurity level as an attribute response since the non-conformance statement made was that a sample had too many impurities.

From this newspaper account, the reader did not know if the underground water response had not met its quality criteria by a small amount or a large amount. A more informative response would have been a continuous-response reporting of the number of impurities in a sample in units in parts per million (PPM). A comparison of the collection sample responses could then have a probability plot assessment against a maximum specification level of acceptable contamination.

Multiple samples drawn from a population, even in a similar time frame, could differ in magnitude. That is, the measurement sampling technique can have variation. For example, two samples from the same time-frame could be different by a small or large amount, for various reasons.

It is essential to keep in mind that there is a primary objective for this underground water testing. This objective is what to do differently, if needed, to address the basic desire of consistently providing water that does not have an unacceptable amount of contaminates, and not just pass a sampling test at a particular point in time.

An additional desire should be to provide acceptable water quality with the least governmental expenditure relative to the amount of required testing from a sampling and not-meeting-criteria-actions approach, including any re-evaluations that may result. The procedures adopted should include the minimization of any governmental employees' time associated with this underground-water evaluation and other similar underground-water evaluations at different locations.

First, everyone needs to agree on an inspection process to follow. This first step minimizes the difference in reported values between who took and then the evaluation of each sample. Secondly, there needs to be an agreement about sampling frequency for the testing. For example, one sample might be drawn daily, weekly, or monthly, depending upon the situation and test complexity.

With this type of data, a 30,000-foot-level chart could then be created, where the x-axis in the individuals chart is the chosen sampling period; for example, weekly. The y-axis in the reporting would then be the level of contamination expressed as a continuous-output response; for example, parts per million of sample contamination.

The individuals chart in the 30,000-foot-level report assesses process stability and provides a statistical assessment as to whether evidence is prevalent that any process-response improvement or degradation has occurred. The chart's associated probability plot presents the distribution of over-time measurements from the processes' responses. When the process response is considered stable, the upper specification limit's use in the probability plot provides a non-compliant expectation frequency for samples relative to the specified acceptable contamination level. An example charting statement for a stable process response is an estimation that 4% of weekly readings will be beyond the upper acceptable contamination limit.

If this 4% frequency level of non-compliance is considered unacceptable relative to a specified limit, there is a need to do something different from a process point of view to reduce impurities in the groundwater.

There would be a 30,000-foot-level individuals chart staging when a statistical indication is present that there was a reduction in water-sampling contamination levels. A new estimated frequency for non-compliant samples after this improvement effort might indicate a 0.1% non-conformance rate, which may be considered acceptable.

For data reporting, this water-supplier-created 30,000-foot-level chart could be updated after every sample and made electronically available to any monitoring government agency. For this situation, the only government-agency audit needed would be a periodic check to ensure that samples are collected, tested, and reported correctly in the 30,000-foot-level water-contaminant report.

Ron highlighted that this described underground water quality testing and reporting process applies to many other current supplier on-site audit situations. The implementation of this methodology could result in a substantial reduction in auditing expense, while at the same time improving supplier quality.

2. Inclusion of Variation in Value Stream Metrics Reporting

A Lean value stream map is to evaluate workflows for situations such as product order to fulfillment. A high-level view of workflow is good in that this effort might highlight areas that should be improved; however, a typical Lean value stream map presents duration times and other calculations as average values.

With an IEE approach, many value-stream metrics can include response variation as part of 30,000-foot-level response reports. The inclusion of variation in a metric response reporting can provide much valuable insight, both for overall value stream output measurements and individual step measurements of the value stream.

Also, the IEE approach of placing created value streams in the most appropriate functional area of an organizational IEE value chain provides much value for future reference and the training of new personnel to various value-stream portions of a business.

3. Diabetic Metrics with a 30,000-foot-level Reporting

Many business and personal situations can benefit from the application of 30,000-foot-level reporting for providing insight into how things are going and where to focus on improvement efforts.

One non-business application of 30,000-foot-level metrics is the reporting of diabetes measurements, as described in an article (Reference Appendix B, Web page 6).

A diabetic friend of the article's author provided his detailed physician visit measurements for the previous 14 years. This person with diabetes also shared four daily measures that he compiled for several months. Presented in the article is a 30,000-foot-level alternative for the reporting of these measurements, which offers more insight than traditional approaches for examining these metrics, including where to focus improvements to improve future measured responses.

Two common diabetes measurements that physicians use for analysis are hemoglobin A1C, which shows a longer-term measure of blood glucose (BG) control, and the readout of a BG meter or CGM (Continuous Glucose Meter) to see more recent short-term trends.

For a person with diabetes, lower numbers are, in general, better for all these measurements, as long as any individual response is not too small.

A 30,000-foot-level report shown in the article indicates that there were two distinct times in the last 14 years when these two physician-diabetic metrics decreased, which is good. The editorial also provided a 30,000-foot-level reporting for the four daily glucose lancet-finger-prick tests that the person with diabetes personally conducted.

The amount of blood sugar in one's blood is dependent upon food intake and throughout-the-day medications. Because of this time-of-day difference, an assessment of this daily-collected data at the 30,000-foot-level should have a daily subgrouping, That is, from a 30,000-foot-level perspective, the source of input variation from a time-of-day reading should be considered common-cause. For this particular set of data, there was a subgrouping of the four daily readings, which provided a process stability assessment from the two individuals charts.

One chart of these two individuals charts tracked daily mean measurement values, while the other followed daily standard deviation calculations. Since there are no individual values beyond calculated UCL and LCL limits, these individuals charts indicated process stability.

Because of this stability conclusion, there was the consideration that all raw data from the individuals chart's recent stable period were a random sample of this person's diabetics sugar-level readings, not only now, but in the future, unless something changed. The normal probability plot in the 30,000-foot-lever report shows the expected glucose-measurement median and 80% frequency of occurrence measurement range for the person with diabetes.

As noted earlier, any specific diabetic measurement is a function of recent food consumption and associated medications timings and insulin injections. Because of this process input variable to a glucose level measurement response, one would expect that there would be a common-cause difference in measured glucose readings at different times of the day.

An IEE Analysis of Means (ANOM) described in the article assessed the null hypothesis that a mean-time-of-day response was equal to the overall daily mean reading value. Sure enough, a statistically significant difference was detected. Bedtime means measurements were significantly higher than the total daily mean response, while the mean evening readings were significantly lower than the overall daily mean response.

What could one conclude from this hypothesis test find? It seems that what this person with diabetes was typically consuming at dinner, and his current medication scheduling could be the reason for this increased time-of-day diabetic-measurement mean response. If there is a desire to reduce the magnitude of this time-of-day response, a change in the dinner-time diet or medication schedule would seem to most appropriate.

Organizations benefit when there is a utilization of the described 30,000-foot-level reporting techniques throughout an IEE value chain.

4. Transitioning Individual Measurements to Systems Thinking

Viewing measurements as the output from processes, when appropriate, can add much to the decision-making process in organizations. This viewpoint is in contrast to responding to the magnitude of individual values.

To illustrate this point, consider the measurement of the amount of electromagnetic noise generated by a computer during regular operation emissions testing. Manufacturers of these products can be periodically required to conduct an electromagnetic interference (EMI) test of manufactured products.

The purpose of these tests is to ensure that the EMI emission level from its various type of computer products is not excessive. In a computer company, a random product-model sample undergoes an expensive EMI test to assess the level of emissions from the computer against an upper limit criterion.

The company produces many different computer products, where an individual computer product is randomly selected and tested at various points in time. If a single product .evaluation is undesirable, the manufacturing process needs to be adjusted to decrease the amount of electromagnetic noise by repositioning cables in a manufacturing process or doing something else differently.

When there is a resolution to excessive EMI noise for an individual failing product, manufacturing incorporates the non-compliant issue resolution in future assembly builds. With EMI testing, over time, many continuous response emission values for various computer models are available.

The fundamental purpose of EMI testing is to provide a safeguard for all manufactured computer products, relative to an acceptable EMI upper limit specification. This line of thinking can lead to a transition from the perspective of what is being sampled and reported onto more than an individual product-model EMI response value. With this new line of thinking, the measured sample is considered a sample from a population of computer products, in general.

This change in perspective would provide a couple of benefits. First, there would be an increase in the overall test sample size from one to many. Secondly, any specific product EMI-fix should be considered relative to what might be done differently in manufacturing computers in general, not any particular computer model offering.

From this random sample of computers over time viewpoint, a 30,000-foot-level tracking chart can provide a prediction statement. From this sampling and evaluation perspective, a test estimate could offer a general computer-non-compliant rate estimate that is, for example, 17% of the manufactured computers exceed an upper specification electrical-emissions limit.

With this form of data reporting, a differing overall computer-manufacturing decision might be made rather than reacting to each testing-response value individually. From this 30,000-foot-level data analysis, one might then conclude that a global product design change is needed to reduce the likelihood of future occurrences of manufacturing EMI product-produced compliance issues.

5. Improvement of Supply Chain and Reported Metrics

Viewing measurements as the output from processes adds much to an organization's supply chain decision-making process. Supply chain metrics for the quantification of product non-conformance and on-time delivery rates gain much when examined from a 30,000-foot-level viewpoint.

As customers of supplied products or services, organizations benefit when their suppliers have a structured approach for undertaking process improvement efforts so that there is an enhancement of current unsatisfactory performance metrics in the future.

Organizations benefit when supplier metrics are measured at the supplier's location and then reported in a 30,000-foot-level format to the customer. A supplier implementation of the IEE system can guide how best to implement any process improvement activity.

Supplier audits could have increased value when targeted focus is given only to the monitoring of the supplier metric data collection and reporting techniques.

There are additional gains when these supplier evaluations include the assessment of the supplier's techniques for executing process improvement for the enhancement of supplier-customer agreed-to metrics.

11.13 TECHNICAL ASPECTS OF 30,000-FOOT-LEVEL REPORTING

Nine discussions related to technical aspects of 30,000-foot-level, 20,000-foot-level, and 50-foot-level reporting are:

1. EPRS-Metrics and EPRS-IEE Software

The creation of 30,000-foot-level charts using traditional statistical and spreadsheet software is not a trivial task for various reasons.

EPRS-metrics software is available for the creation of 30,000-foot-level charts (Reference Appendix B, Web page 13). EPRS-metrics software provides an easy-to-use approach for creating 30,000-foot-level performance metric reports for various types of data.

EPRS-IEE software is available for the implementation of the IEE system (Reference Appendix B, Web page 14). This EPRS software provides an easy-to-use methodology for implementing the various aspects of IEE, including alignment of automatically updated predictive 30,000-foot-level performance metrics with their processes through an IEE value chain, and more.

**2. 30,000-foot-level Performance Metric Reporting
and SPC Control Charts are Different**

Initially, a 30,000-foot-level report may appear to be a traditional statistical process control (SPC) control chart, but it isn't. There are many differences between conventional control charting and 30,000-foot-level reports.

For one thing, unlike control charts, the intent of 30,000-foot-level reports is not to provide *minute-to-minute* or other timely data evaluation for the control of processes through the rapid identification of short-term response differences, which should receive prompt attention.

The time-series portion of a 30,000-foot-level chart is an individuals chart that is to assess process stability from a high-level point of view, where this individuals chart's x-axis time-series increments are typically days, weeks, months, or material-lots.

For a process output response at 30,000-foot-level reporting, and R charts, p-charts, and c-charts are not used to assess the stability of a process. The reason for the exclusion of these traditional SPC charting methodologies in 30,000-foot-level reporting is the mathematical calculation for UCL and LCL lines for the individuals charts. For and R charts, p-charts, and c-charts, there is no mathematical consideration that the variation between subgroups is a source of Y-response common-cause variation in the UCL and LCL calculations (Reference Appendix B, Web page 11).

The time increment to use for the x-axis of an IEE's individuals chart is dependent upon the data and specific situation so that common-cause X-input variation inputs occur within time-series-tracking intervals. It is *critical* to select the most appropriate time interval when creating an individuals chart in a 30,000-foot-level report.

To illustrate how to select x-axis intervals for a chart, consider a 30,000-foot-level tracking of hold time in a call center. In the relationship Y=f(X), the Y response is hold time for individual calls. The duration of a specific call hold time is a function of the Xs associated with the process. For this situation, Xs in the Y=f(X) relationship include time-of-day someone called. More people may tend to call around lunchtime, which could impact hold time. Also, day-of-the-week should be a consideration. Perhaps more people may call on Monday because of the previous weekend's discovered problems. An increase in calls on this day of the week could increase hold time.

In a 30,000-foot-level individuals chart tracking of a call center's hold time response, Y, we don't want to react to time-of-day and day-of-the-week X input variation as though a special-cause Y-response occurred. Because of this, the x-axis increments for tracking a call center hold-time 30,000-foot-level process output response should be weekly.

An implication from this form of tracking is that when an overall 30,000-foot-level response is unsatisfactory, and analysis indicates hold time on Monday is longer than other days of the week, perhaps something should be done differently on Monday. The current process for staffing of personnel receiving calls on Monday may be an excellent place to start an investigation for identifying what to do differently to reduce call-in Monday's hold times, which, if successful, should improve the overall 30,000-foot-level hold-time metric.

When much difference occurs between days of the week, an organization may also wish to create drill-down *20,000-foot-level* charts for each day of the week. This charting would be a subset of the overall 30,000-foot-level report. EPRS software reporting could provide these metrics in an IEE value chain report.

3. 30,000-foot-level Performance Metric Reporting Alternative to Process Capability/Performance Indices Reporting

In traditional Six Sigma training, Cp, Cpk, Pp, Ppk process capability indices describe, for continuous-response data, how a process response is performing relative to a specification. IEE does not use this type of process-capability reporting for several reasons.

For one thing, this process capability/performance indices reporting methodology is confusing. Also, calculated process-capability values are dependent upon the sampling approach used to collect data from a process (Reference Appendix B, Web page 11).

Furthermore, process capability statements are appropriate for stable process-output responses. However, since a process capability calculation is separate from any control chart, process capability calculations can be made on processes that are not stable, which can lead to inappropriate conclusions.

30,000-foot-level reporting resolves these issues. This form of reporting includes an individuals chart that assesses process stability. The added probability plot, for continuous response data in the

30,000-foot-level report, provides a means for the calculation of a process capability statement when the process-output is stable from a high-level viewpoint. For stable processes, the easy-to-understand statement below the report's charting offers not only a current process capability expectation but a futuristic prediction expectation as well.

An example of a 30,000-foot-level capability performance statement is: The process is predictable, with an estimated 5% non-conformance rate. If this non-conformance rate is undesirable, process improvement efforts are needed.

A demonstration of success from process enhancement work occurs when there is a staging of an individuals chart in a 30,000-foot-level report to an enhanced level of performance. When this happens, and the process is considered stable, the statement below the report's charting reflects the new level of expected process-output performance.

4. 30,000-foot-level Performance Metric Report
Alternative to Sigma Level Reporting

In traditional Six Sigma training, a sigma level metric is a quality metric. A 3.4 defects per million opportunities (DPMO) rate indicates that a process is performing at a six sigma level (Reference Appendix B, Web page 11).

Some have said that in Six Sigma deployments this quality-level form of reporting can provide a consistent metric throughout an organization. However, the 1.5 standard deviation shift for the 3.4 DPMO calculation and other aspects of sigma level reporting has issues.

The IEE system does not use sigma level metric reporting. IEE 30,000-foot-level reporting provides an easy-to-understand statement of how a stable process is performing, which can be reported throughout an organization using an organizational IEE value chain. These IEE metric reports can also have automatic updates with EPRS software.

5. Process Capability Reporting for Continuous and Attribute Data: Traditional and 30,000-foot-level Reporting

A process output response can have a pass/fail attribute response relative to criteria or a continuous measurement response, such as 2.34 inches. When a process is in statistical control, a process capability report describes how the process is performing relative to customer specifications.

In Six Sigma, an attribute process capability reporting has a non-conformance rate reporting, such as 233 DPMO. In contrast, a continuous process capability reporting has a process capability indices statement such as Cp=1.3, Cpk=1.7, Pp=1.8, and Ppk=2.3. In Six Sigma, process capability reports for attribute and continuous data are very different.

For both pass/fail attribute and continuous process capability reporting, a process needs to be in statistical control for the calculation to be valid. However, the control charting of a process-output response and the determination of process capability are two separate tasks. Because of this separation of undertakings, a process capability reporting may be unknowingly invalid because the underlying process is not in control.

In IEE 30,000-foot-level charting, there is the inclusion of a process capability statement in the reporting, when a process output response is considered stable. This statement is similar for both an attribute and continuous-data response as an estimated non-conformance rate, such as 1.2 %. This provided statement in a 30,000-foot-level report is easier to understand than process capability indices; plus, this statement will only be included in the report when a process-output response is considered stable.

A requirement for traditional process capability reporting is that a specification exists. However, not all process outputs have a specification. For example, order delivery time, work in progress (WIP), and EBITDA may have targets or goals but do not have specifications like the tolerances on a manufactured part. However, in an organization's overall decision-making methodology, there is a need to describe how stable processes are performing. A 30,000-foot-level report format fulfills this need by providing in its reporting an estimated median or mean response with an 80% frequency of occurrence range, whenever a specification does not exist.

The wording in 30,000-foot-level and satellite-level reports provides an easy-to-understand process capability/performance description both for those in operations and leadership. Besides, when a process is considered stable through a statistical assessment, the provided IEE process capability/performance statement is predictive, where, if this futuristic statement is undesirable, there is a need for enhancing the processes that created the metric.

IEE reporting for performance metric reports offers insight into how a process is performing and what to do when process-output expectations are undesirable.

6. 30,000-foot-level Performance Metric Reporting for Non-normal Data

Many, perhaps even a substantial percentage of those who received traditional Six Sigma training, focus on using a normal probability plot to conduct a normality-of-data hypothesis test and experience a *cold sweat* when data appear to have a non-normal distribution.

The fact is that many process-output responses are inherently non-normal and should be addressed accordingly. Examples of this occurrence are the time to execute a process, flatness of a part, and non-conformance rate. For all three of these situations, negative values are not possible.

Theoretically, data values from a normal distribution have tails extending from minus to plus infinity. When there is a natural boundary in a process, this plus-and-minus-infinity characteristic is not valid. For these natural boundary situations and when the data are close to the limit, a log-normal or other distribution can provide a much better model for describing the expectation of occurrences at various data-response values. If there is a need for a data transformation and one is not undertaken, the reporting is not valid and can give a very deceptive picture of a process-output response.

With a traditional Lean Six Sigma approach for describing process capability when data are non-normal, there can be much confusion and awkwardness. There can also be some fundamental un-sound reporting issues.

However, with a 30,000-foot-level metric response report, this situation and other issues can be addressed quickly using 30,000-foot-level EPRS software-generated reports. If a log-normal transformation is appropriate in this high-level process-response report, the individuals chart in this reporting should incorporate a Box-Cox lambda transformation value equal to zero, which equates to a log-normal transformation of the data. The accompanying probability plot in this 30,000-foot-level report would then be log-normal, where the values from this plot determine the process capability statement below the report's charting. For stable processes, this statement would be an easy-to-understand expected non-conformance rate, whenever a specification exists. When there is no specification, a 30,000-foot-level report will provide a best-estimate mean or median response with an estimated 80% frequency of occurrence response.

As with all 30,000-foot-level reports, the statement below the graphs provides, for stable processes, a prediction statement. An example futuristic statement is: the process is predictable, and the duration of time to produce a product will be higher than ten days, 12% of the time. If this statement is undesirable, there is a need for process enhancements.

A 30,000-foot-level report that has a data transformation can originate from an organization's IEE value chain or elsewhere. Only those who create 30,000-foot-level charts need to understand when and how to address data transformation needs. The person who is examining a 30,000-foot-level report does not need to know whether the chart's data were transformed or not.

FORREST W. BREYFOGLE III

7. 30,000-foot-level Performance Metric Reporting of Attribute Response Data

The IEE 30,000-foot-level reporting approach for creating an attribute pass/fail process-output response utilizes an individuals chart, not a p-chart (Reference Appendix B, Web page 11).

The reason for not using the p-chart in 30,000-foot-level reporting for assessing process output response stability is that the mathematics for calculating the p-chart's UCL and LCL limits has a basis that the non-conformity rate of measurements is the same for each subgroup. P-chart UCL and LCL calculations have a binomial distribution mathematical basis.

From a high-level viewpoint, expecting a constant nonconformity rate between subgroups is not a realistic requirement to set when calculating UCL and LCL for the establishment of a region for Y-response common-cause variability. From a high-level perspective, the expectation is that a common-cause variation of a Y-response can originate from differing nonconformity rates between subgrouping intervals.

The implication of the underlying mathematics for p-chart UCL and LCL calculations can be huge. To illustrate this point, consider a computer company's non-conformance tracking. If the company produces a high volume of product and is daily monitoring a final-test non-conformance rate using a p-chart, the sample size or N for use in a charting equation, for each time-interval reported, would be large.

Mathematically, in a p-charts' equations, N is a denominator variable for calculating UCL and LCL. A high N value would result in upper and lower control limits that are close to each other. A p-chart for the described computer manufacturing illustration would most certainly have out-of-control signals, which could be many.

When there is a reporting of out-of-control conditions in a control chart, actions are to bring the process in control. These actions can be costly and not useful in this situation. The reason for this ineffectiveness of activities is that the primary reason for the out-of-control signals is that the underlying binomial distribution assumption for consistency of

246

a non-conformance rate between subgroups is not appropriate with the high-level tracking of the process's failure rate.

An IEE 30,000-foot-level reporting approach addresses this issue by using an individuals chart to determine process-output-response stability. Unlike the p-chart, an individuals chart mathematically considers between-time tracking intervals as a source of common cause Y-response variation, which is more consistent with real-world situations.

Another benefit of a 30,000-foot-level report is the inclusion of a predictive non-conformance proportion below the graphic for stable processes, where if a predictive statement is undesirable, there is a need for process improvements. A staged 30,000-foot-level report, with an enhanced level of performance statement in the reporting, would be an indicator that there was an enhancement in the process's output response from process improvement efforts.

8. 20,000-foot-level Performance Metric Reporting Data

When evaluating a high-level 30,000-foot-level metric, it is sometimes desirable to create a performance measurement report of a subset source of the high-level metric's performance. For example, for a 30,000-foot-level response tracking of a non-conformance rate, a Pareto chart of data over a recent region of stability for this performance metric might indicate that a specific type of failure has the highest frequency of occurrence.

The non-conformance rate for this particular type of high-failure circumstance could have a tracking using the same mathematics as 30,000-foot-level reporting. Since this metric is a subset of the overall measurement, this metric has a 20,000-foot-level performance metric referencing. This form of metric referencing can be useful when an improvement project is to reduce a non-conformance rate, and, from analysis, it is decided to re-scope the project to give focus to a reduction of the most prevalent type of common-cause non-compliance issue.

A reduction in a 20,000-foot-level non-conformance tracked rate should also result in a reduction of the overall 30,000-foot-level monitored rate.

9. 50-foot-level Metrics

In an IEE explanation, there is frequent reference to the relationship $Y=f(X)$, where Y is the output of a process, and Xs are its inputs. The outputs from processes are the Ys in an organizational value chain and have a 30,000-foot-level report tracking format.

The Y output of a process is the result of its process inputs. When designing a process, it is best to make its inputs error-proof and the overall process response robust to changes from any uncontrollable inputs; however, this desire is often not achievable.

Traditional control charts could monitor 50-foot-level X-metrics over time, where there is an investigation initiation when an SPC X-input-tracking control chart goes out of control. However, there are situations where there is an expectation that a process input will change or drift over time, and an appropriate, pre-determined, intervention is needed to maintain a satisfactory 30,000-foot-level Y response.

Three examples of an X-input-response-intervention need are:

1. Adjustment of the number of attendants actively receiving calls at a specific time of day in a call center; that is, making adjustments for differing calling frequencies throughout the day.
2. Redress, at the appropriate time, a manufacturing grinding wheel that will wear over time with usage.
3. Adjust the number of grocery store check-out attendants to account for changing customer demand throughout a day.

Technically, pre-control charting techniques can provide a means to determine when a previously established intervention action procedure is appropriate for a 50-foot-level metric adjustment need. However, an organization may be able to utilize a more sophisticated means for identifying and then making necessary 50-foot-level adjustments to a process. These metrics could also be available through an IEE value chain drilled down and seen using EPRS software.

11.14 ENTERPRISE PERFORMANCE REPORTING SYSTEM EPRS-METRICS AND EPRS-IEE SOFTWARE

Four IEE discussions related to Enterprise Performance Reporting System EPRS-metrics and EPRS-IEE software are:

1. Creation of 30,000-foot-level Performance Metrics

EPRS-metrics software can easily create a 30,000-foot-level report for various types of time-series, process-output response data, which is available in a spreadsheet format: continuous data that has no subgroups, continuous data that has subgroups, and attribute data.

Appendix B, Web page 13, provides instructions on how to gain access to this software.

2. Creation of automatically updated IEE value chain 30,000-foot-level and Satellite-level Performance Metrics

EPRS-IEE software (or, EPRS software) offers the ability to create an organizational IEE value chain, where there is a structural linkage of 30,000-foot-level and satellite-level performance metrics to the processes that created the measurements.

Authorized users access the software using a web browser. So, no special client software is required. The server software can reside on an organization's server or a Smarter Solutions, Inc. secure cloud server. Installation on an organization's server provides the highest security and direct access to enterprise data. Cloud deployments can offer more flexible accessibility, since there may be easier access over the Internet by any authorized user.

This software needs access to organizational data for the creation of the 30,000-foot-level and satellite-level metric reports. This software provides automatic metric updates; for example, daily at a time scheduled by the organization that is using the software.

The data that the software uses to build the metrics could be in a spreadsheet or comma-separated variables (CSV) format, where the accessed information is automatically or manually updated internally by the organization. The software can also use any modern database that is SQL compatible, including SAP, Oracle, and other ERP systems as a data source.

The organization's IEE value chain created by this software, with its associated metrics that are often predictive, can be accessed by anyone authorized, 24/7.

Appendix B, Web page 14, provides more information about this software.

3. Documentation of IEE Value Chain Processes

EPRS-IEE software (or, EPRS software) offers an IEE value chain structure where is a documentation of processes using the software's flowcharting capabilities. Drill downs of processes provide flexibility for documenting execution detail and proving linkage to appropriate web pages and procedural documents. An IEE value chain offers a *clickable* flowcharting linkage of organizational processes to the 30,000-foot-level and satellite-level performance metric output responses that they create.

Documented organization's IEE value chain procedures using this software can be accessed by anyone authorized, 24/7.

Appendix B, Web page 14, provides instructions on how to gain access to this software.

4. EIP Tracking and Documentation of IEE Projects

EPRS-IEE software (or, EPRS software) offers a simple project tracking function for documentation of an organizational EIP and the status of its process improvement projects with their associated 30,000-foot-level metrics that are to be enhanced.

With this software, the reporting and status of IEE process improvement projects can be accessed by anyone authorized, 24/7.

Appendix B, Web page 14, provides more information about this software.

11.15 IEE TRAINING

Two discussions related to IEE training are:

1. IEE Training Alternatives

Self-paced training and how-to books provide the details of implementing various aspects of the IEE system. Remote and on-site IEE training can target the needs of individuals and their roles in an organization. An IEE trainer's guide is also available.

Appendix B, Web pages 16 and 17 provide more details.

2. MBA and Business School's IEE Training

Josh Kaufman states in his book, *The Personal MBA: Master the Art of Business* (Kaufman 2012):

- Business schools make a fortune forcing their students to take in a huge amount of information. The majority of it is theoretical. The majority of that is useless.
- If you want to succeed in business in any capacity—employee, manager, or owner—you must have a solid, comprehensive understanding of what business principles actually are and how they actually work.
- Every successful business creates or provides something of value that other people want or need at a price they are willing to pay. In a way, that interaction satisfies the purchaser's needs and expectations and provides sufficient business revenue to make it worthwhile for the owners to continue operation.

The IEE system is a practical methodology that includes business principles in a roadmap for making them work. IEE delivers a structure for making businesses successful by satisfactorily fulfilling and exceeding a purchaser's desire with a sufficient generation of revenue for the service or product provider.

MBA and business school students benefit when there is the inclusion of IEE training in their curriculum.

11.16 IEE DEPLOYMENT OPTIONS

Five discussions related to IEE deployment options are:

1. IEE On-site Deployment

The deployment of IEE is most effective using an organizational deployment model similar to the one described in this book.

2. IEE Remote Deployment

The IEE system can be deployed remotely in a company. Reasons for a remote IEE deployment over an on-site deployment include corporate travel restrictions and/or employees working from home or another global region. It is best if an IEE remote deployment follows, as much as possible, the described Harris Hospital deployment. The methodologies described in several IEE books can help guide this implement approach (Reference Appendix B, Web page 16).

3. IEE Do-it-yourself Deployment

An organization may desire to implement IEE without any outside-organizational assistance. A do-it-yourself deployment should follow as much as possible the sequence-of-events as described in the Harris Hospital's IEE deployment.

4. Consultant Company Facilitated IEE Deployment

Both large and small consulting companies can increase their client value through the facilitation of an IEE deployment. EPRS software can supplement a client's ERP software.

5. IEE Enhancement to an Existing Lean Six Sigma Deployment

The value of a Lean Six Sigma (LSS) program can increase by integrating several IEE methodologies within an existing LSS deployment.

A process for addressing this integration opportunity is:

1. List current LSS process improvement projects and the organizational performance metric that each project is to enhance.

2. Document in a blank EIP template a business financial goal and/or another goal that the LSS program is to enhance.

3. Develop this EIP template to show how the improvement of each project's metric would benefit the defined business goal. To create these connections, work from the right side of the EIP chart to the left, instead of the regular EIP development approach that progresses from the chart's left to right. Any LSS project shown on the right side of the chart that cannot be connected to the chart's left side should be considered for termination.

4. Identify the owner for each LSS project metric that has a satisfactory EIP left-to-right connection. These process owners should be actively working with a process improvement team to make process enhancements that show a demonstrated statistical improvement to their strategic-identified performance metric.

5. Create a 30,000-foot-level chart for each LSS project's metric shown in the created EIP. The individuals chart shown in this 30,000-foot-level reporting is what is to transition to an enhanced level of performance through a DMAIC roadmap application.

6. Discuss with leadership what was found in IEE concepts and LSS integration: For example, Developed EIP graphic; Created 30,000-foot-level LSS project charts; Current LSS projects that did not have an EIP project-to-enterprise-as-a-whole-alignment benefit.

7. Share with leadership an overview of the IEE business management system and how IEE techniques might benefit the organization. Items to consider are:

- Discuss IEE one-minute video (Reference Appendix B, Web page 1).
- Share IEE "Positive Metrics Poor Business Performance" overview article (Reference Appendix B, Web page 2).
- Ask for opinions about whether leadership thinks any attributes of the *Effective Management Attributes* on page two of the IEE overview article lack in their organization.
- Discuss the 9-step IEE system shown in Figure 8 of the article with the focus given to the sequence of steps for determining what improvement projects to undertake in step 7 of the roadmap.
- Discuss this book's glossary definition of the terms *Integrated Enterprise Excellence* and *pull for project creation.*
- Discuss the comparison of IEE to other systems charts (Reference Figure 00.01).
- Encourage others to listen to the audio version of this book during travel commutes and/or personal exercise sessions (Reference Appendix B, Web page 19).

8. Make appropriate adjustments to the current LSS program.

12

APPENDIX B: WEB PAGES FOR IEE ARTICLES, VIDEO, AND SOFTWARE

The resource center at SmarterSolutions.com provides information on various aspects of IEE and its implementation details (Reference Appendix B, Web page 21).

The following web pages are a subset of this website's resource center. Provided is a video link and other material, where many of these pages offer a linked-to PDF article at the bottom of the page that contains additional details.

Web page 1: Integrated Enterprise Excellence (IEE) One-minute Referenced Video

- Summary: Provides a one-minute video that describes the benefits of the IEE system with its performance metric tracking methodology over traditional scorecards.
- Web page: SmarterSolutions.com/iee-one-minute-video

Web page 2: Integrated Enterprise Excellence (IEE) Overview Referenced Article

- Summary: Provides the "Positive Metrics Poor Business Performance: How Does this Happen?" article, which summarizes the 9-step IEE system, in a PDF format.
- Web page: SmarterSolutions.com/iee-article

Web page 3: Examples—Converting Company Scorecards to 30,000-foot-level Performance Metric Reports

- Summary: Provides links to eight actual-company-dataset examples that illustrate the conversion of various traditional business scorecards to 30,000-foot-level performance metric reports and the additional insight gained through these conversions.
- Web page: SmarterSolutions.com/iee-scorecard-conversions

Web page 4: The Improvement of Scorecard Management: Comparing Deming's Red-Bead Experiment to Red-Yellow-Green Scorecards

- Summary: Describes how common-place organizational red-yellow-green scorecards have the same issues that Deming illustrated in his 1980's training with his red-bead experiment and how a 30,000-foot-level reporting resolves this RYG scorecard reporting issue.
- Web page: SmarterSolutions.com/red-bead-experiment

Web page 5: Business Goal Setting and Process Improvement—Is there a Conflict?

- Summary: Describes the advantages of converting from a next month or quarter financial specified-value-goal-setting methodology to giving focus to the improvement of a mean monthly response such as organizational profit margins or EBITDA.
- Web page: SmarterSolutions.com/iee-goal-setting

Web page 6: Diabetes Measurement Tracking at the 30,000-foot-level

- Summary: Illustrates the transition of a diabetic's physician-visit and individual-daily readings to a 30,000-foot-level format and the benefits of this transition. Included is an IEE Analysis of

Means (ANOM) that provides insight for making improvements so that future reported diabetic-measurements could be enhanced. The concepts in this diabetes-metrics-tracking example are not unlike many personal and business-metric situations.

- Web page: SmarterSolutions.com/iee-diabetes-metrics

Web page 7: A System to Capture and React to Voice of the Customer

- Summary: Provides a methodology for capturing actionable VOC information in an IEE value chain, which can have whole-enterprise benefits.
- Web page: SmarterSolutions.com/iee-voc

Web page 8: Reports to reduce the Risk of Organizational Problems

- Summary: Provides a methodology for reducing organizational risks as part of an IEE business management system.
- Web page: SmarterSolutions.com/iee-risk-management

Web page 9: Beyond Lean Six Sigma—Why Lean and Six Sigma Deployments Fail and What You Can Do to Resolve the Issue

- Summary: Describes why traditional Lean Six Sigma deployments are not typically long-lasting and how the IEE system addresses this issue by improving functional 30,000-foot-level metrics that benefit the business as a whole.
- Web page: SmarterSolutions.com/iee-lean-six-sigma-issues-resolution

**Web page 10: Organizational Business Management
System Issues—Examples of Managing to the Ys Where
Unfavorable or Destructive Behaviors Resulted**

- Summary: Describes how an IEE implementation and usage might have prevented the publicized, unfavorable, and destructive issues that occurred in many well-respected companies.
- Web page: SmarterSolutions.com/iee-y-management-issues-resolution

**Web page 11: IEE Business Management
and Process Improvement Theory**

- Summary: Provides over 30 links to IEE implementation details and applications theory
- Web page: SmarterSolutions.com/iee-theory

Web page 12: Integrated Enterprise Excellence (IEE) Blog

- Summary: Provides past and current thoughts about business management and process improvement in IEE blogs. Included in this discussion are the concepts and methodologies of IEE and more.
- Web page: SmarterSolutions.com/iee-blog

**Web page 13: EPRS-Metrics Software—30,000-foot-level
and Satellite-level Performance Metrics Reporting**

- Summary: Provides software for the creation of 30,000-foot-level and satellite-level performance metric reports for various types of time-series data, using EPRS-metrics software. The author intends to have a *no-charge* licensing fee for this software.
- Web page: SmarterSolutions.com/eprs-metrics-software

Web page 14: EPRS-IEE Software—IEE System

- Summary: Describes EPRS-IEE software (i.e., IEE software) that, among other things, can automatically update 30,000-foot-level and satellite-level metrics, which have a structural linkage through an IEE value chain to the processes that created them. One approach for an organization to accomplish this automatic metric updating is to install EPRS software on a server that is behind the organization's firewall. For each 30,000-foot-level and satellite-level metric, the IEE implementation team determines an appropriate spreadsheet format that the EPRS software will access nightly for updating all IEE performance metrics. Someone in the organization who is very familiar with the organization's databases will create queries that access the organization's databases to fill in the 30,000-foot-level metric spreadsheets in the appropriate formats before the EPRS software nightly updating.
- Web page: SmarterSolutions.com/eprs-iee-software

Web page 15: Characteristics of Successful IEE Master Black Belts and Black Belts

- Summary: Describes the characteristics of successful IEE Master Black Belts and Black Belts.
- Web page: SmarterSolutions.com/iee-belt-characteristics

Web page 16: IEE Implementation Books

- Summary: Provides information about the books that show the how-to details for implementing IEE at both the enterprise and process-improvement level. *Integrated Enterprise Excellence Volume II* describes the particulars for implementing the 9-step IEE business management system. In its 1100+ pages, *Integrated Enterprise Excellence Volume III* provides the details for executing the IEE Define, Measure, Analyze, Improve, and Control

(DMAIC) process improvement roadmap. *Lean Six Sigma Project Execution Guide* is a tabbed reference that provides IEE DMAIC roadmap drill-downs that can be quickly accessed.

- Web page: SmarterSolutions.com/iee-books

Web page 17: IEE Training

- Summary: Describes IEE training offerings.
- Web page: SmarterSolutions.com/iee-training

Web page 18: IEE Explanation to Others

- Summary: Provides options on how the IEE business management system can be explained to others so that they appreciate its benefits and understand the basics.
- Web page: SmarterSolutions.com/iee-explanation-to-others

Web page 19: IEE Audio Books

- Summary: Provides access to IEE audiobooks.
- Web page: SmarterSolutions.com/iee-audio-books

Web page 20: IEE Two-book Novel Description

- Summary: Provides access to IEE novel description books in all formats; i.e., *Management 2.0: Discovery of Integrated Enterprise Excellence* (Breyfogle 2020a) and *Leadership System 2.0: Implementing Integrated Enterprise Excellence* (Breyfogle 2020b).
- Web page: SmarterSolutions.com/iee-novel-books

Web page 21: IEE Resource Center

- Summary: Provides articles, videos, and other information about the IEE business management system and process improvement methodologies.

- Web page: SmarterSolutions.com/iee-resource-center

Web page 22: Post-Book-Publication IEE Information

- Summary: Provides post-publication information about the methodologies described in this IEE book.
- Web page: SmarterSolutions.com/iee-post-publication-information

13 APPENDIX C: DATASETS, SCORECARDS, AND COMPANIES

The organizations presented in this book are fictitious. The author created situations that companies often needed to resolve. The book's storyline presents fabricated scenarios; however, the author has observed all the described conditions at some point in time in his career.

Except for the four scorecards shown in the "Positive Metrics Poor Business Performance" article, figures presented in this book are from randomly-generated datasets that represent what an organization might experience. A website link provides the conversion and benefits of transitioning the article's four scorecard reports to 30,000-foot-level metrics (Reference Appendix A, Web page 3).

The fabricated IEE 30,000-foot-level and satellite-level report book figures originated from randomly-generated datasets from a normal distribution. The associated book figures illustrate the basic concepts of IEE metric reporting using an easy-to-understand presentation format.

One significant difference between the simulated data used to create these book-figures and what the expectation is for some hospitals and other transactional measurements is the normality of data. Often real data for a hospital or another organizational 30,000-foot-level metric situation could be more accurately represented by a non-normal distribution, such as a log-normal distribution (Reference Appendix B, Web page 3).

To illustrate this normal-distribution-data-generation point, consider the Harris Hospital patient's length of stay dataset, which was created for this book and then reported out as a 30,000-foot-level metric (Reference Figure 6.10).

An internet search for 'average length of stay in a hospital' resulted in 4.5 days. Inputs for generating random data for this figure's dataset were to first convert days to hours by multiplying 4.5 days times 24 hours, which resulted in 108 hours. Secondly, there was an assumption of 24 hours for a standard deviation when creating the dataset.

For most hospital length-of-stay data, a log-normal distribution would probably provide a better data-distribution fit than a normal distribution. The reason for this is that some hospital patients would probably have more difficult situations than a majority of patients, which likely would result in lengthier hospital stays for these individuals. For these more-complex situations, one would expect that these patients experience hospital stays would be much longer than three standard deviations from an overall mean hospital length-of-stay. For this type of skewed distribution situation, a log-normal distribution often would provide a better general representation of actual hospital length-of-stays than a normal distribution.

EPRS-metrics software (Reference Appendix B, Web page 13) can efficiently address non-normal data-distribution circumstances but is beyond the scope of this book (Reference Appendix A, Web page 11).

14 APPENDIX D: HOW-TO-IEE BOOKS AND ASSISTANCE

14.1 IEE IMPLEMENTATION BOOKS

An Integrated Enterprise Excellence (IEE) five-book series (See Figure 14.1) describes the details of implementing IEE both at the enterprise and improvement-project level (Reference Appendix B, Web page 16). These books are a follow-up to the author's ASQ Crosby Medal award-winning book, *Implementing Six Sigma* (Breyfogle 2003).

Figure 14.1: Integrated Enterprise Excellence (IEE) Five-book Set

1. *The Integrated Enterprise Excellence System: An Enhanced, Unified Approach to Balanced Scorecards, Strategic Planning, and Business Improvement* (Breyfogle 2008a): This book describes, from a high-level perspective, the IEE system and its benefits over traditional business scorecard, strategic planning, and process improvement methodologies.

2. *Integrated Enterprise Excellence Volume I—The Basics: Golfing Buddies Go Beyond Lean Six Sigma and the Balanced Scorecard* (Breyfogle 2008b): This book describes in a golfing-novel format the IEE system and its benefits over the traditional organizational deployments of Lean, Lean Six Sigma, and the Balanced Scorecard.

3. *Integrated Enterprise Excellence Volume II—Business Deployment: A Leaders' Guide for Going Beyond Lean Six Sigma and the Balanced Scorecard* (Breyfogle 2008c): This book describes the details of implementing the 9-step IEE business management system.

4. *Integrated Enterprise Excellence Volume III—Improvement Project Execution: A Management and Black Belt Guide for Going Beyond Lean Six Sigma and the Balanced Scorecard* (Breyfogle 2008d): This book's 1100+ pages describe the details for executing an enhanced Lean Six Sigma Define, Measure, Analyze, Improve, and Control (DMAIC) improvement project roadmap. In this DMAIC roadmap, there is an integration of Lean and Six Sigma tools so that the right tool is used at the correct time.

5. *Lean Six Sigma Project Execution Guide: The Integrated Enterprise Excellence (IEE) Process Improvement Project Roadmap* (Breyfogle 2010): This book provides, through its tabbed-book structure, quick access to the implementation detail steps of the enhanced IEE DMAIC project execution roadmap.

14.2 IEE IMPLEMENTATION ASSISTANCE

To schedule an IEE implementation conference-call discussion, contact Smarter Solutions, Inc. at info@SmarterSolutions.com.

15 ACRONYMS

5S	Sort, Set in order, Shine, Standardize, and Sustain
AD	Anderson-Darling (test for normality)
ANOVA	Analysis of variance
ANOM	Analysis of means
BB, IEE	Black Belt, IEE
BG	Blood glucose
BPIE	Business process improvement event
CAHPS	Consumer Assessment of Healthcare Providers & Systems
CEO	Chief executive officer
CCU	Critical care unit
COPQ	Cost of poor quality
CODND	Cost of doing nothing differently
DOE	Design of experiments
DPMO	Defects per million opportunities
DSO	Days sales outstanding
EBITDA	Earnings before interest, taxes, depreciation, and amortization
ED	Emergency department
EIP	Enterprise improvement plan
EPM	Enterprise process management
EPRS-metrics	Enterprise Performance Reporting System metrics (software); Reference Appendix B, Web page 13
EPRS-IEE	Enterprise Performance Reporting System IEE (software); book also references IEE implementation

266

software as 'EPRS software;' Reference Appendix B, Web page 14

ERP	Enterprise Resource Planning
GLM	General linear model
GM	General manager
HR	Human resources
IEE	Integrated Enterprise Excellence
IT	Information technology
IV	Intravenous, which means in the vein
KPI	Key performance indicator
KPIV	Key process input variable
KPOV	Key process output variable
LOS	Length of stay
LCL	Lower control limit
LSS	Lean Six Sigma
MBA	Master of business administration
MBB, IEE	Master Black Belt, IEE
MSA	Measurement system analysis
N	Sample size
OKR	Objectives and key results
OR	Operating room
PDCA	Plan-do-check-act
PPM	Parts per million
R	Range
RN	Registered nurse
RYG	Red-yellow-green (scorecard)
s	Standard deviation of a sample
SMART (goals)	Specific, measurable, actionable, relevant, and time-based
SPC	Statistical process control
TOC	Theory of constraints
TPS	Toyota Production System
TQM	Total quality management
VOC	Voice of the Customer
UCL	Upper control limit

VP	Vice president
WIP	Work in progress
WOTO	Wisdom of the organization
XmR	X (individuals), mR (moving range)
Sample mean	
YTD	Year to date (measurement response)
μ	Mu, population true mean
σ	Sigma, population true standard deviation

16 GLOSSARY

30,000-foot-level metric: Reporting of a process output response or business metric from a high-level viewpoint. In this elevated performance report, short-term variation from the natural variation of input variables will result in an individuals chart or charts that views these fluctuations as common-cause variations. This metric has no calendar boundaries, and data from the latest region of stability are used to provide a predictive statement for stable processes. An undesirable 30,000-foot-level prediction statement suggests that the associated metric's process needs improvement. Evidence that a 30,000-foot-level response has improved is that its individuals chart response has a demonstrated enhancement to an improved level of performance. If this new process response level is considered statistically stable, EPRS-metrics 30,000-foot-level performance metric reporting software will use raw data from the individuals chart staging to calculate a new prediction statement for this reporting. Firefighting often occurs in organizations when there is a reaction to all unsatisfactory outputs as if they had a special cause. The incorporation of 30,000-foot-level performance metric reporting methodology can improve the understanding of process variation and redirect firefighting activities to fire-prevention activities; that is, using a team to systematically improve the underlying process through an IEE process improvement methodology. In IEE, a 30,000-foot-level metric is used for establishing a process response baseline before beginning a project and then for tracking the project-response progress.

50-foot-level metric: A KPIV metric that impacts a 30,000-foot-level response; e.g., process temperature when manufacturing plastic parts. This type of chart can involve frequent sampling since special-cause or process-drift-input issues need timely identification so that problems or process shifts can be quickly resolved without jeopardizing the quality or timeliness of the outgoing product or service. A pre-control chart can be used to monitor 50-foot-level process-input variables.

5S: Refers to five Japanese terms used to describe the steps of the 5S workplace organization method. In Japanese, the five S's are Seiri, Seiton, Seiso, Seiketsu, and Shitsuke. In English, the five S's are translated as Sort, Set in order, Shine, Standardize, and Sustain.

Accuracy: Accuracy and precision are two perspectives that should be considered when evaluating the *drive to a target* of a golfer's swing or business-metric-target achievement. Accuracy refers to how close a measurement is to the true or accepted value. Precision refers to how close measurements of the same item are to each other. To illustrate accuracy versus precision in golfing terms, consider that someone is at a driving range and is targeting his golf-swing for hitting a flag on the range, which is to simulate a golf-course pin location. For this situation, if he takes ten shots and then estimates that the mean of these shots was twenty yards short of the pin, this mean shortage distance from the pin target would be an accuracy estimate for the person's shot. Variation of golfing shot distance around a mean shot distance would represent the precision of a golf swing. In business, an IEE 30,000-foot-level report out probability plot quantifies both measurement accuracy and precision on an overall high-level metric's response—in one chart.

Agile: A continuous iteration of development and testing in the software development process.

Analysis of means (ANOM): A statistical hypothesis testing procedure for assessing the equality of the mean of each group in a population to the overall population mean.

Analysis of variance (ANOVA): A procedure to test statistically the equality of means of discrete factor inputs.

Attribute response: See Response.

Average: See Mean.

Balanced scorecard (the): Initially, the balanced scorecard (Kaplan and Norton 1992) was to track business organizational functions in the areas of financial, customer, and internal business process and learning & growth. In this system, an organization's vision and strategy can also lead to the cascading of objectives, measures, targets, and initiatives throughout the organization. This book describes issues with this system and an alternative IEE approach that overcomes these shortcomings.

Baldrige Award (Malcolm Baldrige National Quality Award): recognizes U.S. organizations in the business, health care, education, and nonprofit sectors for performance excellence.

Benchmark: A standard in judging quality, value, or other essential characteristics.

Benchmarking: Provision of a standard against which something can be assessed.

Best estimate: An estimate calculated from sample data without a confidence interval.

Black Belt (BB), IEE: Full-time IEE implementation practitioner that focuses on improving processes so that organizational IEE value chain 30,000-foot-level metrics are enhanced and the enterprise as a whole and its customers benefit.

Bottom-line: The final profit or loss that a company experiences.

Box-Cox lambda transformation: The core of a Box-Cox transformation is an exponent, lambda (λ), which varies from -5 to 5. The optimal value for lambda is the one that results in the best approximation of a normal distribution curve. When lambda is approximately zero, the original data tend to be log-normally distributed.

Box plot: Describes various aspects of data pictorially. The box contains the lower and upper quartiles. The median appears as a horizontal line within the box. A box plot is sometimes called a box-and-whisker plot.

Brainstorming: Consensus building among experts about a problem or issue using group discussion.

Business process improvement event (BPIE): Functional process improvement effort that is to enhance an associated 30,000-foot-level metric but has not been identified as being an organizational strategic effort and an EIP component.

Capability, process: See Process capability.

Categorical variable: A variable that can be considered in one of a number of possible groups. Examples of categorical variables are gender, race, age group, and educational level.

Cause-and-effect diagram: Also called the fishbone or Ishikawa diagram, the C&E Diagram is a graphical brainstorming tool used to organize possible causes (KPIVs) of a symptom into categories of causes. Standard categories considered are materials, machine, method, personnel, measurement, and environment. These are branched as required to additional levels. It is a tool used for gathering wisdom of the organization.

Cause-and-effect matrix: A tool used to help quantify team consensus on relationships thought to exist between key input and key output variables. The results can lead to other activities such as FMEA, multi-vari charts, ANOVA, regression analysis, and DOE.

C-chart: In SPC, a c-chart is to be the control charting methodology that is used when monitoring subgroups of count data over time. For this type of IEE-metric reporting situation, an individuals chart, not a c-chart, is used to determine if a 30,000-foot-level count-data response is considered stable or not. The reason for using an individuals chart instead of a c-chart for a count-response data situation is that, for a c-chart, common-cause variation between subgroups, there is no mathematical impact on calculated UCL and LCL values. This mathematical truism is an important issue; in a vast majority of high-level 30,000-foot-level tracking responses there will be Y-output common-cause variation between subgroups. Because of this between-subgroup-variation occurrence, a c-chart count data chart could indicate many false special-cause signals that lead to wasteful firefighting common-cause variation as though it were special-cause (Reference Appendix B, Web page 11).

Common cause: In IEE, common-cause variation is viewed from a high-level 30,000-foot-level or satellite-level process-output perspective. Natural or random variation is inherent in most processes over time, affecting response measurement from the process. In IEE 30,000-foot-level reporting, if an individuals chart has no data points beyond statistically calculated UCL and LCL values, the process is presumed to have only common-cause variation. When this condition occurs, the processes are said to be stable and predictable. In IEE, this stability assessment is made using an individuals chart, not a and R chart, p-chart, or c-chart. When a process experiences this high-level common-cause variation but does not meet customer needs, the process is said not to be capable. For non-capability process response situations, there is a need for process enhancements, or input variable changes to improve the condition; that is, this metric improvement need creates a *pull* for an improvement project creation.

Confidence interval: The limits or band of a parameter that contains the true parameter value at a specified confidence level. The confidence band can be single-sided to describe an upper and lower limit, or double-sided to describe both upper and lower bounds.

Continuous data response: See Response.

Control chart: See Individuals chart.

Control plan: A written document created to ensure that processes are run so that products or services meet or exceed customer requirements. It should be a living document, which is updated with both additions and deletions of controls based on experience from the process.

Cost of doing nothing differently (CODND): Unlike COPQ, a CODND monetary value does not require a specification. An example CODND value for a response that has no true specification is work in progress (WIP), where a CODND value could be determined for mean monthly expense cost to the business. In IEE, a CODND monetary value could be determined before beginning a process improvement project and then compared to a post-project value to determine the value of the process enhancements to the business.

Cost of poor quality (COPQ): Traditionally, the cost of quality issues has been given the broad categories of internal failure costs, external failure costs, appraisal costs, and prevention costs. IEE gives focus to determining CODND instead of COPQ.

Customer: Someone for whom work or a service is performed. The end-user of a product is a customer of the employees within a company that manufactures the product. There are also internal customers in a company. When an employee does work or performs a service for someone else in the company, the person who receives this work is a customer of this employee.

Cycle Time: Frequency that a process completes a part or product. Also, the time it takes for an operator to go through work activities before repeating the activities. Also, cycle time can be used to quantify customer order to delivery time.

Dashboard: *See* Scorecard.

Days sales outstanding (DSO): In accountancy, a company determines days sales outstanding to estimate the size of their outstanding accounts receivable. The DSO metric quantifies the size not in units of currency, but average sales days. Typically, days sales outstanding is calculated monthly as a mean value. However, for a DSO measurement from a 30,000-foot-level point of view, one needs to include the variation from individual payments, in addition to a central tendency mean response. This 30,000-foot-level response format for DSO provides individual duration-of-payment days, even if only from a sample of transactions over time. This form of reporting offers much more insight than a simple mean response.

Defect: A nonconformity or departure of a quality characteristic from its intended level or state.

Defective: A nonconforming item that contains at least one defect, or having a combination of several imperfections causing the unit not to satisfy intended requirements.

Design of experiments (DOE): In the IEE DMAIC 'Improve phase,' DOE can be used as proactive analysis methodology where process input variables are changed in a structured fashion to assess whether an evaluated input level has a statistically significant effect on an output response. Factor levels can be assessed in a fractional factorial experiment or in a full factorial experiment structure.

Discrete data: Count information that only has a certain number of values. Examples include the number of attendees in a meeting and number of questions answered correctly.

Distribution: A pattern that randomly collected numbers from a population follows. In IEE, the normal and log-normal distributions are frequently used to model a process output response for determining a predictive statement when a process is determined to be stable in a 30,000-foot-level report. With this high-level reporting for a continuous response, a probability plot provides a data-fit visualization to the distribution where a process capability statement relative to the needs of the business could be determined.

DMAIC roadmap, IEE: An IEE project Define, Measure, Analyze, Improve, and Control roadmap for improvement project execution, which contains a true integration of Six Sigma and Lean tools.

DMAIC, IEE: The five IEE DMAIC phases are:

Define—Define and scope the project.

Measure—Establish current, high-level 30,000-foot-level performance metrics for the process. Consider measurement system analysis (MSA) and the use of Lean tools. Wisdom of the organization (WOTO) assessments are also a part of this phase.

Analyze—Use IEE analysis tools to passively uncover root causes. Evaluate relationships between input factors and output responses and model processes.

Improve—Optimize processes, including the application of Lean and DOE tools.

Control—Institutionalize and maintain gains.

DPMO (defects per million opportunities): Number of defects that, on average, occur in one million opportunities. Care should be taken to assure that all defects, including touch-ups and reworks that previously may not have been recorded, are included in this calculation. Also important is an agreed-upon standard method for counting opportunities.

EIP (Enterprise improvement plan): A system for drilling down from business goals to specific projects (Reference Figure 6.15).

Elephant in the room: An obvious problem or difficult situation exists that people do not want to talk about.

Enterprise Performance Reporting System (EPRS) software: EPRS-metrics software provides a means to easily create 30,000-foot-level metric reports (Reference Appendix B, Web page 13). EPRS-IEE software (also referenced as EPRS software) can, among other things, create an organizational IEE value chain with 30,000-foot-level metrics that are automatically updated (Reference Appendix B, Web page 14).

Failure: A device is said to fail when it no longer performs its intended function satisfactorily.

Failure rate: Failures/unit time or failures/units of usage. Sample failure rates can be presented as 0.002 failures/hour, 0.0003 failures/auto miles traveled, 0.01 failures/1000 parts manufactured.

Failure mode and effects analysis (FMEA): A proactive method of improving or minimizing failures in a product or service. For a process FMEA, wisdom of the organization inputs can be used to list what can go wrong at each step of a process that could cause failures or customer problems. Each item is evaluated for its importance, frequency of occurrence, and the probability of occurrence detection. In an FMEA, this information is used to prioritize the items that most need improving. Recognized items are then assigned a corrective action plan to reduce their risk of occurrence— the opposite of fault tree analysis.

Fault tree analysis: A top-down, deductive failure analysis in which an undesired state of a system is analyzed using logic to combine a series of lower-level events.

Firefighting: An expression used to describe the process of performing emergency fixes to problems where often the reactions are the result of common-cause variation rather than special cause.

Fractional factorial experiment: Design of experiments (DOE) strategy that assesses several factors/variables simultaneously in one test, where only a partial set of all possible combinations of factorial levels is tested to identify important factors more efficiently. This type of test is much more efficient than a traditional one-at-a-time test strategy.

Full factorial experiment: Factorial experiment where all combinations of factor levels are tested.

Functions, IEE value chain: An organizational or business function is a core process or set of activities carried out in a company or its departments. Common functions include operations, marketing, human resources, information technology, customer service, and finance.

Flow chart: Path of steps of work used to produce or do something.

Gage R&R (repeatability and reproducibility): A methodology used in measurement system analysis (MSA). It is the evaluation of measuring instruments to determine their capability to provide a precise response. It determines how much of the observed process variation is due to measurement system variation. Gage repeatability is the variation in measurements using the same measurement instrument several times by one appraiser's measuring the identical characteristic on the same part. Gage reproducibility is the variation in the average of measurements made by different appraisers using the same measuring instrument when measuring the identical characteristics on the same part.

Gemba Walk: The action of observing the actual process, understanding the work, asking questions, and learning what really is happening during process execution.

General linear model (GLM): A statistical linear regression model for a continuous response variable given continuous and/or categorical predictors.

Governance, corporate: The system by which business corporations are directed and controlled. The corporate governance structure specifies the distribution of rights and responsibilities among different participants in the corporation, such as the board, managers, share-

holders and other stakeholders, and spells out the rules and procedures for making decisions on corporate affairs. This system also
provides the structure through which company objectives and the
means of attaining those objectives and monitoring performance
are set. IEE delivers a structured system for corporate governance.

Green Belt (GB), IEE: Part-time IEE implementation practitioner
that focuses on improving processes so that organizational IEE value-chain 30,000-foot-level metrics are enhanced and the enterprise
as a whole and its customers benefit.

Hard savings: Savings that directly impact the bottom-line.

Histogram: A graphical representation of the sample frequency distribution that describes the occurrence of grouped items.

Hoshin kanri: A process used in strategic planning where strategic goals
are to be communicated throughout the company and then put
into action.

Hypothesis testing: Consists of a null hypothesis (H_0) and alternative
hypothesis (H_a) where, for example, a null hypothesis indicates
equality between two process outputs, and an alternative hypothesis indicates non-equality. Through a hypothesis test, a decision is
made whether to reject or not reject a null hypothesis. When a null
hypothesis is rejected, there is α risk of error. Most typically, there
is no risk assignment when we fail to reject the null hypothesis.
However, an appropriate sample size could be determined such that
failure to reject the null hypothesis is made with β risk of error.

Incapable process: A process that does not produce results consistent
with specification requirements or customer expectations.

In control: The description of a process where variation is consistent
over time; that is, only common causes exist. In IEE, an individuals
chart is used to determine whether a process is in control; that is,
stable from a high-level point of view. When an IEE 30,000-foot-
level individuals chart has no data points beyond the chart's statistically determined UCL and LCL values, the process is said to be
stable, and the process response is considered predictable.

Individuals control chart: A control chart of individual values where
between-subgroup variation mathematically affects calculated

UCL and LCL values. For this type of control chart, the difference between the data-calculated UCL and LCL value increases when there is more between-subgroup variation. In IEE, the individuals chart is used to assess process stability in a 30,000-foot-level report. In an individuals chart, when there are no plotted data outside data-calculated UCL and LCL limits, and there are no patterns in the plotted data, the process is considered to be stable and predictable. Mathematically determined UCL and LCL values from the data are independent of specification limits or targets. In IEE, and R chart, p-chart, and c-chart techniques are not used to determine whether a process response is stable or not. *See* and R chart, p-chart, and c-chart.

Inferential statistics: Statements made about a population from the analysis of samples; that is, properties of the population are inferred from the analysis of samples.

Infrequent subgrouping/sampling: Traditionally, rational sub-grouping issues involve the selection of samples that yield relatively homogeneous conditions within the subgroup for a small region of time or space, perhaps five in a row. For a given situation, differing sub-grouping methodologies can dramatically affect the measured variation within subgroups, which in turn affect the distance between the UCL and LCL lines for an SPC chart. For the high-level metrics of IEE, an infrequent subgrouping/sampling approach is needed so that short-term variations caused by KPIV fluctuations are viewed as common-cause issues. A 30,000 foot-level individuals chart created with infrequent subgrouping/sampling can reduce the amount of organizational firefighting; however, this does not mean a problem does not exist within the process. For example, when an accompanying 30,000-foot-level predictive response is unsatisfactory for a stable process output response, this improvement need can *pull* (using a Lean term) for the creation of an IEE improvement project.

Integrated Enterprise Excellence (IEE, I double E): A 9-step roadmap for the creation of an enterprise process system in which organizations can significantly improve both customer satisfaction and their bottom-line. IEE business management techniques can help manufacturing, development, and service organizations become more competitive and/or move them to new heights. The IEE system is a structured approach that guides organizations through the tracking and attainment of organizational goals. IEE goes well beyond traditional Lean Six Sigma and the balanced scorecard methods. IEE integrates enterprise process measures and improvement methodologies with tools such as Lean and TOC in a never-ending pursuit of excellence. IEE becomes an enabling framework, which integrates, improves, and aligns with other initiatives such as TQM, ISO 9001, ISO 45001, ISO 14001, Malcolm Baldrige Assessments, and the Shingo Prize. IEE is the organizational orchestration that moves toward the achievement goal of the three Rs of Business; that is, everyone is doing the Right things and doing them Right at the Right time.

Interaction: The effect of one causal variable on a response depends on the state of a second causal variable.

ISO 9001: An international standard that specifies requirements for a quality management system (QMS) for organizations to use to demonstrate the ability to consistently provide products and services that meet customer and regulatory requirements.

ISO 45001: An international standard that specifies requirements for an occupational health and safety management system with guidance to proactively improve performance in preventing injury and ill-health.

ISO 14001: An international standard that specifies the framework requirements for an effective environmental management system for organizations to follow.

Kaizen event (or kaizen blitz): Kaizen is a Japanese term meaning gradual unending improvement by doing little things better and setting and achieving increasingly higher standards. Kaizen events are short duration improvement projects with a specific aim for improvement. A facilitator leads events, with the implementation team being members predominantly from the area in which the kaizen event is being conducted plus a few additional people from support areas.

Kanban: Pulling a product through the production process. This method of manufacturing process-flow-control only allows the movement of material by pulling from a preceding process. Kanban keeps inventory low, and, when quality errors are detected, less production is affected.

Key performance indicator (KPI): A type of performance measurement that evaluates the success of an organization or of a particular engaged activity such as projects, programs, products and other initiatives.

Key process input variable (KPIV): Factors in a process correlated to an output characteristic(s) important to the internal or external customer. Optimizing and controlling these factors are vital to the improvement of a key process output variable (KPOV).

Key process output variable (KPOV): Characteristic(s) of the output of a process that are important to the customer. Understanding what is important to the internal and external customers is essential to identifying KPOVs.

Lean: Improving operations and the supply chain with an emphasis on the reduction of wasteful activities like waiting, transportation, material hand-offs, inventory, and overproduction.

Level 5 system: Jim Collins' book, *Good to Great* (Collins 2001), describes Level 5 Leaders as leaders who display a potent mixture of personal humility and indomitable will. Level 5 Leaders are incredibly ambitious, but their ambition is first and foremost for the cause, for the organization and its purpose, not for themselves. IEE provides a means to create not only Level 5 leaders but also a Level 5 system that offers a culture that can be formulated, which is long-lasting and works effectively even when Good-to-Great organizational Level 5 leaders leave an organization.

Likert scale: Respondents to a Likert Scale questionnaire specify their level of agreement or disagreement on a symmetric agree-disagree range; for example, one to five, for a series of statements to capture the intensity of a feeling.

Low-hanging fruit: Refers to an action that takes almost no effort.

Master Black Belt (MBB), IEE: IEE expert who is skilled in both understanding and implementing all aspects of the 9-step IEE system in an organization.

Mean: The mean of a sample ($\bar{x}$) is the sum of all the responses divided by the sample size. The mean of a population (μ) is the sum of all responses of the population divided by the population size. For a random sample of a population, $\bar{x}$ is an estimate of a population's mean (μ).

Measurement system analysis (MSA): Assessment of an overall measurement system, including gage repeatability and reproducibility (R&R).

Median: For a sample, the number that is in the middle when all observations are ranked in magnitude. For a population, the value at which the cumulative distribution function is 0.5.

Mistake proofing: The use of a methodology that either makes it impossible for an error to occur or makes the error immediately obvious once it has occurred. An equivalent Japanese term is poka-yoke.

Muda: A Japanese term indicating efforts that do not add value (waste). Some categories of muda are defects, overproduction or excess inventory, idle time, and poor layout.

Multi-vari chart: A chart that displays the measurement differences within units, between units, between samples, and between lots. It is useful in detecting variation sources within a process.

Null hypothesis: See hypothesis.

Normal distribution: A bell-shaped distribution that is often useful to describe various physical, mechanical, electrical, and chemical properties.

Objectives and key results (OKR): Framework for defining and tracking objectives and their outcomes.

Out of Control: Control charts exhibiting one or more special-cause conditions. When an IEE 30,000-foot-level individuals chart has one or more points beyond statistically calculated UCL and LCL values, a default statement in the report will state that the process output response is not predictable.

Pareto chart: A graphical technique used to quantify problems so that effort can be expended in fixing the *vital few* causes, as opposed to the *trivial many*. Named after Vilfredo Pareto (born 1848), an Italian economist.

Pareto principle: 80% of the trouble comes from 20% of the problems; that is, the vital few problems.

Parts per million (PPM): Number of units of mass of a contaminant per million units of the total mass. In Six Sigma, PPM can be used to describe a defective rate; e.g., a PPM rate of 10,000 would equate to a 1% defective rate.

Passive analysis: Data collected and analyzed as the process is currently performing to determine potential KPIVs. Process alterations are not assessed.

P-chart: In SPC, a p-chart is to be the control charting methodology used when monitoring the proportion of nonconforming units in a sample, where the sample proportion nonconforming is the ratio of the number of nonconforming units to the sample size. For this type of IEE-data situation, an individuals chart, not a p-chart, is used to determine if a 30,000-foot-level non-conforming proportion response is considered stable or not. The reason for using an individuals chart instead of a p-chart for non-conformance 30,000-foot-level rate data tracking is that for a p-chart any Y-response common-cause-between-subgroup variation that is occurring would have no mathematical impact on calculated UCL and LCL values. This is an essential issue in that, for a vast majority of high-level 30,000-foot-level tracking responses, there will invariably be some level of common-cause, output-response variation between subgroups. Because of this between-subgroup-variation occurrence, a p-chart for this type of data could show many false special-cause signals that can lead to wasteful firefighting common-cause variation as though it were special cause (Reference Appendix B, Web page 11).

Plan-do-check-act (PDCA): An iterative four-step business management method for continuous process improvement. PDCA is also referenced as the Deming cycle, Shewhart cycle, or plan-do-study-act (PDSA).

Poka-yoke: A Japanese term indicating a mechanism that either prevents a mistake from occurring or makes a mistake evident at a glance.

Precision: See Accuracy.

Prediction statement: In IEE, when a satellite-level or 30,000-foot-level performance metric reporting is considered stable, it is said to be predictable. Data from the chart's recent region of stability is used to determine a best estimate prediction statement provided below the report's charting. When a specification exists, and the process is considered predictable, the report provides a best estimate non-conformance rate statement. When there is no specification, and the process is deemed stable, a mean (or median) and 80% frequency of occurrence rate is reported below the graphs of the 30,000-foot-level performance-metric reporting. This reporting 80% statement provides the chart-reader a quantification of the expected amount of variation from the process; that is, there is the expectation that four out of five reported occurrences will be in the stated 80% frequency of occurrence range.

Probability plot: Data are plotted on a selected probability-plot coordinate system to determine if a particular distribution is appropriate; that is, plotted data follow a straight line. When data follow a probability plot distribution such as normal or log-normal, statements about percentiles of the population can be made from the probability plot. In IEE 30,000-foot-level and satellite-level reports for continuous data, a probability plot is used to determine for stable processes a predictive statement.

Population: The totality of items under consideration.

Pre-control chart: An approach to monitor processes over time, which involves the classification of product measurements into one of three groups depending upon the relative position of the measurement to specification limits. The process is to be adjusted when specific patterns occur in the plot. In IEE, a pre-control chart can be used to manage the Y-response impact from drifting or changing X process inputs at a 50-foot-level.

Problem-solving: The process of determining the cause from a symptom and then choosing an action to improve a process or product.

Process: A method to make or do something that involves several steps.

Process capability/performance indices (Cp, Cpk, Pp, Ppk): For process capability indices, Cp is a measurement of the allowable tolerance spread divided by a short-term 6σ data calculated spread. Cpk has a similar ratio to that of Cp except that this ratio considers the shift of the mean relative to the central specification target. For process performance indices, Pp and Ppk calculations are similar to Cp and Cpk calculations, except the calculation is from a long-term viewpoint, instead of a short-term perspective. A 6σ calculated data spread is used in the calculations (Reference Appendix B, Web page 11).

Pull: A Lean term that results in an activity when a customer or downstream process step requests the action. A home builder that builds houses only when an agreement is reached on the sale of the house is using a pull system. *See* Push.

Pull for project creation: This term is derived from the Lean term, pull. An IEE implementation objective is that performance metric ownership is assigned through the business IEE value chain, where functional performance metric tracking is at a 30,000-foot-level. In the 9-step IEE system, the enterprise is analyzed as a whole in step 3 to determine what performance metrics need improvement and by how much so that whole-organizational satellite-level goals can be met. A metric improvement need would then create a *pull for project creation*. An EIP shows a summary of an organization's *pull for project creation* efforts. *See* Push for project creation.

Push: A Lean term that results in an activity that a customer or downstream process step has not explicitly requested. This activity can create excessive waste and/or inventory. A home builder that builds houses on the speculation of sale is using a push system. If the house does not sell promptly upon completion, the homebuilder has created an excess inventory for the company, which can be very costly. *See* pull.

Push for project creation: This term is derived from the Lean term, push. Lean Six Sigma (LSS) deployments are to create and execute projects that are to be beneficial to the business. When assessing the typical Lean Six Sigma project selection process, either a deployment steering committee or some level of management selects projects from a list that they and others think is important. For this type of deployment, there is often a scurry to determine projects for attendees to work on during their LSS training that starts next week. This system could be considered a push for project creation; that is, people are hunting for projects because they need to work on a defined project during LSS training. With this deployment system, there can be initial successes since agreed-to low-hanging fruit projects can often be readily identified and provide significant benefits; however, this system of project determination is not typically long-lasting. After a while, people usually have a hard time defining and/or agreeing to what projects should be undertaken. Besides, this project creation system does not typically look at the system as a whole when identifying projects to undertake. This system of project selection can lead to sub-optimization, which can be detrimental to the enterprise as a whole. Finally, this LSS deployment system typically creates a separate function entity that manages the deployment, which is separate from operational scorecards and functional units. In time, people in these functions can be very visible on the corporate radar screen when downsizing forces occur, or there is a change in executive management, even though the LSS function has been claiming much past success. *See* Pull for project creation.

p-value: A statistical analysis output. The null hypothesis is rejected when this value is equal to or less than the desired level of significance; e.g. 0.05.

Quality, cost, and time metrics: A frequently referenced description of performance metric for IEE value chain functions. These three categories are to encompass process efficiency, productivity, and customer satisfaction.

Random: Having no specific pattern.

Range: For a set of numbers, the absolute difference between the largest and smallest value.

Red-yellow-green (RYG) Scorecard: Used by organizations to track individual performance metrics relative to goals. A RYG scorecard colored response assesses how well a metric response performs relative to its goal, where green indicates being on track, yellow is an at-risk indicator, and red suggests attention is required. Sometime a RYG scorecard is referenced as a stoplight scorecard.

Regression analysis: Data collected from an experiment are used to empirically quantify, through a mathematical model, the relationship that exists between the response variable and influencing factors. In a simple linear regression model, $y = b_0 + b_1 x + \varepsilon$, x is the regressor, y is the expected response, b_0 and b_1 are coefficients, and ε is random error.

Response: Two basic types of process-output responses are continuous and attribute. A continuous response could also be referenced as variables data. A response is said to be continuous if any value can be taken between limits; e.g., 2, 2.0001, and 3.00005. An attribute response is a measure of the presence or absence of a characteristic. Attribute data focus on numbers, variable data focus on measurements. For example, data on defective products simply classify a process output unit as defective or not defective. This type of measurement could be translated into a failure rate proportion output; e.g., 1 out of 1000 sheets of paper on the average jam when fed through a copier. Continuous response examples include weight, distance, and voltage measurements.

Risk Management: Process of identifying possible risks, problems, or disasters before they happen. IEE includes a means to have a business risk management system that allows leadership to set up procedures to avoid the risk, minimize its impact, or, at the very least, help cope with its implications.

Robust process: A process is considered robust when its output variation is not sensitive to the normal variation from its input variables. For example, a manufacturing process step is robust to different operators who regularly execute the operation step.

Sample: A selection of items from a population.

Satellite-level metric: Similar to a 30,000-foot-level metric except that the satellite-level metric tracks financial metrics, such as profit margins or EBITDA. *See* 30,000-foot-level metric.

Scatter plot: Assessment of the relationship between two continuous variables with the intention of determining a cause-and-effect relationship.

Scientific problem-solving methodology: A scientific approach for the seeking of knowledge, which involves forming and testing a hypothesis. The method provides a logical, systematic way to remove subjectivity when answering questions.

Scorecard: A major difference between the dashboards and scorecards is that a scorecard focuses on a given metric and compares it to a forecast or target, whereas a dashboard will present multiple numbers in different ways. Performance measurement is generally considered to be a regular measurement of outcomes and results, which generates reliable data on the effectiveness and efficiency of programs. Performance metrics are used to measure the behavior, activities, and performance of a business. Satellite-level and 30,000-foot-level metrics track and report performance metrics regularly from a process-output point of view that provides a predictive statement when responses are considered stable. In IEE documentation, satellite-level and 30,000-foot-level metrics are sometimes referenced as a scorecard/dashboard.

Scrum: An Agile product development strategy used to create work products iteratively. Scrum began in the software industry and has spread to universities, the military, the automotive industry, and other entities.

Shingo Prize: An international award for operational excellence that assesses: vision and strategy alignment; employee empowerment; continuous improvement; innovation and development; quality and sustainable results.

Sigma: The Greek letter (σ) is often used to describe the standard deviation of data.

Sigma level: A metric calculated by some to describe the capability of a process relative to its specification. A six-sigma level is said to have a 3.4 DPMO rate. A three-sigma level is about 66,800 DPMO. A four-sigma level is about 6210 DPMO, while a five-sigma level is about 233 DPMO. Sigma level is sometimes referred to as sigma quality level. The IEE system does not use and report sigma level metrics (Reference Appendix B, Web page 11).

Significance: A statistical statement indicating that the level of a factor causes a difference in a response with a certain degree of risk of being in error.

Six Sigma: A term coined by Motorola that emphasizes the improvement of processes to reduce defect rates, decrease variation, and to make general improvements.

SMART goals: Not everyone uses the same letter descriptors for SMART. In IEE, referenced descriptors are italicized in the following list: S—*specific*, significant, stretching; M—*measurable*, meaningful, motivational; A—agreed upon, attainable, achievable, acceptable, action-oriented, *actionable*; R—realistic, *relevant*, reasonable, rewarding, results-oriented; T—*time-based*, timely, tangible, trackable.

Soft savings: Savings that do not directly impact the financial statement as hard savings do. Possible soft savings categories are cost avoidance, lost profit avoidance, productivity improvements, profit enhancement, and other intangibles.

Soft skills: A person who effectively facilitates meetings and works well with other people has good soft skills.

Special cause: Variation in a process from a reason that is not an inherent part of that process; that is, it is not a common cause.

Specification: A criterion that is to be met by a part or product.

Stable process: In satellite-level and 30,000-foot-level performance metric tracking, individuals charts are used to assess process stability. An individuals chart of a process-output that has no data points beyond the chart's UCL and LCL lines is considered stable. In IEE, when a process is deemed stable, a prediction statement is provided below the report's charting for both a satellite-level and 30,000-foot-level reports. EPRS-metrics software offers an option for the chart's creator to override the technicality of any point being beyond the UCL or LCL line because of the belief that the occurrence was by chance.

Stakeholders: Those people who are key to the success of an IEE project; e.g., finance, managers, people who are working in the process, upstream/downstream departments, suppliers, and customers.

Standard deviation (σ, s): A mathematical quantity that describes the variability of a response. It equals the square root of variance. The standard deviation of a sample (s) is used to estimate the standard deviation of a population (σ).

Statistical process control (SPC): The application of analytical techniques in the control of processes.

Test: Assessment of whether an item meets specified requirements by subjecting it to a set of physical, environmental, chemical, or operating actions/conditions.

The balanced scorecard: *See* Balanced scorecard (the).

Three Rs of business: Everyone doing the Right things and doing them Right at the Right time.

Theory of constraints (TOC): The TOC described by Goldratt (Goldratt 1992) presents a systems-thinking process where the focus is on the system's bottlenecks. TOC thinking provides a viewpoint for continual improvement of the performance of the entire system, rather than viewing the system in terms of discrete processes. TOC addresses the larger systematic picture as a chain or grid of interlinked chains. The performance of its weakest link determines the performance of the whole chain. In IEE, TOC is a step 3 consideration in the IEE 9-step business management system.

Total Productive Maintenance (TPM): The TPM process is to increase the Overall Equipment Effectiveness (OEE) of plant equipment. OEE is the resulting product from the multiplication of three equipment factors; that is, performance, availability, and quality.

Total quality management (TQM): Describes a management approach that is to have long-term success through customer satisfaction. In TQM effort, all members of an organization are to participate in improving processes, products, services, and the culture in which they work.

Toyota Production System (TPS): Integrated socio-technical system developed by Toyota that comprises its management philosophy and practices. TPS organizes manufacturing and logistics for the automobile manufacturer, including interaction with suppliers and customers.

Tribal knowledge: Any unwritten information that is not commonly known by others in an organization. This term often references information that may need to be known by others for producing quality products or services.

Utilization review: the critical examination, perhaps by a physician or nurse, of health-care services provided to patients, especially to control costs by identifying unnecessary medical procedures and monitoring the quality of care.

Value added (VA) time: The execution time for the work elements that a customer is willing to pay for.

Value chain, IEE: Describes in flowchart fashion, both primary and support organizational activities and their accompanying 30,000-foot-level or satellite-level performance metrics. An example of primary activity flow is: develop product—market product—sell the product—produce the product—invoice/collect payments—report satellite-level metrics. Example support activities include IT, finance, HR, labor relations, safety & environment, and legal.

Value stream mapping: A Lean manufacturing technique for the analysis, design, and management of the flow of materials and information required to bring a product to a customer. Standard symbols depict various work streams and information flows.

Variance: Has more than one meaning in business. In accounting, a variance is a difference between an actual amount and a pre-determined standard amount or amount budgeted. In a statistical sense, a variance is a measure of the amount of spread in a distribution.

Wisdom of the organization (WOTO): Structured conversations and dialog with people who know a process intimately to describe what is currently being done in the process and what might be done to improve processes. An end goal is to solicit improvement ideas using brainstorming tools such as cause-and-effect diagrams. In IEE WOTO is within the IEE DMAIC's 'Measure phase' drill-down.

Work in progress (WIP): The partially finished goods of a company, which are waiting for completion and eventual sale, or the value of these items. WIP items are either just being fabricated or waiting in a queue or storage buffer for further processing.

$\bar{X}$ **and R chart (pronounced X-bar and R chart):** In SPC, an $\bar{X}$ and R chart is to be the control charting methodology used when monitoring the mean ($\bar{X}$) and range (R) of process samples, which were collected and measured at regular subgroup-time intervals. For this type of IEE-data situation, two individuals charts, not an $\bar{X}$ and R chart, are used to determine if a 30,000-foot-level process-output response is stable or not. One of these individuals charts tracks the subgroup's mean ($\bar{X}$) response, while the other individuals chart tracks the subgroup's standard deviation response. The reason for using individuals charts, instead of an $\bar{X}$ and R chart pair, is that for both of the $\bar{X}$ and R chart subgroup responses any common-cause-between-subgroup variation which occurs will have no mathematical impact on calculated UCL and LCL values. This calculation reality is an essential fact in that, for a vast majority of high-level 30,000-foot-level tracking responses, there will invariably be some level of Y-response common-cause variably between subgroups. Because of this, an $\bar{X}$ and R chart of this type of data could show many false special-cause signals, which can lead to wasteful firefighting common-cause variation as though it were special-cause occurrences (Reference Appendix B, Web page 11).

XmR chart: In SPC, an XmR chart is to be the control charting methodology used when monitoring single data items with X indicating observations and mR indicating moving range. For this type of IEE-data situation, only the individuals chart, not the moving range chart, is used to determine if a 30,000-foot-level non-conforming individual-value response is considered stable or not. The reason for not using the moving range chart of this two-chart pair is that the moving range chart would add unnecessary complexity to 30,000-foot-level reporting since moving range charting tracking is somewhat redundant to the tracking of the individual values. *See* Individuals control chart.

Y-response management: For a process, the output or its Y is dependent upon the inputs that occur in the process's execution; that is, $Y=f(X)$. Organizational management to the Ys through the setting of measurement-value goals that are to be met at some point in time, utilizing techniques such as red-yellow-green scorecards or table-of-numbers reporting, can lead to very unfavorable, if not destructive, organizational behaviors.

17 REFERENCES

Breyfogle, F. W. (2003). Implementing Six Sigma: Smarter Solutions® Using Statistical Methods. 2d ed. Wiley, Hoboken, NJ.

Breyfogle, F. W., Salvekar, Arvind (2004), Lean Six Sigma in Sickness and Health: An Integrated Enterprise Excellence Novel, Smarter Solutions, Austin, TX.

Breyfogle, F. W. (2008a), The Integrated Enterprise Excellence System: An Enhanced, Unified Approach to Balanced Scorecards, Strategic Planning, and Business Improvement, Citius Publishing, Austin, TX.

Breyfogle, F. W. (2008b), Integrated Enterprise Excellence Volume I—The Basics: Golfing Buddies Go Beyond Lean Six Sigma and the Balanced Scorecard, Citius Publishing, Austin, TX.

Breyfogle, F. W. (2008c), Integrated Enterprise Excellence Volume II—Business Deployment: A Leaders' Guide for Going Beyond Lean Six Sigma and the Balanced Scorecard, Citius Publishing, Austin, TX.

Breyfogle, F. W. (2008d), Integrated Enterprise Excellence Volume III—Improvement Project Execution: A Management and Black Belt Guide for Going Beyond Lean Six Sigma and the Balanced Scorecard, Citius Publishing, Austin, TX.

Breyfogle, F. W. (2010), Lean Six Sigma Project Execution Guide: The Integrated Enterprise Excellence (IEE) Process Improvement Project Roadmap, Citius Publishing, Austin, TX.

Breyfogle, F. W. (2020a), Management 2.0: Discovery of Integrated Enterprise Excellence, Citius Publishing, Austin, TX.

Breyfogle, F. W. (2020b), Leadership System 2.0: Implementing Integrated Enterprise Excellence, Citius Publishing, Austin, TX.

Collins, J. (2001), Good to Great: Why Some Companies Make the Leap... and Others Don't, HarperCollins Publishers Inc., New York, NY.

Collins, J. (2009), How The Mighty Fall: And Why Some Companies Never Give In, JimCollins.

Deming, W. Edwards (1986), Out of the Crisis, Massachusetts Institute of Technology, Cambridge, MA.

Drucker, P. F. (2001), The Essential Drucker: In One Volume the Best of Sixty Years of Peter Drucker's Essential Writings on Management, Harper Business, New York, NY.

Goldratt, E. M. (1992), The Goal, 2d ed., North River Press, Great Barrington, MA.

Grove, A. S. (1983), High Output Management, Random House Inc., New York, NY.

Hambrick D. C. and Fredrickson J. W. (2001), "Are you sure you have a strategy?," Academy of Management Executive, Vol. 15, no. 4.

Kaplan, R. S. and D. P. Norton (1992), "The balanced scorecard—measures that drive performance," Harvard Business Review, Jan.—Feb.

Kaufman, J. (2012), The Personal MBA: Master the Art of Business, Portfolio/Penguin, New York, NY.

Peters, T and Waterman R. H. (1982), In Search of Excellence, Harper Collins, New York, NY.

Senge, P. M. (1990), The Fifth Discipline: The Art and Practice of the Learning Organization, New York: Doubleday/Current.

Sullivan, J. (2017), "Ouch, 50% of New Hires Fail! 6 Ugly Numbers Revealing Recruiting's Dirty Little Secret," https://www.ere.net/ouch-50-of-new-hires-fail-6-ugly-numbers-revealing-recruitings-dirty-little-secret/.

Wolff-Mann, E., (2019), "Wells Fargo scandals: The complete list," Yahoo Finance, https://finance.yahoo.com/news/wells-fargo-scandals-the-complete-timeline-141213414.html.

18 ACKNOWLEDGMENTS

I want to thank the many people who helped in differing ways with the creation of this book. I need to first thank my wife, Becki, for her support of my IEE passion over the years and for my continual refinement efforts of how to best convey the benefits of IEE to others.

I do have the concern that I missed someone in this acknowledgement section of the book. If so, I am sorry.

Over many years, I have worked with Rick Haynes, Doug Wheeler, Chinh Tran, and Tri Pham to develop the Enterprise Performance Reporting System (EPRS) software that supports IEE metric reporting and its organizational implementation. This team did a great job creating the software coding for EPRS-metrics (Reference Appendix B, Web page 13) and EPRS-IEE (Reference Appendix B, Web page 14).

The conversations and dialog that I had about general hospital situations and measurement reporting practices with Tim Jones, Earl Maxwell, and Bob Spurck made the book's storyline and situations consistent with what could occur in a hospital.

I mailed draft copies of this book at different stages of this book's development to over fifty people. Some feedback was extensive, but all feedback was valuable! What I thought was interesting is that there was virtually no overlap in the responses. All comments were from a different perspective, which was great! Everyone who gave feedback impacted this book in a positive way.

Detailed draft-copy reviews and many helpful improvement suggestions were provided by Bob Ashenbrenner, Peter Courtois, Mike

Harkins, Andrew Lux, Brian Mitchell, Michael Parrillo, Tony Perez, and Mike Whitescarver.

Others who provided book-improvement suggestions that were very valuable are Manny Barriger, Jim Bennett, Scott Berman, Steven Bonacorsi, Jim Bossert, Fred Bothwell, Evaristo Campos, Rachele Collins, Mark Feller, Ralph Fulwood, Russ Gale, Carrie Green, Jesse Hamilton, Janet Hammill, Cheryl Holden, Arch Holder, Elaine Jennings, John Jennings, Elizabeth Keim, Joe Knecht, Ric Love, Jerry Mairani, Todd Minnick, Lawrence Mossman, Steve Mundwiller, Andy Paquet, Bill Pugh, Dan Rand, Alexander Sasfrass, Janice Shade, Doug Shifflett, Frank Shines, Jerel Walters, and Doug Wheeler.

Thanks go to Adam Hough and his team who assisted with Amazon's launch of this book. Thanks also to Grant Tharp for his narration of the audio version of this book.

For many years, Dorothy S. Stewart has edited my books and articles. Again, Dorothy did a great and timely edit of this book. She also gave much phone guidance for specific conventions to use in the book's text.

30,000-foot-level and satellite-level metric figures were created using a Smarter Solutions, Inc. developed add-in to Minitab*.

Made in the USA
Monee, IL
06 September 2020

41089759R00184